IN THE FIRE OF THE
EASTERN FRONT

The Stackpole Military History Series

THE AMERICAN CIVIL WAR

Cavalry Raids of the Civil War
Ghost, Thunderbolt, and
  Wizard
Pickett's Charge
Witness to Gettysburg

WORLD WAR I

Doughboy War

WORLD WAR II

After D-Day
Armor Battles of the
  Waffen-SS, 1943–45
Armoured Guardsmen
Army of the West
Australian Commandos
The B-24 in China
Backwater War
The Battle of Sicily
Battle of the Bulge, Vol. 1
Battle of the Bulge, Vol. 2
Beyond the Beachhead
Beyond Stalingrad
The Brandenburger
  Commandos
The Brigade
Bringing the Thunder
The Canadian Army and the
  Normandy Campaign
Coast Watching in
  World War II
Colossal Cracks
A Dangerous Assignment
D-Day Bombers
D-Day Deception
D-Day to Berlin
Destination Normandy
Dive Bomber!
A Drop Too Many
Eagles of the Third Reich
Eastern Front Combat
Exit Rommel
Fist from the Sky
Flying American Combat
  Aircraft of World War II
For Europe
Forging the Thunderbolt
For the Homeland
Fortress France
The German Defeat in the
  East, 1944–45

German Order of Battle, Vol. 1
German Order of Battle, Vol. 2
German Order of Battle, Vol. 3
The Germans in Normandy
Germany's Panzer Arm in
  World War II
GI Ingenuity
Goodwood
The Great Ships
Grenadiers
Hitler's Nemesis
Infantry Aces
In the Fire of the Eastern Front
Iron Arm
Iron Knights
Kampfgruppe Peiper at the
  Battle of the Bulge
The Key to the Bulge
Knight's Cross Panzers
Kursk
Luftwaffe Aces
Luftwaffe Fighter Ace
Massacre at Tobruk
Mechanized Juggernaut or
  Military Anachronism?
Messerschmitts over Sicily
Michael Wittmann, Vol. 1
Michael Wittmann, Vol. 2
Mountain Warriors
The Nazi Rocketeers
No Holding Back
On the Canal
Operation Mercury
Packs On!
Panzer Aces
Panzer Aces II
Panzer Commanders of the
  Western Front
Panzer Gunner
The Panzer Legions
Panzers in Normandy
Panzers in Winter
The Path to Blitzkrieg
Penalty Strike
Red Road from Stalingrad
Red Star under the Baltic
Retreat to the Reich
Rommel's Desert Commanders
Rommel's Desert War
Rommel's Lieutenants
The Savage Sky
Ship-Busters
The Siegfried Line

A Soldier in the Cockpit
Soviet Blitzkrieg
Stalin's Keys to Victory
Surviving Bataan and Beyond
T-34 in Action
Tank Tactics
Tigers in the Mud
Triumphant Fox
The 12th SS, Vol. 1
The 12th SS, Vol. 2
Twilight of the Gods
Typhoon Attack
The War against Rommel's
  Supply Lines
War in the Aegean
Wolfpack Warriors
Zhukov at the Oder

THE COLD WAR / VIETNAM

Cyclops in the Jungle
Expendable Warriors
Flying American Combat
  Aircraft: The Cold War
Here There Are Tigers
Land with No Sun
Phantom Reflections
Street without Joy
Through the Valley

WARS OF THE MIDDLE EAST

Never-Ending Conflict

GENERAL MILITARY HISTORY

Carriers in Combat
Cavalry from Hoof to Track
Desert Battles
Guerrilla Warfare
Ranger Dawn
Sieges

IN THE FIRE OF THE EASTERN FRONT

The Experiences of a Dutch Waffen-SS Volunteer, 1941–45

Hendrick C. Verton

Translated by Hazel Toon-Thorn

STACKPOLE
BOOKS

English edition © 2005 by Helion & Company Limited

Published in paperback in 2010 by
STACKPOLE BOOKS
5067 Ritter Road
Mechanicsburg, PA 17055
www.stackpolebooks.com

Paperback edition by arrangement with Helion & Company Limited.

Originally published in 2003 as *Im Feuer der Ostfront: Ein niederländischer Freiwilliger an deutscher Seite im europäischen Schicksalskampf* by Nation Europa Verlag. German edition © by Hendrick C. Verton.

Cover design by Tracy Patterson

Printed in the United States of America

10 9 8 7 6 5 4 3 2 1

Library of Congress Cataloging-in-Publication Data

Verton, Hendrik C., 1923–
  [Im Feuer der Ostfront. English]
  In the fire of the Eastern front : the experiences of a Dutch Waffen-SS Volunteer, 1941–45 / Hendrik C. Verton.
     p. cm. — (Stackpole military history series)
  Originally published: West Midlands, England : Helion, 2005.
  Includes bibliographical references.
  ISBN 978-0-8117-3589-6
  1. Waffen-SS. SS-Freiwilligen-Panzergrenadierregiment "Nordland." 2. World War, 1939–1945—Regimental histories—Germany. 3. World War, 1939–1945—Campaigns—Eastern Front. 4. Verton, Hendrik C., 1923– 5. World War, 1939–1945—Personal narratives, Dutch. 6. Soldiers—Netherlands—Biography. I. Title.
  D757.85.V4613 2009
  940.54'1343092—dc22
     [B]
                                        2008045321

Dedicated to my parents and my brothers and sisters, who because of
my military service in Eastern Europe suffered a terrible penalty in
Holland after the end of the Second World War.

Contents

Foreword

by Dr. Erich Mende

The author (centre) in 1985 with Dr Erich Mende (left) and a comrade.

[Dr. Erich Mende was a Member and Vice-Chancellor of Parliament from 1963 to 1966, and Chairman of the Liberal Party from 1960 to 1967.]

There is a Latin saying, "Vae victis!" i.e. woe to the vanquished, referring to the 'Contempt of the Victor', which Germany was made to feel at the end of World War II. It was confirmed once again, inasmuch that the German population stood under a collective guilt, for which every individual was penalised. The 'victors' released laws in all of the Allied occupied territories, for the annihilation of National Socialism and militarism, and with a total re-education programme. The Germans and their sympathisers had to learn from their mistakes and the error of their ways, and return to a liberal and lawful system of democracy.

A campaign of revenge also began against all those Europeans that had worked hand in glove with Germany, those who had lent a sympathetic ear. It lasted for years. Finally, with insight and common sense, politicians, unions, publishers, and the Church, led by Konrad Adenauer, Kurt Schumacher and Theodor Heuss, won the upper hand against false judgement and targeted insinuation, in order to achieve a balance of the truth.

It took over forty years to reveal to the rest of the world that Russia was responsible for the mass murder of thousands of imprisoned Polish officers and soldiers in Katyn. The Allies, as well as other European countries, despite knowing the truth, blamed the German Wehrmacht. This was done without any hint of a guilty conscience. More than half a million people suffered under the wrath of the 'victors' and their contemptible direction. Being either a close neighbour of Germany, or of the same moral code, many took up arms against Bolshevism, as 'volunteers' in Germany's army. Their actions were regarded as treason, their sacrifices and sufferings in the theatre of war despised.

A Dutchman and his family describe how this really was, in all its shocking reality. European conduct, ideals and neighbourly friendship towards Germany, weave through the whole book, whether in East Prussia or in Silesia. In the defence of Breslau, Hendrik Verton reveals the brave conduct, ethical moral code, and sacrificial assistance given by the European 'volunteers'. Only those who experienced the bitter German-Russian war can testify to the honest and conscientious truth of this book. I can recommend it to students of contemporary history, for its coherent collection of times, dates, and events.

It only remains for me to say that the author and his brother, whose large family stem from Holland, have greatly contributed to the rebuilding of German democracy, in the capital of Bonn, over the last forty years. In every way, my encounter with the Verton family was, at this time, a mutual acknowledgement for an expanded and peaceful Europe of 'fatherlands'.

[Author's Note: Dr. Erich Mende died on 6 May 1998. He had read my manuscript, which had been typed up to that point in time. Being very bitter over the defamation of Germany's soldiers, he supported my work by offering and writing the Foreword to my book.]

Prologue

If one day the world were to open its archives, which in this day and age remain partly inaccessible, we would be able to find out that in the recent past many things were different in reality than how they have been portrayed in the present day. For reasons of power, politics and education, the chroniclers and historians have written according to 'political correctness' that has been manipulated by the 'victors'. Unfortunately, in 'dancing to their tune', historians have hidden the truth. They have therefore prevented any chances of reconciliation.

Nothing can be divided simply into light and shade, and I do not attempt to do this. However, I do wish, as an eyewitness, to anticipate the long awaited glasnost, and to give my account of my experiences of World War II.

My appeal to the reader is, to remember that these accounts of events, together with my feelings, can only be understood when viewed through the perspective of this period of time. Neither do I wish to justify events. My generation neither created nor was able to influence events of that time.

Of those living today, the majority did not live through the war, and even then only superficially. Some day mankind will learn about it only from 'hearsay'. The results of such events however, do lead from that time into the present. I have reported some of these aspects quite extensively and others a little less. The last of the accounts deal especially with historic events, and therefore guilt and reconciliation play a role. The others utilise pressure groups, who from 'time immemorial' pursue a one-sided interest by using every discussion to uphold an old score.

Our family history began in the far distant past in France and Holland, and leaves a lot to speculation. Where, when and why they came, is not fully known. This family history, from the beginning of the 20th Century, is still very 'young', but for my part I have described it exactly, from the beginning of the 1930s. In its composition it includes the description of my own role, of course, and is seen through my eyes. Many had to 'box' their way through this very difficult time. Many lost everything they owned, had to build anew, and not lose their courage. Those born at that time had much to bear and experience. Those born now should be thankful that fate has produced a long peaceful development, and try to understand our role in history a little better.

Our destiny in life is simply a throw of the dice that brings luck for some, and trouble and torment for others.

Our capacity to remember grows ever fainter, therefore time is short. So here is my story, how I and my family experienced it.

Hendrik Verton

CHAPTER 1

Where From?

Early in 1982, 150 families all with the name of Verton, assembled together on the Dutch island of Schouwen–Duiveland. Nearly all came from Holland, except the contingent from Germany who had settled in Bad Godesberg in 1949, and were the only ones with this name in the whole of Germany. Where did they come from and how long had they been in existence?

Decades of research have revealed that the family's roots are to be found in France. The town of Verton, with its population of just 1,200 people, has existed since 'the beginning of time'. The Romans built Vertonu in the 1st century, 40 kilometres south of Boulogne-sur-Mer and on the Channel coast. Today, due to sedimentation from more than one river, Verton now lies 6 kilometres distant from the sea. The astonishing fact is that in the whole of France there are no other families to be found with the name of Verton. So how did the Vertons come to settle in Holland?

Monsieur E. Reas, the former director of the Fromagerie-de-la-Cote-d'Opale, lives in the town of the same name. He relates that those members of the military and religious order of knights, the Templars, were founded in 1119. They migrated from their original abode, their military settlement, and built themselves a massive castle, 'de Verton', a fortress for their protection. Over time, having become very wealthy, there was a fast growing hostility against them. This financial power of our forefathers reached its apex when becoming the bankers to not only very many princes, but also to the Pope himself.

Therefore it was not surprising when Phillip, King of France from 1285 to 1314, decided to break their powerful hold and destroy the Verton knights. He had Jacques de Molay, the Chief of the Order, and many others in high positions, arrested. After an illegal trial, they were sentenced to be burned at the stake. A handful escaped to Holland, probably over the English Channel. They used its northerly flow between Dover and Calais to reach Holland's coast and the shores of the southern regions of Zeeland. The 'Land in the Sea' lay in the fork of the Rhine, Schelde and Maas rivers.

The Vertons very quickly became acclimatised and felt at home, their elegant French language being very quickly replaced with that of the Dutch. They became fishermen, farmers and tradesmen, integrating and becoming honourable members of society in their new home. The majority of them remained on the island of Schouwen-Duiveland, lying to the west, in a delta of streaming waters that flowed from the east.

The Netherlands, including the island Schouwen-Duiveland.

The small medieval town of Zierikzee formed the commercial and cultural centre of the island. From the 13th Century it was the most important centre in the south, as well as being a strategic stronghold throughout the Flemish war. Hundreds of years later, in 1789, with the cry of 'Liberté, Egalité, Fraternité', French soldiers plundered everything of worth to be found in the elegant Patrician houses. In 1810 the whole of Holland was annexed to France. The result was a catastrophe, especially when Emperor Napoleon planned his Russian campaign. Holland's youth were forced to fight in the Russian Steppes, not having the choice to volunteer, as in WWII with Germany. From 30,000 Dutch soldiers who marched to Russia in the summer of 1812, only a few hundred returned in the spring of 1813.

Schouwen–Duiveland has never really recovered from those times. However, life went on for those on the island. They worked along modest lines within the framework of a hard-working, Christian, and very strong conservative tradition and, most certainly, without influence from the outside world. Grandfather Verton was born on 12 January 1850, in a village called Dreischor. It lay 5 kilometres north of Zierikzee and was protected by a massive dyke. The Council Registrar recorded his Christian names as Jan Adriaan Matthijs, upon the wish of his parents. His near relatives were polder wardens. Polder is the Dutch for tiny islands, or pieces of land surrounded by water. Other relatives were dyke administrators, church vergers, council members, and managers of the island's windmills.

Watchmaker and jeweller Jan A.M. Verton was talented in a technical way. His lucrative talent earned him the nickname of 'Goldnugget'. At that time, pocket-watches, grandfather and wall-clocks, were considered to be a status symbol. It was not long before he was supplying the whole of Schouwen-Duiveland. My grandfather married Cornelia Marie Everwijn and moved with her to the large town of Zierikzee. On 30 March 1884, my father, Hendrik Cornelius was born. The technical age moved on, sewing machines and bicycles being asked for, produced and also repaired. The business prospered, with son Hendrik selling sewing machines to customers in the next villages or to outlying farms. He would walk for miles to the next customer, with the machine strapped on his back. My father's memories of 'the good old times' are not filled with an overflow of exciting experiences. Zierikzee was still 'a medieval province where time stood still', which is what the incoming visitors always said. Because of it, the young folk were not offered the chance to expand into cultural, professional or vocational niches.

He then moved to Amsterdam where he found work in the chemical laboratory of a rubber factory. A young 28 year-old woman from Amsterdam won his attention and his heart. So this 28 year-old Zeelander and Louisa Adolphia Lammers were married on 7 June 1912, and she became our mother. In the coming years two daughters and six sons were born, all in different places. The girls were born in 1914 and 1916, and the boys in 1918, '20, '23, '27, '29, and lastly in 1935. The births always took place at home. The stork, with the help of the district nurse, delivered all eight Vertons to the door, as my grandfather had done with his sewing machines!

CHAPTER 2

The First World War and Fragments from Versailles

WWI broke out on 1 August 1914. It was a hugely encompassing and bloody war from which neutral Holland was spared. My father, however, had to defend its borders. Apart from general mobilisation, commercial restrictions, and the influx of nearly a million Belgian refugees, our nation was spared the struggles of war. Due to the concept of the Kaiser's General Staff, German troops could move through France to Paris. But, only by first going through Belgium.

It was in 1917 that the USA, with its mighty reserves, entered the war against the German Empire. Only after four years of bitter struggles, and a blockade that led to famine, did Germany lay down her arms against 28 states, including the six great powers. Kaiser Wilhelm II and the Crown Prince fled to Holland, and the Kaiser's role in history came to an end.

The Allies' proposal of extradition was refused by Holland, pointing out that there was a 'right of asylum'. However, at the same time, Queen Wilhelmina promptly broke off diplomatic relations with the German Monarchy, having strongly disapproved of the Kaiser's flight. Only her husband, Prince Consort Hendrik and his daughter Juliana, fostered a regular contact with their relations from the house of Hohenzollern, to whom she, Juliana, behaved very loyally, after she became Queen.

What were the underlying reasons for WWI? At the turn of the century Germany possessed a commercial monopoly around the whole of the world. Their valuable inventions were being internationally patented. Germany had no agricultural or industrial problems and the first-class quality of the end product was cheaply exported. Germany possessed colonies in Africa, the Pacific and in Asia, their ships travelling the seas of the world. Britain was an export nation, and 'did not like to see this'.

France, since the loss of Alsace-Lorraine, following the Franco-German War of 1870–71, had never come to terms with this. Friendly relations with Germany were never sought. Instead she feverishly armed herself, and her newspapers ordered 'Revenge'. Military pacts against Germany were made, until it was completely surrounded. The result was that the Russian Grand-Duke Nikolajewisch toasted his French military colleagues with "to our joint future victory and our next meeting in Berlin!" After the war, President Woodrow Wilson in America asked, "Is there one man alive who doesn't know that the reason for war, in this modern age, is purely commercial competition?" It was a war of trade and economy!

Between 1871 and 1914 Germany was not engaged in, nor responsible for, any war. However, other 'free-living peoples' at that time, were guiding Germany's foreign politics and their rules. According to Carl von Clausewitz, "War is only, after all, the continuation of politics, but using other methods". Russia was at war with Turkey, and Turkey with Italy. Japan was at war with Russia, and Greece with Turkey. Britain was at war in India, South Africa and also Egypt. Spain went to war against the USA, and the USA against Haiti. France was making war with Tunisia, Morocco and Madagascar, and Holland with Atjeh in the Indies.

Nevertheless, the German Empire, after losing the 1914–18 war was, according to the world, guilty of 'war-mongering' and had to pay for it. The Versailles Pact, signed in the Compiègne forest north of Paris, presented Germany with inflation and poverty. This 'peace treaty' was nothing less than the continuation of the war. The German Empire, as a commercial competitor, had to be wiped out, and reparation, revolution and unemployment were the result.

Without any official agreement, Alsace–Lorraine was immediately returned to France. Poland received the provinces of Poznan, West Prussia and also a promised section of Pomerania. From a section of the torn Imperial and Royal Austrian and Hungarian Empires, an independent state emerged in Czechoslovakia, which included the Sudetenland. Germany's colonies were withdrawn, coming under the law of a League of Nations. Danzig, with its 97% German population, and not only as member of a guild of merchant towns but also the door to the Baltic, was given to Poland. In 1922 it became a part of a customs duty area.

It was therefore not unexpected, when at the outbreak of the next Great War, these developments became an explosive keg of gunpowder! During the course of reparations, if the amount of coal from Germany's coal-mines, or wood from their forests, were not delivered punctually, it was reason enough for France to send five divisions of French and Belgian soldiers to the Ruhr. Many arrests followed, upsetting the cold and starving population. French officers made themselves 'lords of the streets', forcing people into the gutter with whips.

The 'victors' did everything they could to enforce the Versailles Pact, thus being responsible for an atmosphere that festered in the new generation in Germany which was then the torch-bearer of National Socialism under Adolf Hitler. The peace treaty of 1919 could be regarded as responsible for the dictatorship arising from 1933.

In between times, a certain American 'style' in bars and amusement halls, and the sound of jazz music spread over western Europe and the pattern was not confined to such places. To the anger of the conservative-minded it had spread to inner decor and fittings. However, this popularity of everything American suddenly ended in 1929, as Wall Street crashed. The results of 'Black Friday' spread like wildfire around the globe and resulted in one of the worst economic crises of all time. Before the end of 1929 there were already 30,000,000 unemployed. Stockbrokers and profiteers ruled the roost, under the noses of a very limp government. In Germany, it was clear that it had become a land of two classes, the rich and the poor.

Holland, as an up-and-coming land of industry and having become far more independent, was not spared the results of a worldwide recession. With a population of 8.8 million, almost 1 million were unemployed, despite its colonies in the East Indies, known today as Indonesia. The social climate was a catastrophe, as its prosperity dropped continually.

In the families of the unemployed, meat was to be seen on the table just once a month, and then only for the father. A hot meal was eaten just twice a week. In a family with children, it was usual for them to possess just one set of underwear. When the mother washed it they stayed in bed, for the whole day when necessary, until it was dry. When, if unemployed, you were caught visiting the cinema, then your unemployment benefit was reduced. For those under twenty-one years of age and those over sixty, there was no financial support whatsoever. With that, the government worsened the social problem instead of getting to grips with it. More than once, they even radically reduced the unemployment benefit.

In July 1934, in order to protest against this, the workers organised a demonstration on the streets of Amsterdam. The Army and Navy were called in to help the police suppress the protesting masses. There were demonstrations elsewhere, not only in Amsterdam. On that day, the result of people against tanks was seven deaths, and more than two hundred casualties. For those in power there was then nothing left of the widespread Dutch liberal mentality, when the population had dared to voice an opinion!

In 1933 mutiny even broke out within the Dutch East Indies Navy. The crew of one of its warships, the *Seven Provinces*, mutinied in Indies waters, when their pay was drastically reduced. But to no avail. The Dutch government ordered the ship to be destroyed. It was attacked by the Navy. Twenty of its crew were killed.

For us children living with our parents in Zierikzee, that was of no consequence for we had other problems, for instance, school. The school-house seemed to be of gigantic proportions to us, small as we were. Its ceilings appeared to be as high as in a palace, and it had colourful maps decorating the white walls of the classroom. The classroom was dominated by bulky school desks, and the desk of the master on the dais. Behind him was a huge blackboard smeared with chalk. The portrait of 'the mother of our land', Queen Wilhelmina never seemed to age, since she had looked down on her subjects with her youthful appearance, for some years.

Zierikzee

Our teacher, wise and demanding respect, always ruled us with a cane at the ready, to ensure discipline. It was not always warranted, but it did us no harm. Meister Ten Haaf was hard but fair and was our favourite teacher. He knew how to attract our attention, particularly in history. Dramatically, he would stick his hand into his jacket and seize our imagination in portraying Napoleon Bonaparte. Almost without breathing, we would wait for the words of this Corsican general, as standing before the Pyramids in Egypt, he told his soldiers, "Men! Thousands of years are now looking down on you!" All that was missing was Bonaparte's tricorne hat.

We school children literally hung on the words of our teachers. We lived, we feared and we suffered through the experiences of Louis XIV and Marie-Antoinette in the guillotine era, and the dictatorship of the French Jacobins. We followed the glory of the Grand Armée in their battles at Preussisch-Eylau, Friedland, Austerlitz. We 'perspired' in our classroom, in the heat of the Nile. With the modern Genghis Khan we 'froze' in the freezing temperatures of Smolensk and Beresina. We were also proud to know that our grandfathers had also fought with a red cockade on the front of their bearskin caps. Then, in our warm and cosy school-room of the thirties, we could not know that years later, some of us would ourselves be freezing in those same Russian Steppes, and wearing the emblem of the *Totenkopf*, or 'death's head'.

That Napoleon had left behind him a Europe in fragments, is something that we were never told. What we were told, was that as France's national hero and Grand Emperor, his last resting-place was under marble, not far from the Champs-Elysées. Our teacher was convinced that he had been a blessing for the world and held a high position in the world's history.

Our enthusiasm had been fired to re-enact what we had heard about this 'grand army' in school. In wanting to do the same, we marched around with wooden rifles and capes, storming the banks surrounding the meadows. Such banks were for the safety of the sheep and cows when flooded and while I was the only one with an air rifle (no longer functional), I was the leader of the gang. Our ammunition was really what we could lay our hands on, such as lumps of clay or root vegetables. Often, after it had rained, the low-lying meadows were sodden, and we too were sodden and muddy. The cows didn't mind, nor were they disturbed by our war cries. Only when we drove them into a gallop to attack, did they object in bewilderment with a 'moo'.

For us 'children of nature' the island was a paradise, and it was ours. It belonged to us. There were no tourists, and we knew every corner and every backyard. The farmers knew us too. Protected against the wind by tall trees, the thatched, red-bricked farmhouses always stood alone. Framed by water-filled ditches and green meadows, the vegetable gardens always separated houses from stalls and barns. The sweet-smelling perfume of phlox surrounding the vegetable gardens, mixed with that of hay and dung. We played in the sweet-smelling warmth of the hay-barn, springing bravely from the highest bale on to the straw below. It was here that we learned about a taboo subject, that was not taught in school, or at home, and that was of sexual behaviour. We learned from the animals on the farm, from the horses and pigs, and from the hand of 'mother nature'. The story of the stork belonged at home.

All in all, our lives progressed along modest lines. We were happy and without complaints and enjoyed the smallest of surprises. My pride and joy was my old bicycle which shone like new through my own efforts and care. We used to ride all of fifteen kilometres from Zierikzee to Haamstede and West Schouwen, where the widest dunes were to be found, and the largest beach in the whole of Holland. When natural dunes were not to be found, then huge dykes protected our land. One of them was to be found not far away from Zierikzee. Every portion of the coastline with a dyke, was our swimming pool, without tiles, pipes or warm water, very often cold, but to compensate for that, endless and beautiful.

We never had to go to school on Wednesday afternoons. In the fine weather, we played in the water, amongst the seaweed and slippery jelly-fish until the sun went down. The seagulls and crows used to pick between the green-grey stones for dyke mussels, throwing them in mid-flight on to the stones below to break them open. When we didn't have our bicycles with us, then we sprang on to a passing hay-wagon to go home, tired, brown from the sun and exhausted from the water.

CHAPTER 3

Political Revolution

The Allies believed that with their success in 1918, they had set the westerly pattern for democracy. When the truth was known, it was a government reform that endured a gigantic crisis. Worldwide more and more people turned away from it.

Such was the case in Italy – although it had been one of the 'victors', they too suffered from commercial hardship. It had not helped them to suddenly join the side of those 'victors' and also declare war on Germany. It was just such poverty that turned its people to Communism. A Bolshevik uprising in the north, threatened to turn into civil war, only coming to an end in 1922 as the *Duce* Mussolini came to power and ended the chaotic conditions.

A large part of the world was very enthusiastic about that man. In those times of commercial disorder 'strong men' were rare. After visiting Italy, one could report that the trains ran punctually again, that poverty had vanished and above all, there were then no unemployed.

The British Prime Minister, Ramsey MacDonald, visited Mussolini in 1933, and was one of those enthusiasts, as was Winston Churchill. Mahatma Ghandi, the Chief Minister of India's Congress Party, described him as being Italy's 'saviour'. There were many admirers also in Holland, including many prominent people. The result of a survey was published in Holland's leading newspaper, *Allgemeine Handelsblatt*, that in forming this Fascist State, Mussolini was, after the inventor Edison, the 'greatest personality' of that epoch.

However, in Germany, the situation could not continue as it had done. The German Kaiser chopped his wood in Doorn in Holland, and his land was a slowly dying kingdom. After twelve years in which thirteen chancellors had ruled, the land was very near bankruptcy and had nearly 7 million unemployed. The German population was ripe for a radical change in politics. The man, who after years of campaigning, of attending hundreds of party-sittings and who in 1930 entered parliament with 107 other democratically voted politicians, was none other than Adolf Hitler. Not quite three years later, on 30 January 1933, President von Hindenburg named that Austrian-born man as *Reichskanzler*.

The Leader of the National Social German Workers Party, i.e. the *Nationalsozialistischen Deutschen Arbeiterpartei*, the NSDAP, was then 44 years old. Like Napoleon, he was obsessed with his own ideas and the intention of altering everything overnight. It appears that he did just that. The disputes and quarrels, from those in power who had brought Germany to the edge of bankruptcy, were silenced. The authorising laws legalising Hitler's regulations were made without consent of Parliament. Theodore Heuss was among those consenting. He was later to become the Federal President.

The sceptics in the land, as well as those abroad, waited and listened. Millions of idealists, including those wanting to make a career, the adaptable and those who wanted to ride on the turn of the tide, flocked to the new flag in such numbers that membership was stopped. In among the adaptable, was none other than Prince Bernhard von Lippe, who was later to become Prince Consort to Holland's Queen. He allowed himself to be selected as a candidate for Hitler's *Sturmabtailung*, the SA, but joined the SS, i.e. the *Schutzstaffeln* or 'protection squad', which befitted his social status. Driving to many a pleasant NS Rally and 'guard duty' were among his duties, just like any other. He, as a confirmed SS-man however, changed his convictions more than once along the way.

The people saw a 'messiah' in Hitler, who did solve the unemployment problem, who did ban Communism from Germany and who did free the land from the chains of the Versailles Pact. Already by the first days of 1935, on 13 January in fact, the Saar area was resurrected through a referendum. A 90.8% result demanded that it be reclaimed and returned to its homeland. In March of the next year, battalions from the *Wehrmacht* marched over the Rhine and moved into garrisons there. They reclaimed their own western-lying territory, having been declared a demilitarised zone by the former 'victors'.

The defeated, and still lethargic population from 1918, suddenly became self-propelled into social and commercial activities. It became a year of events. Successes were celebrated with brass bands, ceremonies where uniforms could be seen and *Richtfeste*, whereby a small tree with colourful streamers, was placed on the roof-beams of a new building before being tiled. For the very first time a state made it possible for the small man to go abroad on holiday. It was through the organisation *Kraft durch Freude*, or 'Strength through Joy'. Places like Madeira, Scandinavia or Italy, were the targets for the traveller, on board large modern liners. For the majority, it was the very first holiday that they had ever had. The 'Bohemian Private', as Hitler was scathingly called by the envious, had made that possible, whereas kings and the rich colonial powers never had.

Foreigners from all over the world visited Germany and were impressed. Many diplomats and ministers came, including the former British Prime Minister Lloyd George. He greeted the new Chancellor, in Obersalzberg, as one of the 'victors'. Others included representatives of both French and British front-line soldiers from WWI. The famous American pilot, Charles Lindberg, also paid a visit, as did the abdicated King, the

Duke of Windsor. France's Ambassador, André Francois-Poncet, arrived in a highly polished, black Mercedes owned by the state, on his visit to the *Reichsparteitag* in Nuremberg.

In 1938, Winston Churchill wrote the following to Hitler, "Should England ever find herself in a national disaster as Germany did in 1918, we would pray to God that he sends us a man with your strength, will and mentality".

A good percentage of the foreign press did not withhold compliments either. *The Daily Express*, for instance, said "the man has worked wonders". The Dutch newspaper *De Telegraaf* reported that Hitler had destroyed the danger of Communism in Germany, even before becoming Chancellor. A Catholic paper, *De Tijd*, agreed with Hitler "that the fight against Marxism had been a fight for life over death". A Dutch anti-revolutionary newspaper, *De Standaad*, formulated their opinion as, "the freedom In the Weimar Republic had led to extremes, and lack of godliness had increased". As late as 1938, a Dutch Jewish newspaper agreed that "one cannot reject everything that National Socialism creates".

Naturally enough there were other opinions. The Dutch Communist newspaper described Hitler as "the new Chancellor, the farmhand of the German bank capital of the larger industrialists, and an East Prussian country bumpkin". They further suggested that National Socialism would not last long, that Communism would march in, free the working classes and guide them to a socialist 'Soviet-Germany'. The Dutch population looked on in interest at the developments, and waited. It was generally accepted that Germany had done the right thing in freeing itself from the chains of the Versailles Pact. The Dutch Establishment however could not but help envy Hitler's and Mussolini's success. Perhaps, if the truth be known, they were afraid that certain sections of the population doubted their capabilities as protectors, which had been loudly proclaimed.

To combat this, negative campaigns were broadcast that Germany was approaching bankruptcy and Hitler about to die, being incurably ill. Those who lived in the border areas did not believe those stories, or allow themselves to be influenced, in view of flourishing employment possibilities. They peddled to and from their work over the border. In fact, when as unemployed you rejected work in Germany when offered it, then the Dutch authorities stopped your unemployment benefit. They damaged their prestige by such action, but in part it solved their unemployment problem, even when they did not want to admit it. To offset this criticism, the Dutch press was always ready to propagate negative stories about Germany, and to publish public opinion in detail. The success of Germany's new government was being deliberately ignored.

That cannot be said for the Dutch businessmen and the commercial representatives who were impressed with Germany's industrial creativity and who wanted a closer working relationship. They saw vast opportunities for their own land. Through the *Buro Ribbentrop*, named after Germany's Minister for Foreign Affairs, Joachim Ribbentrop, the German-Dutch Association was formed. It concentrated on the traffic of business, not only with one another, but specialising in western Europe.

My father visited Germany too, buying machines in Mönchengladbach, and negotiating with IG Farben AG. He was fascinated with the modern technology presented at the exhibitions, in both Hannover and Leipzig. As a director of a rubber factory, he then engaged two Germans to work for him, one as a 'master' and the other as an engineer. Both were 'old school' diligent workers. The constant contact between my father and those treasured workmen, being examples of German discipline and enthusiasm, won father's sympathy for the Hitler 'fans' and the 'new order'.

For us young folk, Germany was a large and distant land. It stretched far to the east, with its rich countryside of gentle hills, dark forests and high mountain ranges, and to the south. That is how it was described to us in our school, none of us having seen it with our own eyes. Germany was also the 'land of birth' of those wonderful model railways and metal cars, from the firm Märklin. For us boys it was 'Märklin land'. The model soldiers with their authentic, decorated and highly coloured uniforms and the 'Made in Germany' label, fascinated us. The significant uniforms of the German *Wehrmacht* were more familiar to us than those of our own Army.

We were also impressed with the sporting idols of our next-door neighbour, such as the BMW motorcycle rider George Schorsch Meier, the World Champion boxer Max Schmeling, and our favourite Auto-Union racing driver Bernd Rosemeyer. We gladly changed to Radio Bremen to hear martial music, or the songs of Marika Rökk, such as *On a night in May*, which represented Germany for us. Otherwise there were, in comparison, the Anglo-Saxon songs of Louis Armstrong, presented for hours on end by Radio Hilversum.

The successful developments of the Republic, under Hitler, had a political influence on Holland, in that the National Socialist Movement (*Bewegung*) the NSB formed in 1931. An independent associate party of the NSDAP had a sensational increase in membership. Their Party programme was very similar to that of Benno Mussolini's party, being "true to the King, Social Rights and anti-Marxist". At the beginning they showed no signs of anti-Semitism. In the mid-thirties, there was a total of 56 parties in Holland, nearly all quarrelling with one another.

The leader of the NSB, a water-engineer called Anton Mussert, was a 100% conventional Dutchman, with strong ideals. In 'better circles' his party was fully accepted, because of its strong anti-left character. It drew in businessmen, officers, retired Colonial officials, those from the middle classes and free-lance individuals. Baron de Jorge, Holland's Governor General and former Colonial, did not reject the National Socialist Movement either. The disillusioned unemployed also gave it their support. The NSB held 8% of the indirect Parliament Election of 1935, being 300,000 votes with which Mussert was more than content. In the cities of Amsterdam, the Hague and Utrecht, the party held 10% and 39% in the eastern border counties adjacent to Germany.

The success of the NSB shocked the government in the Hague and they had to deal with the consequences. It was, from that moment on, forbidden for officers and officials to be party members. Some obeyed this rule. It must be pointed out that, for those unemployed to be engaged in a permanent position as an official, it was a treasured one. Other Mussert fans stayed true to the NSB and so the movement had its first 'martyrs', which they used to the full for propaganda purposes. The world of the 1930s in Holland was comparatively peaceful in view of the commercial situation, and was practically uneventful for us boys in the country. Much appeared to be petit-bourgeois conservatism. We boys wanted a challenge or two. Singing songs around the Boy Scout camp fire or playing games was fun, but did nothing to fulfil our ambitions. We saw photos of German youths in uniforms, with short trousers, sitting in gliders of the Hitler Youth, or being able to race DKW motorbikes, which we could only envy. This was smart, dynamic and paid for by the state and held our admiration, for who could afford a motorbike or a glider at our age?

CHAPTER 4

War in Sight?

On 14 March 1919, the National Assembly in Vienna agreed that Austria annexe itself to the German Empire. In Germany it was a sensation. But it was immediately refused by the 'victors'. This had to wait for twenty years.

The pro-German movement had steadily grown as in the years before. In the end, it could not be suppressed and came into power, but not without some bloodshed, or spasmodic opposition. The Ostmark region laid itself at Hitler's feet and he readily accepted the new duty. The *Wehrmacht* marched from Bavaria, over the borders, to be showered with flowers from the enthusiastic Austrian population. Street after street was made free for what was thereafter to be called the 'Flower Campaign'. A month later, 99.75% of the Austrian people voted for annexation to Germany and the church gave its effusive blessing.

Only a few months later, and under the motto "The Right of Referendum" from the League of Nations, the Sudetenland, deprived of its right of self-government, was the target of the German government. Having been suppressed, lived in extreme poverty and been persecuted for the previous twenty years by the Czechs, Sudetenland held the highest rate, not only of suicides but also of infant mortality, in the whole of Europe! The borders however were hermetically sealed, not allowing migration. It is not to be wondered at, when the slogan 'Home to the Reich' grew from day to day, and the immediate areas behind Germany's borders experienced an economic boom. The same situation arose therefore as it had in Austria, and came to an inevitable head. German troops marched in on 1 October 1938. Flowers, cries and tears of joy greeted and accompanied the marching troops. By September, Britain's Prime Minister Neville Chamberlain, as representative of the western powers, met Theodore Heuss in Berchtesgaden, and then others in the Rhine hotel Dreesen in Bad Godesberg, along with representatives of the German government. All agreed with that union.

Abroad, it was acceptable as a natural step for Germany to gather its leaders into a Pan-German league and the world's press reported positively. *The Times* wrote on 4 October 1938, "the first Czechoslovakian State has been destroyed, through its own politics from which it was born. They had never survived a war and its destruction was automatic, even without the reality of war". Already in January 1938, nine months before the affiliation of the Sudetenland, the Amsterdam newspaper *Het Nieuwe Nederland*, criti-

15

cally stated that "the shameful treatment of National minorities in Czecho-slovakia must be destroyed, in the interest of freedom. The Benes-clique must also be dealt with".

Till then, Hitler's foreign policy had been peaceful and successful and the explosive situation caused by the Versailles Pact had been defused. However, that did not mean that the German government accepted the existence of the Czechs. The policy continued in the rest of Czechoslovakia. Hitler felt very strongly about that. He found a friend and ally in Pierre Cot, the French Minister for Aviation, when voicing the opinion that, in the case of war, German towns and centres of industry could be bombed from Czechoslovakian aerodromes. Did France want to place her planes at Germany's borders? In order to avoid this dilemma and also win enough living-space for Germany's self-sufficient politics, the Czech President of State Emil Hàcha was prevailed upon to "re-instate internal order in his land", which he did. In March 1939, the *Wehrmacht* marched into Prague, the oldest German university town, without a shot being fired. Bohemia and Moravia having belonged to a Germanic empire for a thousand years, was declared a Protectorate under German supreme command. Slovakia declared itself independent.

After marching in, and in order to avoid being attacked by Poland, the German troops had to take up defensive positions along the Czech/Polish borders. There was no help forthcoming from Russia, on the contrary, they were waiting for a piece of the booty.

Reaction from Britain was surprisingly quiet. On 15 March, Chamberlain gave a speech in the House of Commons saying, "although the State has given certain guarantees to guard these borders, these have now come to an end, having been settled internally. His Majesty's Government can therefore no longer be bound by these duties". Many in Britain did not share this opinion and demanded that a 'Note of Protest' be sent to Germany, as did the French.

Ernst von Weizsäcker, who was State-Secretary in the NS Foreign Office, returned the protest, defending the move as "Politically, morally and lawfully necessary, in order to correct the foundations of privacy". This drew enormous protest over Germany from the Press abroad, and one could smell gunpowder.

Although Hitler's own principle was to give the population the right of referendum, he did not follow his principle at that time. With the success of his latest coup, he set about removing the last and largest injustice inflicted by the Versailles Pact, the 'Polish Corridor'. Arbitrarily it separated East Prussia, with its 2.5 million population, from their fatherland. It was only by plane, or with sealed railway wagons, that one could reach the north-east province of the land, formerly West Prussia, by using a 30–90 kilometre corridor. The rail connections, meaning everything essential to life, were used as harassment, to the full, by the Polish authorities. For every authoritative party within the Weimar Republic, the division was an impossible situation.

Hitler tried to find a solution. He started to bargain with Poland by suggesting that a motorway and stretches of railway be built through the corridor to West Prussia, this being a long-term guarantee for the German/Polish borders. That guarantee was in earnest. At that time a strong Poland, as a buffer against Russia, was a necessity for Germany.

Poland's reaction was one of dismissal. Despite every political reception for German politicians in Warsaw, and friendly speeches over drinks, the efforts were without success. In the end, Poland's Minister for Foreign Affairs, Beck, threatened Hitler with war, should the existing statutes be altered. By March 1939, with guarantees from France and Britain, Warsaw mobilised for the protection of the corridor. The call for war could not be ignored.

Without inhibition, campaigns in the press started against Germany. At events for the masses and at parades, the cry "off to Danzig and to Berlin" could be heard. Propaganda postcards in extraordinary numbers reached propaganda centres, with an enlarged 'new' Poland, its borders stretching over Berlin and Leipzig to Lübeck.

Retribution began against German nationals in Poland. Out of five hundred schools, three hundred were closed. German cultural centres and associations were forbidden. Tension grew in the summer months, resulting in incidents, bloody clashes and gruesome torture of those German nationals. Under the motto "Harvest-festival of the Shining Knives", very many who had lived in good neighbourly harmony, living and working alongside the Poles, were without reason suddenly arrested, transported away and/or murdered. Out of 2.1 million German residents, 70,000 fled to Germany, reporting their shocking experiences to the German *Wochenschau*, or newsreels.

Hitler's speeches became harder and more merciless and with them the menace against the German population increased. Under the cloak of protection from the west, Poland became more pig-headed. At last, in August, came the shameful incident of Lufthansa's civilian planes, on their way to East Prussia from Hela and Gdingen, being fired on by the Polish Air Force.

For weeks, French and British Military missions had talked with their Russian counterparts in Moscow about the situation for Germany becoming more than critical. Just as had happened twenty years before, Germany's enemies were circling around her. In order to avoid this, Hitler endeavoured personally to coax goodwill from the Kremlin. They gave it. In August 1939, a State contract was drawn up with signatures from Stalin, and the ministers for foreign affairs, Molotov and Ribbentrop. The Red 'Tsar' drank to Hitler's health.

Seldom was such a Treaty sealed with so many malicious resolutions as the pact between National Socialism and Communism. The unbelievable had happened and the generals of foreign affairs, who had criticised him fearing a two-front war, had to wonder at Hitler's stroke of genius.

The Dutch watched this military leadership with many a worry about the explosive tension in Europe. Holland had reason to worry with its own army in such a desolate state, due to years of merciless saving, thus producing a grotesque situation. Dutch artillery had to use artillery dating from 1880, and the infantry had rifles which had been produced in 1895. The cavalry used carbines and sabres. Some hundred machine guns from the First World War had been left in south Limberg during the war by retreating German troops. Those then had to be restored. Many of those 'antiques' seldom worked properly, and mostly never. The machine guns, weighing a huge amount, were often just as dangerous for those using them as for the enemy.

Things were no better for their Air Force, the accent being on 'air' rather than on planes and weapons, which on paper, had the sum total of 130 aircraft, many obsolete. France in contrast, possessed nearly 1,000 fighters. A modernisation for their forces was decided upon, but as it turned out, far too late. Only a small percentage of the modernisation programme was achieved.

Because there were no volunteers, the conscripts, by drawing 'lots', were housed in uncomfortable and empty barracks for five and a half months, some not even possessing a canteen. The basic tasteless menu was cooked in the open air, in field kitchens or in cattle-feed stoves. The soldiers found their military education boring and without reason, their uniforms old-fashioned and impractical. All in all they were devoid of any sort of morale. They also had to cope with an unpopular image from the general public, being accused nastily of being 'murderers'. Very strong anti-military groups demanded the dissolution of both Army and Navy. The active demonstrators displayed banners with a broken rifle, with the words "no men, and no money", being their solution to the problem.

Only with the general mobilisation of 1939 did the government appeal to the brave defenders of their land to make sacrifices. It was much too late. Once more in gear, the training unfolded, but nowhere was there to be seen any hint of the expected and wished for military effect. Both the government and the army reckoned on the military help of both France and Britain, when it came to the crunch.

Till then the 300,000 strong Dutch Army would take up their positions behind 'the waterline'. Always their enemy, water was about to be their saving grace. The 'waterline' plan was designed to hinder any entry into their land by flooding the canals to a height of 50cm on the water-gauge. That would make them invisible, and thus ideal traps for tanks. They would be

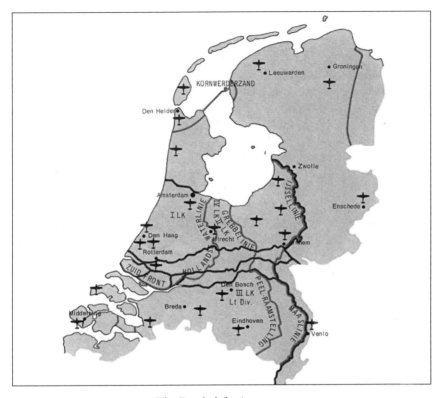

The Dutch defensive system

too low for the passage of amphibious vehicles and boats. Amsterdam, Utrecht, Rotterdam and the Hague were the most populated and important areas, making up Holland's 'fortress'. The cities would receive the maximum defence that such a plan could give. Concrete bunkers were manufactured and erected as quickly as possible, from Ijsselmeer to the south-west of the land. Many miles of barbed wire and trenches were to be seen in the rolling countryside, time however, not allowing for their camouflage. The bunkers were therefore noticeable for miles around, naked of trees, banks or bushes.

That was not the only problem with the plan. In various areas fruit plantations hindered the rotating barrels of the stationary weapons of defence. The government refused permission for the felling of the fruit trees because the compensation for their owners had not been calculated into their defence budget.

Returning to the situation on Germany's easterly borders, Hitler's demands began to take shape, with the non-aggression pact with Russia. However, his patience with the blindly chauvinist Polish attitude, that had been strengthened by support from France and Britain, was wearing very thin. He demanded a referendum under an international guarantee for the 'corridor' area. The advantages in solving the 'Macedonian situation' representing a 'continued peace' not only for Germany, but for the whole of Europe, being his personal view. Negotiations therefore criss-crossed with breathtaking speed between East and West in the last, politically heated, days of August.

On 29 August 1939 there were alarming news reports of strong rioting in Poland aimed at German nationals. London warned Warsaw to stop using weapons aimed against the increasing numbers of refugees wanting to leave the land. On the same day the hypocritical British negotiations were welcomed and accepted by the Germans. They failed due to Poland's stubbornness and Hitler's impatience. The Polish Ambassador in Berlin explained that he had no authority to act, apart from obeying instructions from his government that he was 'not to enter into discussion'. It was a fatal mistake.

CHAPTER 5

War

The dice between war and peace had now been thrown. It was on 1 September that fifty-four German divisions, supported by two squadrons of planes, marched over the Polish border. True, that portion of the German Army was not expecting to be there for a long-term war. According to their estimation, it would not come to that. But at 10 am, Hitler announced to his government in Berlin, that Polish troops had begun their attack at 5.45. The same morning, Germany had returned their fire, with a 'bomb-for-bomb' tactic. The 'local' war between two countries then extended at an alarming rate.

3 September was a lovely sunny Sunday. It was the day that France and Britain declared war on Germany. They created world tension from a central European quarrel into which they drew their forces from their colonies. After twenty years of peace, the Second World War now sprouted from the roots of 1914 to 1918, the First World War.

From the beginning, the two million strong Polish Army suffered very heavy losses. However, this did not give the western powers second thoughts. In the first twenty-four hours, the Polish air force was practically destroyed on the ground, the whole German air force making a massive lightning attack which was like a hot knife cutting through butter. Poland's cavalry, with 70,000 riders including the death-defying Uhlans, who had wanted to push Germany's 'cardboard tanks back to Berlin's door with their lances', had also been destroyed. Their remnants were marching 'to Berlin's door', as prisoners.

One cannot say that the success was due to overwhelming numbers. It was all due to co-ordination and co-operation of the motorised armed forces and air force, together with the impetus of the German soldier. It baffled the world. It had also given the field-grey uniformed and élite troops the Leibstandarte, i.e. LAH, their 'baptism of fire'. Those 'long lads' of the Waffen SS fought in death-defying style, in bold and sweeping attacks. With tough fighting, they pushed the enemy back over Lodz to Warsaw. At the end of the fighting, a *Wehrmacht* General commented that "the LAH had been an example, as a young unit", but had to add, "despite their go-getting, unabashed élan, they had suffered heavy losses".

Three days after the outbreak of war, the German population of Bromberg had to live through the day of the 'Bartholomew March'. That event has been described as 'Bloody Sunday' in the annals of history. The German troops found over 5,000 bodies, whole or hacked to pieces, on the streets, in houses, gardens and in the woods. The indescribable barbarity was not for publication, declared the Swedish newspaper *Christa Jäderland*. This was not the only case. Polish military and civilian murder commandos, and other lynch mobs, took the law into their own hands in other areas, and thousands of innocent people lost their lives.

Three weeks later, the fighting in the Vistula bend was coming to an end and hundreds of thousands of Polish soldiers found themselves prisoners of war. It was 25 September when Poland's fate was almost decided, that German troops marched on Warsaw. Radio messages, sent over two days, ordered the city to be given over to the German Military who offered free passage to the whole civilian population that wanted to leave Warsaw, in order to avoid unnecessary bloodshed for the innocent. German troops moved forward with less opposition, but Polish commanders were still waiting for the promised help from France and Britain. It was help that never came. The Poles received only comforting words, for what was already a lost cause. Warsaw, defended from an entire army with a strength of only 100,000 men, was attacked on the ground and from the air. Two days later, the whole army surrendered.

As agreed in the Hitler-Stalin Pact, thirty divisions of Russian infantry, twelve motorised brigades and ten of cavalry, moved secretly over the unprotected eastern borders of Poland, at the break of day, on 17 September. All in all, a total of one million men from Russia's Red Army moved in. They also took over the Baltic states of Estonia, Latvia and Lithuania, the Western powers refraining from declaring war on Moscow.

One has to ask, did two sets of rules apply here? Did the guarantee of help only apply in the case of an attack from Germany? Was it an excuse? Was it a case of a strong competitor taking up a position, exactly where he was wanted, in a military dispute?

France and Britain did nothing to help Poland. To allow Russia entry into Poland without intervention however, held a very large advantage for them in Europe. After all, their economy had not been endangered before those events. Russia's Minister for Foreign Affairs Wjatscheslaw Molotov declared afterwards, "an attack from the German *Wehrmacht*, followed by the Red Army, was enough to destroy what was left in Poland of the monstrous product of the Versailles Pact".

German and Russian officers shook hands when meeting one another on the agreed demarcation lines, just as the Russians and Americans were to do on the banks of the Elbe five years later. A joint German/Russian victory parade in Brest-Litovsk ended the Polish campaign. Then the suffering of the Polish people began.

The Germans declared that their territory would be ruled under a 'General Government'. With that, Hitler returned to the doubtful practice of 'colonial politics'. The occupying forces ruled, just as the former Russian

Tsar did, or as France had ruled Morocco as a protectorate. One could not speak of the freedom to vote or of a referendum. The Poles, having had enough of the suppression and injustice to German nationals, could not however escape the consequences. The continued existence of Germany, and the war which was to come, contributed to the hard régime in Poland under which they then had to live. That does not excuse it.

The Soviet Union pushed their borders a further three hundred kilometres in a westerly direction, annexing to the east Brest-Litovsk and along the river Bug, being a vast area with a population of 12 million people. On 'bestowing' Russian citizenship upon the younger generation, the male citizens were then promptly conscripted to the Russian Armed Forces. The NKVD, Russia's Secret Service, transported 1,650,000 of the population from that area to Siberia. There until 1942, 900,000 died. In 1940, there were already 15,000 Polish officers alone, in prisoner of war camps. They were shot. It was in the spring of 1943 that German troops discovered a massive grave area, twenty kilometres from Smolensk, in Katyn. It was the area where those Polish officers were buried and the blame was put at Germany's door. That lie was deliberately nurtured until the early 1990s.

After the "destruction of the most dangerous aspect of the Versailles Pact", to quote Hitler, he made 'moves' towards Paris and London. With his suggestions for peace Hitler did not understand why France and Britain wanted to interfere in a military argument between two other countries. They continued with their declaration of war, which would escalate with worldwide results. Poland had to be used to suppress Germany's competitors, was the ensuing political comment. "Was that so wrong?" was the question then asked.

The French soldier was already tired of the war and it had really not begun. For them, politics were a fraud and they had no intention of 'dying for Danzig'. As the first allied British Expeditionary Forces landed in Cherbourg, in September 1939, the sum total of a reception committee consisted of one naval representative, two policemen, a couple of old 'market women' and a fisherman. There was not a hint of the 'brothers-in-arms' support, as was expected at that time. The higher ranks of the French Army, sitting cosily in their concrete bunkers on the Maginot Line, made jokes about the British. "The British will fight to the last soldier, the last French soldier"! They behaved as if there was no war and their Allied counterparts from over the water had the impression that the French had already acquiesced.

The war now threatened Holland. At the end of August 1939, the government announced over the radio, as well as in the press and by distribution of posters, that special trains would take the assigned conscripts to their military designations 'somewhere in Holland'. The morale of those soldiers was mixed, the best of which could only be described as 'good'. Many thought that the measures were a false alarm and all hoped that Holland would be spared the shock of war, as it had been twenty years before.

An ordnance officer had his hands full, his duty being to take the incomplete uniforms out of their mothballs for distribution. At first sight, the combination of uniform parts did not give a uniform fit for a soldier defending his country. Knitting committees were formed in every corner of the country to knit warm socks and gloves for the army. The absence of uniforms and weapons was a catastrophe, the soldiers wearing any sort of civilian hat and carrying wooden walking sticks for weapons, when on guard duty. Five days after reporting for duty, sailors belonging to five 'older' age groups, were sent back home, there being neither barracks, cooking facilities nor equipment for them. During mobilisation, the deficiency in qualified officers was very noticeable. The general disinterest in the Army, nurtured by the politicians, had not produced one single application for the Royal Military Academy in Breda during 1935–36.

The Dutch protected the whole of their coastline with floating mines. The estuary of Zierikzee and Schiermonnikoog was closed to shipping, and the ferry service to Britain was cancelled. The Army placed explosives on all of the important bridges and strategic points on the easterly border. It was only when 100% completed did the population begin to feel a little safer behind their 'water-line', should the war begin earnest. The military however, began to doubt the measures of defence for their land, having been taken completely unawares by Germany's 'lightning' attack on Poland. They knew next to nothing about Hitler's newest weapon, his airborne troops. None of the western powers had airborne troops and only Russia possessed such units besides Germany.

Far behind the Rhine, on the Maginot Line, with its impenetrable system of concrete bunkers, one had the sense of security. Strong men such as General Heinz Guderian, the designer of the modern and independent *Panzer* regiments, were few and far between, or non-existent. So Charles de Gaulle found no one to listen, as that young army captain also suggested this strategy of modern warfare. His commanding officers, staid and wary of new methods, declaring among other reasons, that 'oil is messy, horse-manure isn't'.

No one from my family had been conscripted. My father had protected Holland's borders in the First World War. So now he was exempt, as were Jan Adriaan Matthijs, the eldest of the six sons at 21, and Evert nineteen years old, because he was apprenticed in the Merchant Navy at that time. The other sons at 16, 13, 10 and 4 years old were of course too young.

The whole family used to sit together in the evening sun on the terrace, throughout September 1939, to listen to the latest news issuing from the Bakelite radio that we possessed. We had no clue as to the future fate of the members of the family, as soldiers or civilians. How could we? We were part of a land which, apart from their colonial politics, had never been to war. Neither our father nor our uncle could describe to us how awful the reality of war was. So we found such reports sensational rather than fatal and we, in our naïvety, wondered at the 'sporty' achievements of this modern German Army. The continuous and very negative campaign against the Third Reich by the media, at that time, created a very defiant opposition in us, and in other young people too.

The Dutch fought for their official neutrality, in the hope of being spared this war, and at the same time played with fire. It would appear that foreign Secret Service agents 'romped' around Holland. Its General Staff sought military contact with the Allies without knowing of such contacts. This did not escape Germany's notice and they objected. They declared that France and Britain intended a military thrust to the Ruhr, using reconnoitred positions, not only in 'neutral' Belgium, but in Holland as well.

It was after all an open secret that the French and British received reports about Germany's Armed Forces from the Dutch General Staff, through its Intelligence Service. They had a very good source. He was Hans Oster, a Prussian Officer and a very influential major, but in counter-intelligence. He continually delivered to the Dutch Military Attaché in Berlin all the newest secret military plans made by Germany. However, he was always mistrusted by both the Dutch government and their Military Directorate. They could not envisage a Prussian officer betraying his fatherland and sacrificing the security of his comrades, but they used him, with reservations. One commander-in-chief, General Winkelman described him as a 'wretched traitor'.

The 'good' relationship between Holland and Germany, as neighbours, suddenly clouded over. The German Secret Service kidnapped two very active British intelligence agents who were working in Venlo. They were whisked over the Dutch border into Germany in November 1939. They spent the rest of the war in a German prison. Meanwhile, Holland's neutrality had been horribly damaged.

Although Churchill, then Minister for the Navy, had done his best to encourage the neutral states of Europe and the USA against the 'Third Reich', many retained their good relationships with Germany. Sweden enjoyed very many good business contracts with Germany, much to Britain's annoyance. Its iron-ore, for instance, was being continually transported by ship, to the south, using the Norwegian port of Narvik. After receiving no response to close their port to such transport, the British Navy mined the Norwegian territorial waters.

A very critical situation then developed in Hitler's headquarters. On one side there were those against extending the war in the north, but on the other side they were very dependent on the ore from Sweden. Secondly, Allied military bases there had to be avoided, at all costs. It was a race against time. Hitler won. He took the initiative on 9 April 1940 with his *Weserübung* campaign using his *Wehrmacht*. This 'one-off' campaign was brilliant in precision and audacity, being complimented with support from both Navy and Air Force. On his 'journey to the north' he beat Churchill by just a couple of hours, and occupied Narvik. Norway resisted, manning the 28cm calibre guns positioned in coastal batteries. But those were quickly overcome and the most important harbour was then occupied.

In the next few days there was hard fighting with French and British troops who had landed, supported by exiled Polish troops and joined by Norwegian units. General Eduard Dietl, with a very mixed bag of para-troopers, mountain troops and sailors surviving their ships being destroyed, held his position for weeks, despite the overwhelming numbers of the en-emy. It was not until the beginning of June therefore that the Allies with-drew their troops and Norway capitulated. Germany's 'spring to the north' was successful by a hair's breadth in preventing the Allies landing. Both sides violated Norway's neutrality.

The battle 'under the heavens of the North Pole' had ended successfully for Hitler, the *Weserübung* enforcing the undefended occupation of Den-mark. Its government saw the uselessness of resistance and submitted to the forced 'protection' of the Greater Germany.

While Belgium and Holland waited for an invasion from their easterly neighbours, Germany was worried much more about the 'compliance' of its western neighbours. They had allowed the Allies to march through their land to the Ruhr, rather than wait for an independent attack from them. Germany had to combat that at all costs. Both those countries made efforts to contact the secret services of the Allies. It was not only those efforts that strengthened the assumptions of the German leaders, but also the predomi-nantly one-sided defence measures directed towards the east. At a later date, that assumption proved to be correct.

Street plans could already be found in the department of National De-fence, as to which main roads had to be evacuated for the smooth passage of French/British troop movements. Not only that, French regiments had al-ready received provisional operation orders, in April 1940, for their advance through Belgium and Holland. The 'Siegfried Line', that wall of protection against France, was not quite completed. It ended at the Belgian/Dutch borders. The open flank offered itself as the area of concentration for the Allied Armed Forces.

It was Duff Cooper, later Minister for Information in Churchill's cabi-net, who said, "We cannot afford to have any scruples. We must take any step necessary, and without consideration of the neutrality of the land". At the same time, in the House of Commons, Chamberlain declared, "The campaign can take place anywhere else, as in the north, and with far more power and results. We British can distribute our attacks as and when we wish". Hitler decided not to give his enemies the chance of any initiative.

Plan 'Yellow' was being planned, designed to destroy the Allied Armed Forces within Europe, the main emphasis of that planned offensive being the 'seam' between France and Belgium, where the Maginot Line ended. To prevent the sequential access of the British into Holland, as in the case of Denmark, it had to be occupied. The breaking of 'Rights of Neutrality' were not considered by Germany, in view of the far from neutral behaviour, not only of Belgium, but of Holland as well. For the last time, and more than once in the evening before the offensive, the German Major from the Resistance informed the Dutch Military Attaché in Berlin, who in turn informed his government, of the exact time of the attack.

The Hague gave the alarm and the Army put their last defence arrangements into action. They blew up their bridges, built road barriers with felled trees, closed their ports, and ordered their ships out to sea where they could hopefully avoid an attack. Along the coastline submarines waited in ambush.

For the whole Western offensive, the *Wehrmacht* consisted of 89 divisions, amongst which were 10 *Panzer* divisions, with another 45 divisions as reserves. The Allies had 144 divisions, supported by Belgium and Holland, although with their deficiency of front-line experience, one cannot say that they could contribute much, their worth having been over-estimated. Although the German High Command held Holland to be a secondary theatre of war, 160 modern bombers and 240 fighters were to be used, in addition to transport planes. The Dutch Air Force as already mentioned, had a total of 170 machines, the majority obsolete. Their ground forces did not possess one combat tank which they could use against the Germans, not one.

CHAPTER 6

The War in the West

Hitler started his 'Plan Yellow' campaign to the west, with the following speech to his troops. "The hour has come, for you, which will decide Germany's fate. Do your duty! Go with the blessing of the German people".

On Friday 10 May 1940, this major offensive took its course from the North Sea to the southern border of Luxembourg. Weather conditions had caused postponements on more than one occasion. The 19th Army, with its 22 divisions, was under the command of General George Küchler. He had support from General Albert Kesselring's *Luftflotte 2*, who positioned himself as the northern flank of the attacking force to the west, through Belgium to France. With the first morning light, at 5.30 am, German 'summer time', and in an early morning mist, the first advance troops marched over the eastern border of Holland.

From their air bases in Westphalia, German bombers started in a westerly direction, at 1.00 am, in clear moonlight. The experienced pilots wove their way around Holland's searchlights and anti-aircraft fire. In a northerly curve over the Ijsselmeer, they reached their objective. At about 3.00 am, at a pre-determined point, they turned in an easterly direction, in close formation, over the North Sea to Holland. An hour later they reached their destination, i.e. Holland's westerly aerodromes. The transport machines, the Junkers 52, fully laden with paratroopers, had another destination, the important strategic cities of Dordrecht and Rotterdam.

Nearly a year before, on 20 April 1939, on Hitler's fiftieth birthday, paratroopers filed past in a massive military parade in Berlin, marching past the High Command, as the Air Force's youngest achievement. The world saw for the first time, this 'élite' troop in a new type of uniform. In military jargon they were called jump smocks, with aerodynamic steel helmets. A great many of the invited foreign military attachés present, at that parade, underestimated the efficiency of these troops in combat.

Despite Holland's military experts having seen the performance of Germany's paratroopers in Narvik, they stated, "We will skewer them on our pitchforks, in mid-air". The nearer the Junkers came to their target, the stronger the anti-aircraft fire became. For the heavy slow-flying aircraft, it was dangerous. Already with the first approach, there were casualties. The company leaders jumped first, followed in seconds by the whole squad, the last man giving the cry of 'Horrido', and following his companions with the elegant spring of a fish out of water.

Hundreds of parachutes blanketed the earth like a meadow full of over-large white flowers. Everyone was his own assault-leader upon reaching the ground, until later they stormed the most important bridges and aerodromes together. During this mission, many of those courageous young men sprang to their deaths. Although the majority carried out their orders, it was there that the 'Green Devils' suffered very heavy losses.

Within the same hour, another *Fallschirmjäger* unit overran the 1,000 strong garrison within the mighty Fort Eban-Emael, in Belgium's theatre of war south of Maastricht. Modern thinking held this to be an impenetrable 'bastion', at least from the ground. The Germans conquered the problem from the air, with two secret weapons. One was troop-carrying gliders, the other, 50 kilo hollow-charges to blow up the armoured defences, 25 cm thick.

The *Fallschirmjäger* had started from their base in Cologne-Ostheim and were towed close to Aachen, landing silently on the roof the fort. Within 24 hours, that Stormtroop 'Granit' made the bulwark non-operational. With dare-devil courage, they put the most important key position of the allied defence system out of action. 1,200 Belgians were taken prisoner and the advance into the heart of France, through Belgium, could now take place.

Many other strategies of war, some not so straightforward, were used to achieve a smooth passage, for instance, the removal of explosives from Dutch bridges. That was the immediate objective. The first groups, dressed as Dutch railway workers, went to work after dark. In other places, 'Dutch Resistance' escorted German 'prisoners' over the bridges, without being challenged. The Dutch suspected nothing.

There was another case, called a 'trojan-horse'. A commando group hid in the hold of a Rhine-barge, using the 'down valley' stream of the river Waal, to destroy the Nijmegan bridge. One cannot say that those methods were 'fair' tactics of war. The Dutch did not behave any better when opening fire on German soldiers waving a white flag, as they were approaching a bunker that they were guarding. 'A la guerre comme à la guerre'. War is war, was the motto at that time.

In our new home in Soest, we could not but notice the signs of war. Before the night had ended, we were half-wakened by the monotonous drone of plane engines, becoming so loud that we were wide awake. We went to the window, to see a show in the sky that we had never seen before. Uncountable planes flew in close formation in a westerly direction over our town. With the flight-path coming from the east, we were convinced that there was a forthcoming attack on Britain.

More and more windows were opened by our neighbours. They looked in amazement into the skies where the stars were slowly fading. In great excitement, many gathered in the streets to talk to one another, with rumour and presumption making the rounds. As darkness faded we could recognise the black swastikas on the tails of the planes, flying like migrating cranes to the west. It was not until we saw individual fighters, those small, lightning machines, leave the formation, that it dawned on us that we were the target. The planes circled over the military aerodrome of Soesterberg, six kilometres away.

Very soon we heard confirmation over the radio. Radio Hilversum broadcast a Cabinet-formulated proclamation, a flaming protest against the German 'raping' of Holland's neutrality. Wilhelmina ordered her people to do their duty, as would she and the Dutch Government. The Dutch Minister for Foreign Affairs had received a memorandum from Germany, with a long list of accusations that I will explain later. Who was right?

While bombers and troop-carrying squadrons flew at dawn to their destinations, *Panzer* and infantry regiments prepared for their advance to the West. The German High Command ordered the motorised units of the Waffen SS, as spearhead, to overrun the Dutch border forces. From their starting positions in Eltern-Westphalia, the 'Der Führer' regiment reached the river Ijssel, east of Arnhem, shortly after 7.00 am. Dutch engineers had however, destroyed the bridge in good time. Crossing the river had to be carried out using rubber rafts which they had brought with them. Without a moment's hesitation, the men started to cross the river under very heavy fire, reaching the other side and landing on a very flat, barbed wire barricaded riverbank. They suffered very heavy losses.

For the young Austrians among those men, it was their first campaign and also their baptism of fire. Perhaps the Catholic archbishop, Count von Galen, had a premonition as to the high price in blood that the Waffen SS would pay with that campaign. He withdrew his consent to give the troops his blessing, shortly before the fighting began.

Resistance however was not encountered everywhere. In some parts of the border areas, the war began like a day's outing in May for the German soldiers. Some of the Dutch commanders learned about the war beginning only hours after it had started. The news transmission, despite the short distances in that small land, left a lot to be desired. So the invaders only met farmers in many villages, on their bicycles on the way to milk their cows. They looked surprised, as they were greeted with "good morning!" from the soldiers.

As daylight came, people gathered on the streets to stare in astonishment at the kilometres-long military column. They sat on chairs to sunbathe in front of their houses, as the Germans marched by. Some of them, not knowing any better, mistook them for the British. Others, in their naive way, offered them bread and coffee, for they thought that the 'boys were certainly tired, having come such a long way'.

There were many, who having been influenced by many years of campaigns against Germany, were suddenly overcome with panic and burnt their anti-German literature. It was very noticeable, during that warm May weather, that days later smoke was to be seen coming from the chimney-pots in Holland. Five years later, also in May, Hitler's book *Mein Kampf* was to be the cause of the smoking chimney-pots.

Almost unhindered, the German advance was precise. It progressed rapidly, with only a few exceptions. Already on the first day, there was the impression of the disbanding of the badly equipped Dutch Armed Forces. The Dutch government confirmed with the Commission of Enquiry, set up after 1945, that the failure of large parts of their troops, in particular when having to fight against the Waffen SS, had been a catastrophe.

A totally unnerved Dutch general placed machine-guns and entanglements of barbed wire, behind the backs of his defenders, in order to prevent the panic-stricken flight of that 'pitiful and cowardly bunch', which was how he described them. Similar hair-raising cases of defeatism or neglected duty, were compiled in books of official 'war-reports' and skilfully detailed by the Dutch Imperial Institute of War Documents. In his research, a chronicler found that it had been Dutch troops and not the accused German soldiers who had plundered articles of gold from jewellers in the evacuated border areas. "One saw soldiers walking around with watches strapped on their arms, and trouser pockets full of gold rings". However, to lay that military 'fiasco' only at the door of the Dutch soldiers, in those tragic and critical days, would be unreasonable.

The results of twenty years of that 'broken-weapon' propaganda, by Government and press, had chiselled away the will to fight, and produced that catastrophe. All at once, the insufficiently trained Dutch soldier, the subject of defamation, should be the perfect and morally upright attacker and an example of steadfast fighting spirit.

Despite this, there were some units under the command of courageous officers. They put up dogged resistance, despite the German air-raids and concentrated artillery attacks, thus delaying the advance of the German troops. They found bitter resistance, for instance, from well-built casements at the entrance of the 30 kilometres long dam, separating the Ijselmeer from the North Sea, and hindering their entry. The bitter resistance of that strategically important barrier was the only military accomplishment that emerged from the three northern provinces. Like an egg without its shell and just as defenceless, the green lush flatland provinces of Groningen, Drente and Friesland, fell to the invaders. From Friesland to Ijsselmeer, the hunted Dutch soldiers fled on bicycles or buses, and in private cars. Those they had commandeered, in order to flee over the narrow, now congested end-dam to try to reach the province of North Holland, not yet endangered from the war.

As in Poland, the Dutch were then left to their own devices, with the excuse from 10 Downing Street, that "Unfortunately, we do not possess a flying carpet". In this precarious situation however, British assistance presented itself in great haste, in the form of 'demolition groups'. Their machines of destruction destroyed the Dutch harbours, locks and sluices, and burnt their gigantic oil reserves. But the ultimate form of their support came in the form of transportation of Holland's gold reserves and politically endangered persons, to Britain.

Although geographically in a better position than their British brothers-in-arms, French troops did not produce an effective military performance in their efforts to stand at the side of their Dutch counterparts. A joint effort to take and hold the strategic bridgehead of Moerdijk bridge, collapsed under the tough defence of German paratroopers, who had already landed. On the evening of 11 May, the demoralised *Poilus* retreated over Breda to Antwerp, accompanied by chaotic conditions. The inhabitants in the southern border regions came to recognise very quickly another side of those French and Belgian warriors. They were 'freed', not from the German invader, but from their gold and silver. It is not to be wondered at, that they longed for the German advance, in order that the plundering by the Allied soldiers stopped. They did not have to wait long. Hitler's tank formations rolled through the Ardennes with an unbelievable speed on a 'Tour de France', in the direction of the Channel coast.

Although surrounded by simple field positions, we were endangered, by being within distance of one of the most strategic and important defence-lines, the Grebeberg Wall. Therefore a total evacuation was ordered by the authorities.

Instead of the shopping in preparation for the usual Whitsun holiday, we hurriedly packed the 30 kilos of essentials per person that we were allowed to take for that journey into the unknown. Nearly ten thousand inhabitants, walked, cycled or used the bus to reach the station in Soest-Soestdyke, where special trains waited to take them to safety. Already underway on our bicycles, we ducked our heads, as high above us, we heard the rat-tat-tat of the machineguns, as fighters fought with one another, leaving lightning tracers in the sky.

My brother Evert had gone to war the day before. The events of war in Rotterdam however had caused him to miss his ship, in which he should have departed as an apprentice of the Engineer School. He shakily told us of his 'horror trip' when returning to Soest on a motorbike. He passed dead paratroopers hanging in trees, and the wounded from shot down transport planes, or those having made an emergency landing. 'Lady Fate' had held her hand over him, for we were to learn later that his steamer had been sunk.

In overcrowded and darkened compartments, our train journey took us hours on end. We passed through a polder that had been flooded for defensive purposes, appearing almost ghostly. Seldom with any pause, our train steamed its way over the miles to the North Holland province, into safety. In passing Amsterdam, we had seen a red horizon of flaming oil-tanks, set alight by the British, and illuminating the sky. The last station of our journey was the small, sleepy town of Enkhuisen, nestling directly on the Ijsselmeer. Our family of ten had to be billeted separately, the small picturesque houses not able to house us all. That was where we spent those May war-days of 1940, in safety. But our peace of mind was clouded with fearful rumours about the situation in Soest.

The German Military Directorate decided to send their most recently formed units, the Waffen SS, to the Grebbe-line. Just three days after marching over the border, they managed to break through the core of the Dutch fortress, which Holland's military experts had estimated would be their strongest form of protection. They believed it would withhold an enemy invasion for up to two and half months. After the attack, a Dutch soldier gave the following account of the German soldiers. "They gave a devilish impression in their colourful 'camo' uniforms, with stick or 'potato-masher' grenades stuck into boots and belt". That description was to be confirmed later by a Dutch officer who said, "with an iron discipline and unprecedented fighting morale, this 'go-getting' modern force, although being at a numerical disadvantage, were in comparison to us, far, far superior". Around 5,000 Dutch soldiers were taken prisoner at the Grebbe-line, having fought with two divisions against the 'Der Führer' Regiment. Those two divisions consisted of the cream of Dutch-Colonial troops, who with few exceptions, fought bravely, and with tough determination.

During those turbulent times a newsflash shook our land to the core. Queen Wilhelmina and the whole Cabinet had deserted and fled to England! Her plea to her people, 'to do their duty, as she and her Government would do', was forgotten. They had left the day before, being the second day of the invasion. On command of the mother-in-law of the active Prince Bernhard and his wife Juliana, together with her two other daughters, Beatrix and Irene, they boarded the British destroyer *Codrington*.

The population was shocked and angry at the desertion of the House of Orange. Demonstratively, officers tore their medals from their uniforms and soldiers threw down their weapons. It was an advantage that not all of the front-line soldiers were so quickly informed. General Winkelman of the High Command described the situation as "shameful", in referring to the desertion of those controllers of state, who had left the already burdened General complete power of government.

In contrast, we were to learn a few weeks later that the Belgian King, Leopold III, although capitulating on 28 May 1940, had not left his soldiers or his people, to their own devices. He allowed himself to be interned in the Laeken Palace near Brussels, according to his status and the interests of his land, and according to the conditions laid down by the 'victors'. This honourable and moral code of behaviour, was however turned against him after 1945, he being made responsible for Belgium's defeat. Worse still he was accused of collaboration with the Germans. He was made a scapegoat, and forced to give his crown to his son Baudouin. One can only say, 'unusual morals, unusual politics'.

A bridgehead was made by German soldiers during the night of 10 May. They had taken off from Zwischenahner Meer near Oldenburg, in twelve He 59 seaplanes, and flew into the heart of Rotterdam, where they landed. The heavily laden biplanes landed on the Nieuwe Maas, the river in the middle of Rotterdam, and in front of astounded inhabitants. It was what can only be called a 'suicide mission'. A battle flared around the most important Maas bridges. Very soon, the mission was given support from paratrooper comrades, many landing on the green spaces between the tangle of houses and the Feyenoord football stadium. There they gathered together before the attack. Speed was the order of the day and without further ado, they commandeered a tram parked in front of the stadium. They 'roared like the devil' through the empty streets, fully loaded, to the shrill ring of the tram's bell. They went to one of the disputed war zones at the Wilhelms Bridge. Not long before, paratroopers had sprung from the Junkers' transporters to their targets, ready to begin their battle.

Very strong Dutch resistance hindered the advance of the Germans into the core of the town. In order to avoid unnecessary bloodshed, the deploying *Wehrmacht* General ordered the Dutch commander to surrender, threatening air-bombardment if he refused, but also relieving his own hard-fighting soldiers.

The 'tragedy' of Rotterdam ran its course through more than one misunderstanding. The ultimatum was not accompanied with the necessary name and rank from the German General. So, that order was refused by the Dutch commander, who did not know that it was done to veil the strength of the enemy troops, nor that it was the usual code of conduct.

The slow-moving terms of 'capitulation', plus the bureaucratic conditions from the Dutch commander, led to a catastrophe in the end. The deadline of the hand-over, was cancelled however, as the bombers were already underway. Through insufficient communications, the taskforce could not be stopped.

An ocean liner that had been burning for days in the port, had produced a blanket of smoke for the pilots above, obscuring their view. The red flares, lit by the Germans to prevent them jettisoning their bombs, were seen therefore only by a few. Their own soldiers down below were also not spared from the oncoming bombardment.

In order to attack their target, but spare the civilian population, the bombers flew at the very low height of 750 metres, despite strong anti-aircraft fire. It was especially tragic that in one part of the town, where not even one bomb had fallen, damaged gas-pipes caused fires which spread rapidly through the old and closely built houses in a storm of fire.

It was a chain of unlucky circumstances which had caused the deaths of 600 innocent people. The Dutch Government however declined to prosecute, on charges of war crimes against Germany, after an investigation in 1947. After 1945, it had not been easy to assess who had caused the most damage to the Rotterdam Haven that was one of the most important to Holland. Five bombardments had followed that of the Germans, from both British and American bombers, that were far heavier.

In order to avoid the enormous consequences of further defence measures, which really were without hope, General Winkelman ordered an immediate surrender. He asked for 'Terms of Surrender'. They were sealed with his signature and that of General von Küchler, for the whole of Holland, on 15 May 1940, in Rysoord. In that 'five-day' war, 2,032 Dutch soldiers lost their lives, nearly 20% falling in the defence of the Grebbe-line.

In Rotterdam, the town which had experienced the shock of war in all its reality, the inhabitants danced in the streets with relief and happiness. It was only natural after such an inhuman experience. After a few weeks Hitler released the Dutch prisoners of war from a north German prison, allowing them to return to their homeland. There they were enthusiastically greeted as if they were the victors.

Paris has fallen! The headline of the *Hamburger Fremdenblatt* on 14 June 1940

The operations of the *Wehrmacht* then progressed, concentrating on Belgium and France. 'Lady luck' threw her dice to their advantage, allowing them to break through French lines, with an army of tanks, which in size, mass, manoeuvrability and power had never been seen before. On the fifth day of the invasion, they advanced into the rear of the Allies in haste, to the English Channel.

On 24 May, German divisions would squeeze together both the surrounded British and French armed forces at Dunkirk. There is no doubt that they could have either destroyed, or have taken, the whole of the British Expeditionary Force prisoner. Among them was the core of the professionally trained army. There were also 400,000 French officers and men, but something extraordinary happened, 'the miracle of Dunkirk'.

It was for friend or foe, an unexpected and fateful turn of events, as Hitler himself, in a love/hate relationship and as an admirer of Britain's Empire, who stopped the offensive, giving the British the chance to escape. An enormous fleet of 'sea-goers', large and small, rowing-boat and ferry, boat and ship, answered the call to evacuate the British Expeditionary Force from the beaches, to take them back to England and to safety. All that was wished for from Britain, was that they recognised Germany's place on the Continent. The target of coming to peace with Britain, in all honour, had motivated Hitler to spare the British, had however clashed with the opinions of his generals.

The English military historian, Liddell Hart wrote after 1945, that the German Reich had absolutely no plans for war against Britain. Hitler always believed in the significance of the British Empire's structure, representing world discipline. Germany had imagined itself as a very important partner for Britain. Together they could oppose the Kremlin's global machinations. Britain could have been an important ally to them, in a critical moment in their history, with which they could be content.

After the expulsion of the British Armed Forces from the continental mainland and the Belgian capitulation at the end of May, the second phase of the Western Offensive, the 'Battle for France', began on 5 June. Once again it developed into a 'Triumphal March' which was without precedence.

In what appeared to be a seamless combination between tanks and dive bomber squadrons, they advanced in sickle-like, semi-circular movements, closing in on the enemy forces, until they were surrounded and beaten. The German concept of *Blitzkrieg* had been perfected in the western theatre of war. Co-ordination imperfections and other mishaps, which had happened in the Polish campaign, were improved to near perfect co-ordination between Army and Air Force. The demoralised French could do nothing to stop the powerful advance of the German Army. In less than two weeks, the

German infantry marched by the 'Arc de Triomphe' in Paris, it having been declared an 'open city'.

They had a daily march behind them of between 50–60 kilometres, in the dust and the heat of a strange land. (Napoleon's troops in comparison, managed only half as much in a day). Only a few days later, Marshall Philippe Pétain, France's national hero from the First World War, asked for Terms of Surrender, after the occupation of his land.

On 21 July 1940, Hitler and his high command, waited to receive the French Peace Delegation, in the forest of Compiègne. The negotiations took place and were sealed in the same fox-red, railway salon-wagon as had been used on 8 November 1918 for the Surrender Treaty of the German Empire. However, it was certainly no repeat performance of humiliation as had happened on that autumn day. Then, the German envoys were treated with abuse, and already as prisoners of war, by the French Marshal, Ferdinand Foch. However, in July 1940, Germany's 'brave opponents' were treated with military honour, the negotiations were handled correctly, and with a view to the future.

Incidentally, it was the same Marshal Foch who had, after the signing of the Versailles Pact declared, "This is no peace, but a laying down of arms for twenty years". He was right. War had begun again 1939, but now, the roles were reversed.

In a campaign which had taken no less than seven weeks, three countries had been defeated by the German Armed Forces. Europe's coastline from the North Cape to the Pyrenees were now in German hands. However, that did not mean they had held the upper hand with a 3:1 superiority of strength in the west, which military experts had assessed to be the ultimate requirement. Germany had fought with 136 divisions against 144 of the Allies, and with 2,245 tanks against 3,063. Only in the air was Germany supreme, with approximately 4,000 planes in comparison to 3,400 enemy machines.

War was at an end in the west and the German people now hoped for peace. The fighting forces were rewarded with holidays and it was suggested that no less than 35 divisions be demobilised. The return of Hitler's forces from the western battle-zone was celebrated with a triumphal parade through Berlin. Every bell in the city was rung and an indescribable cheering from the population accompanied the column of cars driving over a carpet of flowers, from the Anhalter Station to the new Chancellery. The German people were overjoyed. In the few weeks of the war, very few had fallen, in comparison with the awful years of First World War which had cost the lives of millions.

On 19 July 1940, Hitler tried once more for conciliatory negotiations with his British opponents, in order to avoid unnecessary suffering and misfortune. But Churchill remained resolute. The war moved into the next round, Churchill being determined to fight for a 'knock-out'.

German submarines were having one success after another at sea. The Royal Navy suffered considerable damage and losses. In the first year it was at a rate of 10 to 1 to the Germans. Instead of concentrating their efforts at sea, Britain became active in the air.

The first bombing mission by the Royal Air Force took place on 4 September 1939, 24 hours after Britain's declaration of war. From aerodromes in East Anglia, the target of 29 bombers was Wilhelmshaven and German warships, which they wanted to destroy. Weather conditions were far from ideal and ten of the planes returned to their base, not having found their target, because of rain and heavy clouds. Three other planes wanted, mistakenly, to attack British warships but recognised their signals and turned around. One plane jettisoned its load on the Danish town of Esbjerg, being 180 kilometres off target through a navigation failure. In the actual bombardment of Wilhelmshaven from the other fifteen machines, five Blenheims and two Wellingtons were destroyed, from a heavy anti-aircraft barrage. All in all, they had only produced the minimum of damage. In broad daylight, those bombing crews were faced with flying a distance of 430 kilometres, from the British coast, in order to find their targets, which half the bomber force had not managed to find. It was a very disappointing beginning, luckily without heavy loss of life, but Britain learned very quickly from those mistakes.

When Churchill came to power, the air-warfare escalated. Liddell Hart's comment was, "the world has not seen such an uncivilised form of warfare from the War Office, since the devastation by the Mongols".

The 'Blitz', i.e. the air raids on London, began only after Britain had continuously bombarded German cities for three months. The first German bombs fell on the Island Kingdom from the German Air Force in June 1940.

Pointless restraint was at an end. At the opening of the Organised Winter Relief on 4 September 1940, Hitler declared, "they come in the night, indiscriminately dropping their bombs on residential areas, and I have, after three months, not retaliated. I believed that such madness would be stopped. We are now answering night for night. If the British Air Force drops two, three or four tons of bombs, then we will in one night drop 150, 250 or 300 tons. If they declare that they will increase their attacks on our cities, then we will raze their cities to the ground". He then secretly lifted the embargo on London.

In the aerial battle of Britain, the 'Battle of Britain', it very quickly became clear that the young German Air Force was not equipped for aerial warfare, particularly for bombing raids on a large scale. They just did not possess any large bomber-type aircraft similar to those of the British, or

those that the Americans used later against Germany. The bomber squadrons were very quick to recognise that they had a problem. They and their
accompanying fighters could only cope with a tenth of the range needed to
reach Britain's island territory, in which, almost undisturbed the production of planes continued, as well as the training of their pilots. The war, as
far as the German Air Force was concerned, was ill-timed, its conception
not having been completed. They really did not have a very good chance to
fulfil all that was expected of them.

Despite this, the air raids in the late summer and autumn of 1940,
caused fear and anxiety for the 7 million inhabitants on and around the
Thames. London, as the nerve-centre of the War Office, the Royal Wool-
wich Arsenal and munitions factories, with the Battersea power station,
commercial docks, warehouses and trade centres, was of a very high strategic importance. In the first attack, 306 Londoners were killed.

We boys often cycled to the neighbouring aerodrome in Soesterberg,
from where the German squadrons flew their missions over the Channel.
We wanted to take a look at those gigantic birds. We were just fascinated by
both flying perfection and technique. There were no security measures as
such and we were able to walk over the grass to the crews sitting in the shade
playing 'skat', to while away the time, the sun shining on the glass cockpits
of the He–111s. Somewhat amused, but always friendly, the crews talked to
us, giving information for which we had a real thirst. Enthusiastic and just
as relaxed as those heroes of the air, we listened intently, as they told their
stories of the battles with the 'Sons of Albion'.

With the extension of air warfare, the Royal Air Force began to attack
the small aerodromes in the Netherlands, including that of Soesterberg. Gigantic searchlights, shooting fingers of light in the night sky, encircled
heavy 8.8cm calibre anti-aircraft guns standing in the middle of our village,
for our defence.

The 'ack-ack' went into action at the approach of the British planes,
flashes of fire spitting from the muzzles over the darkened houses. We heard
shrapnel hitting roofs and tarmac quite clearly and night was turned into
day for minutes on end, from parachute flares, silently floating down from
the enemy planes. We saw flashes of lightning in the distance from exploding high explosive bombs and when the nightmare ended, we boys returned
quite happily to our beds. It did not however quite end there. The 'God of
War' gave encores, with a devilish plan, in every sense of the word, for the
next day. He had another iron in the fire with a delayed reaction. Phospho-
rous strips, dropped by the British, ignited in the rays of the hot sun, which
set harvest and hay stacks alight and which was a positive danger for us
living in our thatched roof houses.

The air battle over Britain was not decided with bombs, but with dog-
fight duels between the fighters. In this, the British had a clear advantage.

Although the German planes were quicker, they suffered from the handicap of only being able to operate for no longer than 75 minutes. As accompanying support, they could only operate for between five and fifteen minutes, even when over London, their primary target. This amount of time was definitely too short. There was no absence of death-defying courage on either side, the opponents proving to be equally matched in their mercilessness. Without doubt the brave Royal Air Force pilots in their Hurricanes and Spitfires were the saviours of their country. Churchill said, "Never in the field of human conflict, was so much owed by so many, to so few".

CHAPTER 7

The European Volunteers

Very many Europeans, at the beginning of 1940, began to see a new National Socialist Europe, through Germany's successes. It was an opinion being broadcast without restraint. The Bolshevik world revolution, but for some had been a binding element, had been suppressed. It corresponded with some people's opinions and feelings. Such people hoped for, and imagined, a new Europe as another Commonwealth of equal partners, the most competent on the continent being the leader. It could just have easily been France or Britain but at that time it was Germany.

France had been beaten. The British had retreated to their island and now seemingly cared only for their own welfare. Apart from that, how should sovereignty be reinstated for those defeated lands, other than by a reconciliation with the Third Reich, and with those who were willing? The idea of a new Europe provided many alternatives and solutions at the same time, or so it seemed, and the younger generation was in agreement. The shock over the surprisingly quick defeat of their lands left them comparing one with another, producing a plus for Germany. The enduring chaotic political relations, unemployment and commercial misery in their homelands could not be ignored. They had been witness to it long enough and saw with jealousy the German State's interest in the promotion of its own country's youth. Meanwhile, other countries were showing only the slightest interest in the stimulation of their younger generation.

It was certainly not just a few who were gripped by Hitler's eloquence and dynamism, many believed his frequent pledges for peace. Then there was also the personal experience with the German soldiers, with their correct behaviour in their occupied lands, which made an impression. "The perfect military machinery not only shocked but had fascinated many youths and adolescents in the German ruling sphere". (Hans Werner Neulen, *Europa's Verratene Söhne*).

For the majority of German soldiers, with their march into the western and north European lands, a new world had opened up. They found no hate from the Danes, Norwegians, Dutch, Belgian or French. They regretted their show of arms, deep in their hearts, which they saw more or less as a war between brothers. As the relationship deepened between each land, the populations were astounded to find that the customs, style of living and feelings even, were very similar to those of the 'victors'. The German soldier made efforts to give consideration to those who suffered from a damaged

A recruiting poster and page from a recruitment leaflet aimed at recruiting Dutch volunteers for the Waffen SS.

national pride, and in general wherever they could. The war with Britain was an unpopular theme with the majority.

It was with the formation in the summer of 1940, of the Waffen SS *Standarte* 'Westland', ordered by Hitler, that young Dutch and Flemish men had the chance to volunteer and show their willingness, by their actions, to fight for the new Europe. The call of the Waffen SS was not without an echo for Europe's youth. I will now take this opportunity to explain to the reader a little more about the term 'SS', without the usual defamatory polemic. Today, decades after their disappearance, this ancient Germanic letter of the alphabet, this mysterious symbol is representative of everything evil and wicked. I will permit myself to give an even more objective explanation to this 'myth'. For better or worse, the term 'Waffen SS' was, especially after the war, used as the slogan. Similarly, the title 'Criminal Organisation', was used to force into oblivion the enthusiasm with which Germany's youth, in fact Europe's youth, had 'hurried to the flag', to quote the résumé from an expert, Günter Drescher.

In the turbulent, political struggles of the 1920s and '30s, in which bloody terror ruled, the '*Schutzstaffeln*', i.e. SS, was formed. Joseph 'Sepp' Dietrich, Hitler's personal bodyguard, became its commander. At the beginning, this small troop wore no uniform. Their highest military leader was none other than Heinrich Himmler. After the NSDAP came into power, this small troop was the 'Elite of the Nation'. They enjoyed the title of 'SS Honorary Leader' this being the visiting card to High Society, such as ministers, high officials, managers of industry, and leading athletes of the time. Membership was on a par with a state award or medal.

To quote Helmut Treffner, from his book *Geschichte der Waffen-SS*:

> In comparison with the SA, i.e. *Sturm Abteilung*, the Waffen SS impressed at first sight, in their black uniforms in sharp contrast to the unattractive brown garb of the SA. Far more important was their reputation, which appeared to be as an unquestioning, obedient élite of fanatics who, to Hitler's admirers, also appeared to be a mysterious and terrifying band. The SS commanders in contrast, appeared to be of a superior intellectual class to their heavily-built and hooligan-like SA brethren. The SS were the 'finer' troop, their size denoting quality and not quantity, boasting only 50,000 men at the beginning of 1933, the SA having 3,000,000.

The troop budded and grew very quickly from this offshoot. They and the 'Leibstandarte Adolf Hitler' were joined by three regiments for special duties to the Reich, being known as the VT, i.e. *Verfugungs Truppe*, a troop detailed for special assignments, namely the 'Deutschland', 'Germania', and 'Der Führer'.

In 1940, non-German nationals were also allowed to join the Waffen SS, by which time the 'Black Guard' had changed the colour of their uniform to field-grey. Reputable Prussian officers, with a steel-hard apprenticeship behind them, had produced the former General Staff Officer from First World War and later General, Paul Hausser. In its formative stages, the military reformer and former *Reichswehr* officer, Major Felix Steiner, was also involved, training his soldiers almost to the level of top athletes, to think for themselves, to take decisions, and to be individual fighters with initiative. The very sharp cleft between soldier, non-commissioned officers, and officers, was evened out and with it a solid fighting unit was achieved.

In the first years of the war, the Waffen SS recruited only young men giving at first sight a good impression. If found to possess a first-class character, mental flexibility and very good physical condition then they were accepted. Those with a criminal record and hoping to avoid their sentences by joining the organisation were rejected, as were those with financial problems, unless they had been resolved. One's 'confession' did not play a role, nor were political convictions explored, even the sons of former Social Democrats being accepted. The field-grey clad men of the SS did not want a political army and, for that reason, removed themselves from Himmler.

"They wanted professional soldiers and not those who viewed world politics", according to Helmut Treffner. However, at the same time some traditional Germanic convictions were present and approved, not only by Himmler but also by 'Berlin dogmatism'. It was acceptable when being a cultural bridge from man to man, but it had to stay within certain limits. Hitler also rejected Himmler's religious zealousness. He commented to

Speer, his personal architect, on one occasion, "when we have almost achieved a day and age without mysticism, he, Himmler, starts it all over again!" (Quote from the French historian Jacques de Launay)

For the Waffen SS it was no problem, their very sober and professionally trained superiors taking care of this. "Much later, this cleft between the Waffen SS, constantly at the heart of heavy fighting on the front, and the inexperienced 'home-guard' could not have been greater", to quote Felix Steiner, from his book *Die Freiwilligen*.

"Produce a fully functional motorised division to our present quality and in six months!" was the order received by General Steiner in 1940, in forming the 'Wiking' division, to be made up mostly from volunteers from west and northern Europe. "This duty was a novelty, the planning of which in face of the heavy psychological fundamentalism, being a venture in itself," wrote Steiner later. That he was the right man, in the right place and time, was with the trust and devotion of his men proven, at a later date, with his military success.

The cadre of the new division was made up of non-commissioned officers and officers from peacetime and two campaigns. They cared for their westerly comrades in an almost brotherly fashion, without any signs of arrogance towards their men. On the contrary, frankness was nurtured and they moulded their young volunteers, who were willing 'to go to hell and capture the devil', into iron-hard soldiers, not only in a professional way but also as comrades.

Munich was the training centre for the first of the Dutch and Flemish recruits. That was a good decision. The town, situated on the river Isar, with its happy rhythm of life and cultural attractions, would suit the 'full of life' Dutchmen. But not all who applied were accepted. The very strict Commission refused the majority of applicants, only accepting 45 from the first 455 Flemish volunteers. Hans Werner Neulen wrote, "The European volunteers were, in the majority not adventurers, foreign legionnaires, mercenaries or private soldiers." They were from amongst the sons of diplomats and officials, from industrial families, aristocracy and high society, or gold medallist students from the Jesuit schools. In amongst those candidates, was the leader of a Belgian catholic students' society, with the name of Leon Degrelle. More than half the recruits, from 1940/41, were aged between seventeen and twenty-five.

My brother Evert followed the dictate of his conscience and belonged to those willing to make a sacrifice for his fatherland, in the Europe of the future. So he donned the uniform of the enemy, taking the opportunity offered to him by the Waffen SS and in September, arrived in Munich, at the Freimann barracks. At the turn of the century Ezra Pound, the American poet, had written, "when a man is not willing to take risks for his convictions, these convictions are of no worth and neither is he". Those were the words of this idealist who was popular in the forties.

For the Christmas of 1940, Evert, after three months of very hard training, marched through our garden gate in his field-grey uniform, a death's head adorning his cap and on a black arm-band, the silver regimental emblem of the 'Westland'. It was to be the first and the last Christmas that he spent at home, as a soldier. He passionately related how the previous three months in far-off Bavaria had been, to us his younger brothers and sisters, who listened intently.

Despite strict Prussian drilling, which extracted the very last reserves that the men could give, my brother was very enthusiastic about everything that he had seen, from his superiors and from the comradeship among those young men. He told us just as passionately, about the motives of his comrades and brothers-in-arms and those motives corresponded with my own opinions. There was definitely no connection, for the volunteers, with National Socialist ideology. Political lessons were given, just once weekly, for an hour.

For my brother Evert, it was very doubtful that I, his younger brother would, or could withstand this very hard training. I was not grown up enough, an opinion which I would not accept. I decided to follow him and nothing would deter me. My parents did not object although, naturally enough, they had their worries. At the same time they decided that a form of training with the accent on athletics would not do any harm. The war was not in fifth gear by any means. The majority thought that it would end shortly, but nonetheless Evert and I did not want to miss out. Our ambitions for a new Europe, we knew, would not be realised by lounging around in dressing gowns and slippers. A few months later, I presented myself at the recruiting centre at number 60, Queen's Canal and was received by German Waffen SS Officers, experienced in front warfare. They were a very strict selection board, every second candidate being rejected.

Ten days later, on 30 April 1940, the recruits had to muster at the Zoo in the Hague, with their cases, rucksacks and cardboard boxes, where they were given a farewell with an official speech and flowers. Only a few days before, I had taken part in my mother's birthday party, decorating her chair in family tradition with green leaves and flowers, then going my way after a happy celebration. The sound of martial music mixed with that of the whistle from the steam-engine, as our train pulled out of the 'Staatsspoor' railway station, in the direction of Germany. My war-wandering years had begun.

CHAPTER 8

My Training in the Waffen SS

Although the British Air Force had not produced any significant damage up to the spring of 1941, the BBC broadcasts exaggerated reports of successful bombing raids over Germany. According to those reports, the Reich's armaments industry had been destroyed and the cathedral in Cologne razed to the ground, although when travelling in the Ruhr, everything was just as normal as the day before. Happy farmers smilingly waved as they worked in the fields, smoke issued forth from factory chimneys and when driving over the Hohenzollern Rhine-bridge, the cathedral could be seen stretching into the sky, as usual.

A scene that never ceased to impress us was that of the Rhine banks, the 200 kilometres between Cologne and Mainz in particular, with its steep rock cliffs on either side, medieval ruined castles and the picturesque wine-producing villages, nestling on the river bank. When surrounded by the cherry orchards in full bloom in the spring, it was particularly beautiful. So was the region around Sennheim in upper Alsace. Our destination for our battalion's training was at the foot of the Vosges, not far from Mülhausen, our barracks being a converted, former psychiatric hospital. One of the seven large stone houses surrounding a towered building became our home.

After a welcoming speech, we were separated into companies and our colourful civilian clothes exchanged for the field-grey, Prussian, 'straight-jackets'. We took care that every button and hook was fastened, even when the collar was too tight and rubbed. Sport played a very large role in Sennheim, sports clothes being issued too and suddenly we realised why we volunteers had been so rigorously selected. 'Praise be to all that toughens!' being the favourite saying, which we were to hear time and time again from our instructors. They were all very experienced athletes, never expecting anything from us that they could not demonstrate themselves. This not only gave them a strong air of authority, but it spurred us on as well. Needless to say, by boxing, my first injury was a broken nose and it was not to be the last, by any means.

Throughout our training as recruits, individualism and common initiative were not wished for and were forcefully suppressed, our 'backs being broken' and carefully put back together again, piece by piece. We understood that we belonged to a military unit in wartime and everyone could not 'cook their own soup', but it was not easy at the beginning. It was the reality of being a soldier and our idealistic dreams being miles apart. We had to grit

The author as a recruit in 1941

our teeth to come to terms not only with our spartan lifestyle, but also the bodily and mental stress. On the other side of the coin, we knew what it meant to belong to such an elite organisation and so we took one step at a time.

Every morning, on the stroke of five, we were wakened by a non-commissioned officer with a very shrill whistle, who drove us to the wash-rooms in the barracks, to wash in cold water and a very sticky soap. After our hurried wash, we had to muster for morning gym, in a cold May morning mist in shorts and T-shirts, shivering through our teeth. After a trot around the block a few times, we were rewarded with a sparse breakfast of bread, artificial honey, and artificial coffee made from chicory, to us however, welcome and tasty.

So the order of the day was gymnastics, sport and theoretical studies. Up at the crack of dawn, it was not to be wondered at when sometimes an eyelid dropped, in a warm and airless room. A verbal crack of the whip aimed at one of us, woke us all and made us pay attention once more. Hour after hour, the commands rang out over the barrack-square from zealous instructors, mercilessly driving the panting recruits, in whirling dust and in the burning sun.

We had another problem at first, which was our 'schoolboy German', which simply was not good enough. The commands in Prussian-German could have been Spanish for all we knew. Only by hearing them repetitively, learning them off by heart, and learning the songs that soldiers sang, did this improve. After only a few weeks, we had no more problems in understanding what was said, or of communicating. Our German instructors had their hands full with us too. Our typical Dutch liberal mentality caused comments. There was a refusal here and there, instead of the quiet acceptance and wished-for obedience that was very important for the instructors. Our suitability had to be proved, and to fit in with their unspoken choice that was forming for choosing future officers. However, not all the 'ambitious' ones were chosen. Transfers and exchanges were made.

"Pre-conditions for suitability are, heart, passion, capability of solving even the extreme and unusual of problems, and of personal example." (Quote from Felix Steiner). General Steiner's comments on leadership, in 1942, on the Russian front were, "With the foreign replacements within the division, the diversity of mistakes that can be made in forming a close comradeship, will have far more dramatic results, than with a German unit ". He meant us. "The most important pre-requisite for human leadership, is untiring and enduring care from commanders for their men, ensuring complete faith in them and to convince them that he is their best friend. His men should love him. In particular, platoon and company commanders should always be an example to their men. When reasonable, thoughtful, and with a warm heart, then the stronger will be the solidarity and fighting spirit. I beg of all my officers, to nurture a human relationship within their companies, and I mean that most earnestly".

In Sennheim, we did not possess any weapons. We only had our bayonets attached to our belts and the 'front' atmosphere, naturally enough, was not present. It was our basic training, consisting of exercising, drills and

The author (far left) during training on a heavy machine gun

marching, by day and by night, which increased from week to week. Up front, the columns were led by our superfit sportsmen as instructors. At the rear came a medical orderly who marched with us, to give first aid to the 'new-born' in this test of maximum resilience and constitution! In searing heat, marching for anything between 20 and 40 kilometres daily, we no longer sang 'It's so great to be a soldier', as we marched with taut muscles back to the barracks. Our shaking legs took us, totally exhausted, through the gate, at the end of our strength, but not for a well-earned rest. Shortly after we had to muster once more, to the whistle of the orderly, freshly washed for the evening distribution of orders on the barrack-square.

The toughening process under open skies and in the lap of 'mother nature', did not allow however for time to appreciate the magic of picturesque Alsace. We could climb, for want of a better word, the 957-metre-high, Hartmannweilerskopf in the south of the Vosges for instance. It was clearly to be seen from our barracks, but only in the course of duty in a hurried march, and when bathed in sweat.

Sightseeing could only be done when we had permission for free time, which we used among other things to visit towns that were historic to the 1914–18 war. In particular, we saw the 18 metre memorial surrounded by bunkers, showing signs of the bitter fighting between French Alpine and German troops. Our barracks was no cloister and its inhabitants no pillars of holyness. Theme number one was the longing for feminine company, for the daughters of Alsace. At our age it was natural and for us no taboo. But weeks went by before our company officer released us to follow the 'lust for life', and not before he 'talked' to us for hours on end, on how to behave in the civilised world outside! We patiently listened to the preaching we heard, about our intimate bodily hygiene, and dangerous and doubtful sexual relationships. The language was sober, factual, everything in its place and being named. The guards at the barrack gates also had a part to play within the framework, for they inspected us before we enjoyed 'Happy Hour'. They saw that our boots and leather belts were polished like mirrors, that we had a freshly washed and ironed clean handkerchief, and a condom.

When, at last, we were no longer under control and inspection, we swarmed like bees into freedom. We explored our surroundings, singly or in small groups. Alsace was a land torn constantly in the past between Germany and France, between their cultures. It resulted in a split personality of French nonchalance and German exactitude. The inhabitants, in answer to the question as to were they an imprinted folk because of it, said that in the years in between, they had found their own identity, of which they were proud. The relationship between them and the Waffen SS recruits was nothing but the best.

Sunday was a day when we stormed the bakers. It was no surprise that the few bakers open on Sunday in Sennheim and Mülhausen were quickly sold out of their delicacies, cakes etc. We followed our instincts and found what we were looking for. After the doors of the barracks were opened we hungry soldiers were let loose, for the Sunday bakers sold their wares without the obligatory food coupons. Once our stomachs were filled, the 'attractive' lads in the field-grey uniforms then went on an amorous patrol. In the few hours of freedom at hand, it did not take long for them to make contact, even when the somewhat strange mixture of French and Alsace-German dialect, was a 'palaver' to their ears.

I had no problem with Annette, a pretty girl with hair the colour of chestnuts, who came from Thann. I had a stroke of luck, inasmuch as her older sister was the flame of my platoon-leader and her youngest sister a sympathetic ally and girlfriend of our sergeant. She organised many an exceptional pass to visit. The sisterly solidarity for romance determined that our longed-for meetings were therefore not confined to just Sundays. The romance with that pretty 'amourette' in the peaceful Vosges nearly made me forget about the war. Together with Annette, walking along 'lovers lane' and with the ring of her gentle Alsace dialect I decided that without doubt, the land of Alsace was the *pays d'amour*. The spit and polish atmosphere however, very quickly sobered 'this romantic' upon his return to the very unromantic barracks!

Decades after my recruitment, the description "the volunteers from Sennheim were adventurers and criminals", was to be found in an official war document. It came from a Dutch historian, who most probably was the only one who knew the truth, whilst turning chronicler and whiling away his time as an exile in England. As such, he could not have been further away from first-hand knowledge. One should remember Friedrich Nietzsche's philosophy that "The historian is spoilt, for he has the power to alter the truth which the gods cannot." It cannot then be said, by those who regard the duty of a soldier as defamatory, that it was the generation of the twenties who had kindled a war.

It was in 1966, in his book *Soldaten wie andere auch*, that General Paul Hausser, a man worshipped by his men and respected by former opponents wrote, "I respect the opinions of others and of authors, who write against the Waffen SS because of their convictions. I object, when their work is taken as "pure knowledge", "sober and objective" or "the matter fair and just", and is discussed or examined as such. In particular " when they gather only discriminatory material and/or compensate everything of a positive nature, with defamatory comments, which is unmistakably evident".

Within two years of the end of the war, unqualified and damning literature appeared, such as in the National Socialist newspaper *Het Parool*. This important instrument of the movement wrote, "since our liberation, there is a chasm of hate and contempt between the National Socialists and the rest of our people. The right to hate, when allowed, is the right of those who personally suffered under the occupation, or were actively resistant. It is noticeable however, that the hate was never as strong with that group as with the average citizen who remained untouched by the invaders. During the war the true resistance members, who chose their own destiny, themselves stood psychologically closer to the Dutch volunteers who also risked their lives, as they had done."

Our training slowly came to an end in Sennheim, which was not the case with the war. Although we could not say that we had lived like a god in France, to leave its land and people was hard; in particular, to leave the daughters of Alsace was very hard.

In between times, Germany's theatres of war had extended to North Africa, which was not particularly desirable. Often during the war, Germany's allies such as Italy, were not, as expected, competent enough to perform their military plans, either due to leadership or quality of troops.

Mussolini's 'sword' proved to be somewhat 'blunt', in his lust for expansion, and turned out to be nothing but a burden. Hitler was forced to give him military support in Africa and the Balkans. Still eager for some of the bounty, Italy found itself on the side of the victors during the last hours of the war in the West. After a successful lightning attack during three weeks in southern Europe, German soldiers hoisted their flag of war in Belgrade, and in the Acropolis in Athens. From Tunis, and nearly to the Nile, the Swastika fluttered in the wind, but only after Erwin Rommel and his *Afrika Korps* had rescued Italy's warriors from a military catastrophe. On the Mediterranean island of Crete, German soldiers were also the 'victors', after their paratroopers under General Student suffered terrible losses against overpowering odds of 6,000 Greek and 27,000 British soldiers.

Standing in the wings and before we could act in that war, we had another very hard 'Weapons and Terrain Course' before us, in the mountains of Austria, in Carinthia. Lendorf, near Klagenfurt was our new posting. In the summer of 1941, our train steamed over Munich and Salzburg into, for us, a strange land, with its Alpine folklore dress of felt hats and leather trousers. We had assumed however that we were destined for the Balkans. Underway and when stopping, the teams of Red Cross nurses quenched our thirst with chicory coffee at the railway stations, and wished us 'brave soldiers' a healthy return.

We had been impressed with the hills of Alsace, but we 'flatlanders' were overwhelmed with the gigantic mountain world of Carinthia. Standing in front of them was for us an alpine nightmare, one which cut us off from our homeland and was unimaginable from pictures seen in school. In comparison however to our makeshift quarters in Sennheim, our barrack here at the foot of the Ulrich mountains consisted of modern, two-storied buildings of pristine-pure cleanliness, and conscientiously placed against an idyllic background. Specially built for the Waffen SS, the exaggerated and monumental expression of power was missing. Only the huge dining room, which was also the assembly room in the main building, offered the appropriate martial radiance of architecture of that era. Gigantic wall-paintings of battles showing the new German army, decorated the walls between the tall windows and were certainly intended for the motivation of the recruits. I made a return visit to those barracks, used by Austrian mountain troops in 1959, and the wall-paintings were still there.

We were finally issued weapons and with that status, in Klagenfurt. Just as in other armies, we were to be sworn-in as soldiers. It was noticeable that none of the volunteers were forced to take those vows of allegiance. Anyone could then leave without disadvantage, if of the opinion that they were not grown up enough for service to their country and the responsibility thereof, or if they had reservations concerning the conditions of the oath they were about to swear. Their point of view was respected and without any attempts to persuade or convince from their superiors, they could at that point return home as civilians. After duties of the soldier, disciplinary measures, honour, oath to the flag, as well as other regulations were read to us in detail, we then stood under the military, penal law of the *Wehrmacht*.

The battalion was assembled for swearing-in on the barrack-square in groups of four, and flanked by small upright stacks of machine-guns. With our right hands raised, and our left hands on a drawn sword, in chorus we repeated our oath after an officer. "I swear to you, our leader Adolf Hitler, faithfulness and bravery. I pledge obedience to you and my superiors until my death, so help me God". It was done in front of our highest commanders.

The pledge was sealed with the tattooing of everyone's blood-group on the inside of their left arm. It was done as a medical insurance for a quick and life-saving blood-transfusion on the battlefield. However, after the war, it proved to be a stigma for tens of thousands. It was known as 'the mark of Cain'. They were made lepers of society. It cost them, in many cases, no less than their lives.

Now I was officially a soldier of the Waffen SS and my unit was the 4th Company of the surrogate battalion 'Westland', belonging to the 'Wiking' Division. This Division was one of the armoured divisions, equipped with rocket-launchers and machine-gun squads and we bore the burden of those machines. We had to carry them, which we did, willingly. In this way, we could stay together as the former unit from Sennheim. New members arrived in numbers, from other northern countries, such as Scandinavia. Things did not always run smoothly for our instructors, having to adjust to the mentality of those young men from the north.

There were problems right from the beginning with the blond northerners, especially with the Danes. They were stubborn, coarse, critical, and loved good drink and food. They complained about the menus from the military kitchens, the food not being to their liking at all. Now and again such criticism even reached obstinacy and defiance.

The German instructors did win their faith, after what seemed to the Dutch, with their strong national sensitivity, to be nothing but harassment and humiliation, which they hated. After a dose of encouragement, they were found to be approachable and, despite everything, showed a wide-awake sense of justice and a spirit of comradeship.

The Norwegians were to be more difficult, more earnest and contemplative. Once you had won their trust too, however, then you had it forever. Most came from villages or small towns from that sparsely populated land, having grown up in comparatively close-knit, down-to-earth communities. They were calmer, possessed a youthful, carefree light-heartedness, which within their military sphere developed their instincts to almost carelessness later, in particular where their own personal safety on the front was concerned. Those young men could also be a joy to their instructors and many were to show how much they were prepared to offer in their first operation as soldiers, and what magnificent comrades those volunteers would prove to be.

With the standard commands, the verbal chaos between the Danes and Norwegians, Flemish, Dutch, and Germans, was gradually overcome. Just as the French 140 years before, Germany had after-all a function in Europe and through their language, especially in the evening after duty, the communication 'barrier' of the new 'European Army' collapsed.

The language of weapons was foremost in Klagenfurt and demanded from those who carried them, the utmost from every man. We had believed, in our naïvety, that the military 'polish' suffered in Sennheim could not be improved upon. We were to learn very quickly, how wrong we were. It was all part of a procedure in supplying the 'Wiking' division with front-line combat-ready troops.

Our instructors were upright, strapping soldiers from the Ostmark, a new region won from the Polish Campaign, and who were often more Prussian than the Prussians themselves. We had to be professionals, and follow in the footsteps of the front-experienced soldiers and their praiseworthy actions. "Every soldier should be an athlete. He must run with lightning speed, jump as wide and as high as possible, throw as far as he can and march quickly, with stamina and staying power", said Felix Steiner. The target was to train a modern grenadier who was stalker, hunter and a fierce storm-trooper at the same time.

The privates shouldered the heavy 8cm mortar, dismantled the barrel, strapping the carriage, weighing no less, on to their backs. Others carried the ammo boxes with the rounds, accompanied by the company's heavy machine-gun squad. After an extensive march, we practised approaching the enemy, for hours on end, using natural protection, when at hand. We chose spots on the edge of woods, hollows or large rocks to erect in haste and with a practised hand, the MG 34 onto its tripod mount. After brief instructions from our instructor, we heard the command, "Sights at 250. Fire!" Twenty-five rounds of blanks per second burst from every barrel. Then we heard, *"Volle deckung! stellungswechsel!"* and we had to take cover, and change our positions.

When the exercise was not executed with the desired speed, 'gas-mask' practice was then on the agenda. Made from rubberised tenting material, breathing through gas-masks was twice as difficult when executing the above-mentioned activity! We thought that we would suffocate. We could not expect pity from our instructors, and received none, for we had to run like greyhounds as the 'Elite', be as tough as leather and hard as Krupps steel, which was for us at that moment in time, very, very unimportant. With the pressing weight of the weapons, we climbed the slopes, up and down repeatedly in the searing heat, to then wade in full uniform into an ice-cold river and cross to the other side, because an imaginary bridge had been blown. The torture did not end on the return march, for suddenly a cry "plane from the right", or left, rang in our ears and we had to dive for cover in a ditch, when one was there, or take flight into the nearest wood.

As a reward and as relaxation, when one could call it that, a visit to the cinema or to the theatre was arranged for the evening. Once again, after our evening meal, the company marched the seven kilometres into Klagenfurt. We found, that with the going-down of the burning sun and marching on tarred roads that the seven kilometres were not so bad. However, we had the seven kilometres to march back to the barracks, after sitting in the warm, dark cosiness of the cinema. Not even the magical Marikka Rökk had kept us awake, in *A Night in May*. After such an exhausting day our marching feet took us back, practically in our sleep.

The Ufa-films in Klagenfurt were much more to our taste. The 'films', from the projector on to the screens in the barracks, were about sexual diseases, for our education, and to shock us! Explained to us in detail by the company doctor, pictures were shown to us, mercilessly impressing the dangers of infection upon us. Examples from the First World War were shown to us, whereby syphilis and gonorrhoea infections were deliberately used as weapons, to put careless soldiers out of action. Somewhat confused by such drastic and extreme measures, in connection with loose sexual practices and their results, the impression made on us, as we young men left the class, did not go unnoticed.

During the day, we were once again to be found on the shadowless barrack square, exercising for hours on end in the merciless sun, which for us had nothing, but nothing to do with the acts of heroes. "Present arms!

Tempo one! Tempo two!" was to be heard for weeks on end, and we practised, and practised, until our presentation of arms was exact. Even our 'goose-step' for march parades was to become our special talent. We, the 4th Company, were to become the 'presentation unit' of the battalion, the honour of which, in the face of things we had fought hard for with our sweat. The punishing drilling in Klagenfurt, which tore at one's strength, the blunt but necessary hitting the ground, standing up, running to crawl over muddy ground in helmet, with weapon and knapsack, followed us into our dreams, although it did us no harm.

This bodily strengthening was to be our saving on the battlefield and was to prove the saying 'sweat saves blood', time and time again saving our skin. The iron discipline and growth to manhood that we had to learn, was to our good stead in tight situations and not only in war, but also in POW camps and the troubled years following the war. Even today, very many of the old comrades have profited personally from their strict military upbringing.

Naturally enough, our lives in Klagenfurt did not only consist of moans and groans. We also had our hours of pleasure on Sundays, gathering together by the well-known stone 'Lindwurm' fountain, in the 'old town' of the city in order to meet, this time, the 'daughters of Austria'. Well-groomed and dressed to kill, sometimes our caps a little too slanted over our very short back-and-sides, we 'lads from Lendorf' were eagerly awaited by the *dirndl*, the folk dress of Austria and other Alpine lands. That was how the Ostmark population got to know us, the 'volunteers' of the Waffen SS, and that was how we courted the young and feminine of their land. The soldier-lads, quick-witted and intelligent, with their unmistakable native accent when speaking German, were very certain of a response from the 'maidens from Carinthia'.

Our sergeant-major knew this too. How could he not know? He was from the Ostmark. He warned us every time we had free time against developing a serious relationship. He warned us that we were too young and about to be sent to the front. But he also told us with a grin, that there were never as many illegitimate children to be found in the world, as in Carinthia! It was said that the 'Lindwurm' himself would wag his tail, when a virgin were to walk past him, and that has not happened in Klagenfurt, 'till today!'

Despite the warnings, nothing was going to spoil our fun, including comrades, or those with contact with middle-class young ladies, who were certainly no novices from the nunnery! So it was that in not wanting to part from our 'flame', or end our enjoyment in our local on each Sunday evening, we noticed very often, that the time had slipped by and we would arrive at the barrack-gates later than was allowed. In order to avoid house-arrest, or even worse the dreaded extra drill, we chose a spot furthest away from the nearest guards and hopped over the barrack walls and crept in, in stockinged feet, with our boots in our hands, to creep into our beds. We escaped the guards and we escaped the punishment for such an escapade, when in reality it would have been character building and better to have obeyed the rules!

CHAPTER 9

Solstice in the East

The offensive named 'Barbarossa' began in the early morning hours, just before daybreak, at 3.15 am. The German Army had begun their march into Russia, on 22 June 1941. Thousands of guns thundered over a 2,500 wide front, from Finland to the Black Sea against the East, on that fateful June night.

At 5.30, a fanfare burst over every German radio channel heralding a broadcast from the Minister for Propaganda, Dr. Joseph Goebbels. In minutes, not only the German people but the whole world knew about Hitler's campaign against Russia. Supported by the Air Force, a *Blitzkrieg* operation was underway, with regiments of tanks which were to eradicate the Red Army that was massed together just behind their borders. The plan rested on speed and surprise, and it appeared to work.

Was Stalin surprised by this German offensive? "Yes", said Victor Suvarov, from the former Red Army General Staff. However, the peaceful impression that Russia had given was the lull before the storm, the storm on Germany. Stalin was about to attack Germany and everything was being prepared. The massing of his army was not for defence purposes. In his book *The Icebreaker*, Victor Suvarov states that "Stalin would have used Hitler's advancing troops to crush the whole of Europe, if he had chosen another time. Hitler however was too early, by two weeks".

The following was published in 1989 in the magazine *Der Spiegel* from an eyewitness:

> Hitler's attack coincided with the deployment of the Red Army. Suvarov's revelations confirm what was crystal-clear to every German soldier on 22 June 1941, in crossing over Russia's border. Their units found makeshift airfields, uncountable store-houses, divisions of airborne troops, and gigantic numbers of tanks. Woe betide us, had we waited until the Red Army had fulfilled this operation.

It was certainly no coincidence that over two and a half million Red Army soldiers, together with those from White Russia, were stationed where they were in Ukraine, at the time of Germany's attack. The *Wehrmacht* captured enormous amounts of weaponry, even in the first weeks of the war. The hundreds of thousands of Russian prisoners from this powerful army were proof enough to convince every German soldier down to every private, that the 'Barbarossa' operation was a preventive measure against an obvious act of aggression aimed at Germany. "Russia was in every

measure prepared for a western offensive, at every conceivable moment."
(Quote from General Franz Halder the German Chief of Staff)

Alexander Werth, correspondent from an British newspaper, and in
Moscow during the Second World War, wrote in his book *Russia at War*,
that "in his speech from 5 May 1941, Stalin stated that "war with Germany
is unavoidable, with the existing international situation. The Red Army can
expect a German attack, or take the initiative itself."

In Hitler's proclamation of 22 June 1941 he stated,

> The responsibility of the largest formation of fighting forces of all times, is
> not only for the safety of individual lands, but the safety of Europe and we,
> the German Reich, do not stand alone. Many states, who with certainty do
> not want to remember their former call to arms of yesterday, are today
> joining the crusade against Communism.

After Hungary had joined forces with Germany in Yugoslavia, their
army also took part in the eastern offensive. Italy also sent divisions to the
Russian front, proclaiming their unity with Germany. On 23 June,
Slovakia, after taking part in the Polish campaign in 1939, also appeared on
the front. Spain's government declared their sympathy with the Axis powers, allowing the formation of the volunteer division called the 'Blue Division', but declining any part in the leadership of that offensive, in
comparison with other western powers. Finland, although having conducted a doubtful winter campaign against Soviet invaders in 1939/40,
now operated together with German mountain troops in northern Russia.
Bulgaria and Rumania were natural brothers-in-arms from the beginning,
their relationship with Germany over time having become very close. In
1940 Rumania had to cede both Bessarabian and Bukovinian territories to
the Soviet Union, and now they wanted to recover their old rights.

The military worth and reliability of those brothers-in-arms who stood
under our command, was varied. Leon Degrelle, a Walloon and East Front
fighter, remembered after the war that,

> we had very noisy neighbours, the Rumanians, who ensured hellish noise,
> more than 20,000 lying on our left flank. They shot at everything and
> nothing, the unending 'rat-tat-tat' making the Russians wild and inviting
> them to retaliate. In one single night, the Rumanians used two whole weeks'
> supply of ammunition that the whole sector could and would have used.
> We lay in the defensive lines, and worthless and senseless counter-reactions
> were the result, in which we were involved. It was not war anymore but a
> disturbance of the peace! They did retrieve their Bessarabian territory and
> conquered Odessa too. They fought their way through to the Crimea and to
> the Donets basin, making a name for themselves.

Unfortunately, the Rumanians possessed much of the basic characteristics of the Russian, including a very wild nature and we had to suffer for their
measures of revenge on the prisoners they took and slaughtered. Nonetheless,

the German non-stop march brought them to Smolensk within the first three weeks of the war, then to the outskirts of Kiev and the Leningrad perimeter, giving the Russians a paralysing shock and causing panic and confusion.

There were many *Wehrmacht* generals who were convinced that, by the second week in July, the war was nearly won, nearly. However, it was not at an end. The American General Staff had already offered their opinion by 23 June 1941, on the situation in the East. "Germany will need between one and three months to conquer Russia". A week later the opinion of the British General Staff was, "It is possible that this 'lightning' war still needs six to eight weeks, before final victory". The euphoria of the German 'victors' infected the population of the annexed Baltic countries, Estonia, Latvia and Lithuania, who had had much to suffer in the recent past. They greeted the *Wehrmacht* heartily as liberators. Even in 'old Russia' the situation was the same in many towns, the people having had more than enough of Communism. Since the October Revolution in 1917, they had suffered expropriation, ethnic cleansing and mass-murder, through deliberate starvation, bitter poverty, robbery of personal freedom, not to mention the suppression of their religion and churches.

The expectations of the local residents from the Germans were fulfilled by the service given in the Smolensk Cathedral in August of 1941, and in churches that had been used as party-archives, warehouses or cinemas. "Former Ukrainian clergy donned their long-hidden robes once more, and blessed the people of all ages streaming into their churches". (Erich Helmdach, *Überfall*)

The Orthodox Bishop of Archimandrit, Bovis Jokubovski, thanked the commander of an engineer battalion for the resurrection of the Russian Houses of God, and the Cathedral churches, on 5 October 1941. He said, "It is our duty to give our heart-felt thanks to you, your engineers and Adolf Hitler and we will never forget".

When possible, farmland was divided and returned to the villagers for them to manage the field cultivation themselves. But that good relationship, nurtured by the front-line troops failed unfortunately, being absent later in the National Socialist Eastern politics.

At home, the churches in Germany were carried away with "the crucial course of military action against the mortal enemy of Christian Occidental culture" [taken from Statutes of the German Evangelist Churches 9 July 1941]. "The Reich's Christianity give you, our Führer, the guarantee, in these moving hours, of our unwavering faith and willingness". In the edition from 10 August 1941, the newspaper *Kirchliche Rundschau*, produced for the entire group of Evangelist churches, it was stated that they prayed for a victorious result in the battle in the east. "Dear God, we praise you, we thank you for our leader, and for the men that you have given us to lead our army to victory".

Following the typical spirit of today's political atmosphere, they now vehemently deny that they gave their blessing then, in fact they now try to convince us that they rejected National Socialism. It was definitely not as they state. To quote, "It is true that there were exceptions, but in the majority, many influential men of the church, or circles of both confessions, definitely supported the Third Reich. Dr. Joseph Goebbels, Minister for Propaganda, distributed worldwide, every printed declaration of support appearing in church publications." (from Nicolaus von Preradovich and Joseph Stingl's *Gott segne den Führer*).

Neutral States also supported Germany's 'just war' alongside the church, such as Turkey, who put it in 'black and white' in a memo which it sent to the Ministry of Foreign Affairs, on 22 June, shortly before a German/Turkish Alliance had been formed. There were groups in Britain and America too who welcomed and encouraged the bravery and audacity of Germany in tackling Stalin.

The governments in London and Washington however saw things differently. Due to the pressure of the situation, Britain agreed to an alliance with Stalin, not with foresight, for after the war Churchill was to say, "we slaughtered the wrong swine". Stalin received gigantic amounts of war-material from the western Allies that were despatched over the Persian-Gulf and the polar sea routes. From reports from the United States War Ministry, Stalin received during WWII enough war material to equip 200 divisions, including 400,000 lorries and 1,500 planes, for his Red Army. The very alliance between Capitalism and Communism was a very unnatural one. It ended, after the war, in a 'cold war' that lasted decades.

In deciding to join the fight against Communism and with their enthusiasm for a new Europe, thousands of young foreign 'volunteers' enlisted for the Waffen SS in 1941. 135,000 men all-in-all, from the western European lands in the four years of the Russian campaign. They were made up of 55,000 Dutch, the largest portion, followed by 23,000 Flemish and 20,000 French and as many Walloons. Among those volunteers, were the sons of the Norwegian Nobel prize-winner for Literature, Knut Hamsum and Iceland's President Sveinn Björnson. By the end of the war, 1,123,700 non-German nationals had served in the German *Wehrmacht* (quoted from Hans W-Neulen *An Deutscher Seite*), statistics that are not generally known, never broadcast, and are even suppressed.

The thought of a new crusade fascinated not only National Socialists but also the conservative and ultra-clerical in the occupied lands. They marched with the enemy in their homelands and in doing so were bound closer together with them, than with the anti-Christians in the Soviet Union.

CHAPTER 10

On the Eastern Front

Autumn unfolded over Klagenfurt as the successful attack on Russia was coming to an end. The hay was dried in the summer sun and stacked in the hay-barns, and the summer having been a good one offered a very good harvest. The colours of the flowers paled and 'Mother Nature' prepared herself for a winter sleep. However, sleep and leisure were begrudged us soldiers of the Lendorf Battalion. For us, life meant training and drilling, and drilling and training, repeating everything that we had already learned. It was cemented with visits from officers and the non-commissioned, who were posted away from the Russian front from the Wiking Division. We listened intently and in wonder to the decorated soldiers as they related to us their experiences and encounters against the Soviets. Soldiers were constantly posted to the Division in Russia, including those who were in Munich-Freimann before us and who had ended their training in Klagenfurt.

The send-off of the graduates of war, with their thirst for action, was indeed a wet one, with 'elbow exercise' in our canteen, as we wished them "all the best", including my brother Evert. It was not a sad send-off. On the contrary, we made it a celebration in festive mood, giving vent to our high spirits. We were really jealous, and desperate to be included in the Victory Parade to take place on Red Square in Moscow!

The volunteers from the lands of Europe had become not only companions, but very good friends. A friend of mine, also Dutch, was Robby Reilingh from Groningen. I looked upon this twenty-year-old student almost as a brother, our friendship beginning in the first few days in Sennheim. All-in-all we were a happy bunch of wide-awake young men, who could and did laugh a lot about ourselves, as much as our daily lives allowed. We were always ready for a joke.

We didn't usually take it too seriously either when something went awry, or we overstretched ourselves. Nor were we nasty with one another, or ridiculed each other when one of us found ourselves in an embarrassing situation. We laughed it off, in a friendly manner mostly, as in one particular exercise copied from the *Fallschirmjäger* divisions. In rows they fell forwards on to the grass, necessary exercise for their parachute jumps, with their feet together and hands held behind their backs. We did too, or at least we tried. This sporty exercise was not easy and we fell around laughing. It was not everyone's cup of tea. It cost us more than a little pluck and/or a dislocated joint or two.

Another exercise produced a far more serious and macabre scorn in us. One of our chums turned out to be a 'walking disaster' when practising with chemical agents. We had practised this exercise time and time again, in the open air. The time came however, for us to practice changing the filter on our gas-masks in an air-tight room. We felt more than a little apprehension. Nervous tension caused our chum to fumble with the screw when changing the filter and in that moment he forgot to hold his breath! Our nervous friend had to hastily leave the room, with streaming eyes, coughing and spluttering endlessly.

Our hour of probation eventually came. Over the summer months the Wiking Division, in stubborn fighting, had pushed the enemy back to the south of the western front. In September of 1941 they were in Dnjepr. In the hundreds of miles that lay behind them, the Division had suffered very heavy losses and needed replacements of highly-trained combat-ready men. The enemy had proved to be unexpectedly tough opponents, not to be compared with the Poles in 1939, or the French in 1940. The first wave of volunteers had already proved themselves in the field. With their front experiences, in the tank and motorised divisions under General von Kleist, they had proved that they could be relied upon. The Dutch, Danish, Norwegian and Finnish soldiers had earned themselves a reputation among the General Staff. The task of the second wave was "to hold the headway made by their predecessors", wrote Felix Steiner. We were the second wave, the graduates of the SS surrogate battalion 'Westland' from Klagenfurt.

The days became shorter and frost was in the air as the first powdery snow fell on the rooftops. The roads were somewhat slippery too. Marching with our backpacks, we slipped now and again on the cobbles, as we entered the old town. In the early morning hours the battalion marched from Lendorf to Klagenfurt. The route went over the long Feldkirchener road, leading to the main railway station. As we marched we took a long, last look at the Lindworm fountain. The picture-book houses with their arcades and courtyards were imprinted on our minds. Passers-by waved to us, as company after company we entered the railway station, the last 'native' station for us. At the station there was a lively throng. The girlfriends and sweethearts made in Lendorf, were waiting with bouquets of autumn flowers, usual for a farewell.

They stood in sharp contrast to the parents of soldiers, who lived near enough to have made the journey of farewell to their sons before they made their way to the front. Farewell parcels, containing sweet delicacies and something warm to wear, were presented by many a helpless and weeping mother, to sons who tried to comfort them with promises that they would see one another again soon. It was a moving scene.

We 'volunteers' from the western and north European countries did not have this problem. Our parents were too far away to travel to southern

Carinthia. This moving scene came to an end, with the increasing noise of the waiting steam-engine. We had to take our seats, and settle down in one another's trusted company. The waving girlfriends and family members disappeared in a cloud of white steam, as the train slowly pulled away to the shrill whistle of the porter.

It was to be a journey into the unknown, into a strange world. It was to be the world of war and a powerful crusade in which we were small fish. Some made themselves comfortable, lying in the luggage racks over the seats in the compartment. Soon after the departure of the train some others were speculating as to our destination. The wheels rolled over the tracks with a monotonous rhythm, so monotonous that it silenced the speculation. Few noticed the gradual change in the countryside after leaving Carinthia. We travelled slowly from the west to the east, leaving behind a friendly and magical idyll.

We passed the Wörthersee, a lake in which we had bathed, and picturesque farmhouses, where long rows of maize cobs were hanging to dry. Later in the evening, in Vienna, we crossed the Danube. Shortly after, we left behind us the Ostmark and Austria, a land then united with the Pan-German Reich. Bratislava was the next borderless checkpoint. Not long after, we passed through the Protectorate of Bohemia and Moravia, an unspoiled land in the middle of Europe, set between the forests of Bohemia and Tatra.

In the grey, early morning hours we reached Poland. Poorly-built shacks for houses, built upon clay or sandy soils, flashed by the window. Two years before, Poland had been the prelude and the first eastern theatre of the Second World War. Now it was the central government of the Germans. The Slavic people, from the plains between the Baltic and the Caparthian mountains, who were so often separated in the past, were now divided and mercilessly ruled in old colonial style, by both Hitler and Stalin. Krakau, i.e. Cracow, was to be our next in-between stop, *en route* to the Russian front. We stayed there for some weeks, for an unknown reason. At least if our officers knew, they kept it to themselves. We were found quarters in a former Polish barrack, old, uncomfortable and plagued with fleas!

Cracow, the old Polish seat of kings, was now the capital of the General Government, which in the six years of war had hardly been damaged. Poverty, however, had become rife and could not be overlooked on our trips into town. Polish prisoners of war, working for the local farmers, had much better living conditions than anyone else. Those in the Officers' camp could study, and even further their education. Who ever believed that the lull before the storm was going to be a holiday, was very wrong. Our old lifestyle ruled our lives once more with old drills, old rules and control. Even the payment in *zloty* of the Polish girls, engaged in the *Wehrmacht* brothel, was controlled by a sergeant-major. He resided in the rooms of the former house-master and inspected our pay books, and our condoms too.

During that time our battalion was to receive a special duty, that of bodyguards, so to speak. We had to ensure the safe passage of the Führer's train as it passed through Cracow. We stood for hours on end on either side of the railway tracks, in the biting cold, with loaded carbines, waiting for the night train. The Commander-in-Chief and his staff had their quarters in two locomotives and it was our duty to save them from any planned assassination attack. Our superiors hid themselves in the darkness and randomly threw stones to check that we were awake, and that we reacted. At around midnight the rolling stock with the curious name of *Amerika* (from 1943 renamed the *Brandenburg*) with the two locomotives and two armoured anti-aircraft wagons, raced by in a white cloud of flying snow. Had he even been on the train?

Our own 'front-express' was on the rails again and heading in an easterly direction. Some of our master-sergeants had already been sent to the Wiking Division, which had lost many men in the fighting on the southern Russian front, in the Donets basin. We travelled alongside the river Vistula. Dams were to be seen in low-lying stretches, built against flooding. That is all that one can say for the Poles and the care of their river. It was gradually filling with sand in places, and clear to see. Two years before, many railway and pedestrian bridges across the river had been destroyed and replaced with provisional ones, built by German Army engineers.

The journey was unending and it was hours before we crossed over the San, an arm of the Vistula, and reached Lemberg. The German/Soviet demarcation-line was in that area somewhere, but there were no obvious signs of it. In fact it was very hard for us to orientate ourselves, with former state borders having disappeared in the fury of war, and former territories having been returned to the Reich. Our train had no corridor and so we had no room for movement. The compartments were small, airless and sticky. It was no wonder that we were tired and mostly disinterested in our surroundings.

The countryside through which we travelled was really no different to the eastern Polish plains. In the so-called 'endless Soviet paradise', the very thinly populated areas and colourless view offered only a lonely farmhouse now and again. It was depressing. The lights went out for the night, but for many of us sleep did not come in the darkened compartment. The continuous and monotonous sounds of the train intruded and disturbed us, making it impossible to sleep. In that twilight sleep our minds nudged the pangs of home-sickness, and a premonition or two. Innermost apprehensions came to the fore, leading to doubts as to our courage. There was nothing for it but to conquer the creeping depression, take the bull by the horns, stand by our voluntary sacrifice, and follow the dictates of our conscience.

With daybreak and our soldiers' songs, we were our old selves especially after our first fight with snowballs. Yet again our journey had been broken for some unknown reason. We remained for several hours in a half-destroyed railway station. Our opponents were Hungarians, but our 'fight' between the railway tracks with those sons of the Hungarian plains, was jovial and bloodless. Their train had been held up for some days. While we waited men who were obviously prisoners, from the look of their tattered clothes, whether Jewish or Russian being unknown to us, cleaned the compartment. They used over-large and primitive brooms, and were under the supervision of older, uniformed men. In very crude tones, they drove the prisoners to hurry. When those in our compartment were denied the crusts of bread left by us, and which we were not going to eat, it annoyed us, to the extent that one of our *SS-Untersturmführer* tore the overseer off a strip, for his inhuman behaviour. It was our very first experience of the fate of prisoners. Was that in store for everyone, for us too?

Once more underway, we saw wooden huts along the line, housing armed *Wehrmacht* guards. We also saw a message for the homebound trains along the side of the track. "Say 'Hallo' to the Rhine for us", was written in black stones. The further east that our train took us, the colder it became, especially for those guards on the running-board outside the compartments, and in the icy wind of the moving train. They were on the look-out for partisan activity. Tracks and bridges were very often mined and so our locomotive pushed a goods-wagon filled with sand in front of it. The theory was that it softened the impact of an explosion and lessened the damage to train and men. Some days before, the guards of a transport train travelling on the same line, shot warning shots into the air to warn the driver of a visible explosive charge. But instead of stopping he accelerated, in the belief that partisans were attacking. Thirty men lost their lives in that explosion.

The extent of what we were to see in Tarnapol was unavoidable. The signs of encirclement and the bloody battle of the summer months were a taste of what was to come. It was almost like seeing a newsreel, with scenes of that legendary battle opening up before our eyes, in all its original bitter and savage reality. There were uncountable numbers of burnt-out tanks and other war machinery. Outlying destroyed villages showed the bitter fighting that had taken place in the area between the Carpathian mountains and the Pripyet marshes.

We then had another break in our journey for no explainable reason. It lasted for three weeks, in Vinnitsa, a middle-sized town in Ukraine. The population was passive and resigned, showing us no hostility. The reason for that undoubtedly was the social misery that they had had to endure under Stalin. One could not fail to see the utter poverty. You were not able to distinguish the men from the women on the streets. They all wore the same grey, ugly, wadded clothes, which they held together with string or suchlike. There were no buttons and no shoes. Leather shoes and fur boots were seldom to be seen. Most wore the 'local shoe', made from sail-cloth or raffia.

The poorest of the poor had bound a piece of an old car tyre to the soles of their feet. Those conditions were hardly the outcome of the first few months of the war. In a fatal light it illustrated a classless State and was in sharp contrast to the 'Soviet paradise' as loudly proclaimed by the Russians.

The lack of housing in Vinnitsa was also very noticeable, as was probably true in the whole of the Soviet Union. For instance, we knew of a three-roomed house built in the twenties. The largest of its rooms measured five metres by five metres, in which no fewer than nine people were housed, not all of the same family. They all lived, slept, cooked and ate in that room, cooking on a paraffin-stove. There was a married couple with two small children, a bachelor engineer, a 'worker', and an older woman with two unmarried daughters.

Under those living conditions and as the product of the Bolshevik Regime, it is not to be wondered at that sexual morals sank to the lowest imaginable, without boundaries or control. The situation grew out of all proportion. It had its roots in inhumane politics. Year after year thousands of illegitimate children, in exploding numbers, without parents or state to look after them, gradually became a danger to the land and its people. We could assess it for ourselves. The picture was of orphans dressed in rags, without having washed or bathed for months on end, with boils, other skin infections and festering wounds. All of it made a mockery of everything and everyone who possessed a healthy, hygienic and normal standard of life.

In large numbers, those bands of orphans wandered from town to town to beg, steal and rob, in order to keep themselves 'above water'. Already in 1941, the numbers could be assessed by non-Russian experts at some millions. The state that had caused the catastrophe, sought to solve the problem with a law that permitted youngsters from the age of twelve to be given the death sentence. As a result, the gangs armed themselves and then battled with the police. Such scenes made a very grave impression upon us. It confirmed to every one of us that Communism had to be repulsed at all costs. It also justified our presence in that land.

My friend Robby had a close contact with a Russian family, or perhaps it would be better to say, with the daughter of the family. He was very much enamoured. I had orders to accompany him on his visits and, more often than not, a loaf of bread found its way into the very modest wooden house of the family. That charitable 'fraternisation' released a very moving response.

To digress briefly, I would point out that six months later, in the middle of July 1942, and with the advance of the southern army groups, Hitler's headquarters was moved to fifteen kilometres north-east of the town and on the road to Zhitomir. The new headquarters named 'Werwolf', was nearer to the front-line and ensured a far more efficient direction and organisation of troop movement, formation and liaison.

Underway, once more, after our stay in Vinnitsa, we journeyed undisturbed, reaching the town of Uman, in the centre of Ukraine. It was not far from the airfield. We were in primitive but warm wooden barracks. Suddenly everything was hurried. Our transport to the front was no longer overland by train, but by plane.

However, bad weather delayed the flights. Day after day we marched with a full pack on our backs to the airfield, but could not take off. As the bad weather cleared, Junkers 52s of the transport squadron landed one after another, on the snow-covered airfield. Marching to the planes, we noticed two wolves, totally unimpressed or disturbed by our presence, until the noise of the starting engines drove them back into the forest.

There was a weight problem to be solved, much to our disgust, by being told that our food rations had to be left behind! We, with our insatiable appetites, were indignant at such a suggestion, and they were not going to do that to us. We solved that problem by making short work of our rations very quickly. Despite the hard and icy-cold sausages we did not give a thought to the weight, inside or outside our stomachs.

Like excited schoolboys waiting to board the bus, we finally took our places in the *Tante Ju*, Auntie Ju as they were called, the word *Tante* not always having a nice meaning. We had to sit on our rucksacks. The seats had been removed because of our numbers, but we didn't mind this lack of luxury for were we not flying at the cost of the State? With their 600PS, BMW star motors, the Junkers prepared for take-off. It was not only the motors that started to throb. Many hearts of us first-time flyers started to beat in time with the engines too. It was a sluggish take-off for a Ju, loaded to full capacity. They headed in an easterly direction, flying over the low-lying clouds at first. Then, in order to shake off any enemy fighters, the formation reduced their height and we crowded at the large portholes.

The Russian Steppes, covered in snow, unfolded like a map beneath us. It was unending. We were astounded at the view from above, seeing dark forests and black craters in sharp contrast to the white snow. Destroyed bridges were clear to see. Now and again, an air-pocket lifted the Junkers, with its thirty metre wing-span, a foot or two into the air. We were like children on the switch-back at the fair. We let out a cry as the metal bird dropped again, like a stone. Unconcerned and naive we soaked up this new experience until, during the course of the hour-long flight, small dark spots appeared in the sky, approaching our formation rather quickly. Enemy fighters! Then our radio operator rose hastily, and dressed in a thick fur-lined jacket, brown leather cap, goggles, and with a cartridge-belt slung over his shoulders, went to take his position at the rear of the plane, at the machine gun position. It was open to wind and weather. Only then did we realise how serious the situation was. The slow and clumsy Junkers, with a maximum speed of 270 kms per hour, would have been a very easy target for the Soviets. But luck was on our side that day, for suddenly they turned and disappeared into the horizon. We, as flying infantry, somehow had a feeling of being the 'victors of the air'.

Our joviality was to disappear very quickly with the increased turbulence. Face after face lost its pink colour, slowly turning to an ill-looking white. Many rued the hasty consumption of their rations, which now landed undigested in hastily emptied gas-mask cases. There was nothing else available. There were no exceptions, all of us, but all of us were horribly air-sick. Busy only with ourselves, we did not notice, some time later, when our Junkers approached a landing strip with very provisional markings.

With the motors still running, we sprang from the ice-cold Junkers. I cannot impress enough how good it was to have the earth under our feet once more. Shivering with the cold, we ran through flurries of snow to a large, open hangar. There a log-fire burned in an empty oil-barrel, to warm our frozen joints. At that time, we had no clue as to where we were, only later did we learn that the airfield had the name of Orel. Shortly after, it was clear to us that the town did not lie in the south, near Dnjepr, but in the centre of the Soviet Union and on the river Oka. We had flown in a straight north-easterly course over Kiev and had landed roughly 250 kilometres from Moscow. It meant that we were not to fight with the Wiking Division, and the question was 'why'?

The English historian, David Irving, in his research for his book on Hitler and his generals, came up with the answer to the question that we were then asking. In a tense situation caused by the bitter Russian winter, Hitler had taken over as Commander-in-Chief of the Armed Forces, from Field-Marshal Walther von Brauchitsch, just before the attack on Moscow. His orders were for fanatical resistance, and no consideration for the enemy who had broken through the flanks or at the rear. He had given the order for replacement troops to be sent from the Waffen SS and at the shortest notice possible, by air. They had to act as 'flying firemen' to support the troops who found themselves in a very tense and dangerous situation, in the middle sector of the front.

In his observations David Irving summed-up by saying, that in those dark months of the winter of 1941, Hitler displayed his determination, combined with the legendary strength of the German soldier, who bore every hardship. On the evening of our arrival in Orel we witnessed, from the edge of the airfield, a huge fire-ball, followed by a hefty explosion. Upon landing, a four-engined Focke-Wulf-Condor plane had crashed, killing all of the passengers, mainly Generals, but it had not been attacked.

The Junkers 52 were no luxury machines and had deficiencies, in comparison with today's planes. There was no heating and no toilets. One of those deficiencies endangered the take-off of the Junkers that we had just used, upon its turn-around. One of our chums, in his moment of need during our flight, had used a half empty petrol canister in the rear of the plane as a *pissoir*, not knowing that the mixture of urine and petrol was not digestible for a Junkers, robust as it was. It gave the pilot a couple of uncomfortable minutes.

We spent the night in that hangar, with temperatures of minus thirty degrees. Our journey the next morning was in goods wagons in which we had an iron stove. We could huddle around and thaw our deeply frozen joints with the added small comfort of fresh straw covering the floor. It did not therefore take very long before we oiled our vocal cords and were singing our old songs. More than once, snowdrifts stopped our train and we had to alight and shift the snow. Those who were first to jump from the wagons unexpectedly landed in chest-high drifts. It happened more than once. So we shovelled ourselves free for the rest of the journey, from one drift to another.

CHAPTER 11

War in Winter

In the north, a bitter winter with minus 52 degrees was recorded. Such temperatures for this latitude had been known, but not for the previous 140 years. There has never been a soldier born, nor a weapon invented that could combat those extreme conditions. The result was devastating.

The Red Army used that situation and prepared a counter-offensive to stop the German army at Moscow's doors. They thanked 'General Winter' for the 'Wonder of Moscow', as it was called, for being an eternal ally to Russia. For the first time, Josef Stalin sat in the Kremlin and enjoyed the first glimmer of hope. Till then nothing, be it weather or enemy, had managed to bring the 'victory' march of the *Wehrmacht* to a halt. In the October of 1941, 'General Morass' succeeded in hindering the offensive. Then the frosts of November solved the problem.

In the summer, as the German army crossed the Beresina river, a right-hand offspring of the river Dnjepr, the Soviets lost all their confidence. That river held a 'nimbus', a storm-cloud, i.e. a threatening portent for the Red Army, knowing that Napoleon had had very heavy losses, on his retreat in 1812. The river gave his *Grande Armée* an insurmountable problem. The flow of the river simply had to stop all other attempts to cross it. The German spearhead had reached the last tram-stop of the outlying districts, 18 kilometres from Moscow. Privileged Russian officials packed their cases and left. Government and diplomatic corps members were then taken to safety, behind the Volga.

Many of the population were convinced that the *Wehrmacht* was about to march into Moscow. There was much unrest, leading to shops and flats being looted by evacuees. Some Communist Party members even burned their party membership books. Groups of the NKVD, the People's Commission of Internal Affairs, took a hand, shooting mutineers. They also opened the doors of the prisons.

Soviet General Georgii K. Zhukov formed militia divisions from over 100,000 members of the population, to defend Moscow. Over half a million citizens built street barriers and anti-tank trenches. The same military laws now applied to civilians, as if they were fighting on the front, with 'panic-makers, cowards, and traitors', being shot. There was no return.

The seizure of Moscow however, never took place. A German Communist played a decisive role in that phase of the war. He was Dr Richard Sorge, Russia's correspondent and agent in Tokyo. He gave unquestionable information to the Kremlin, that the threatening war between Japan and

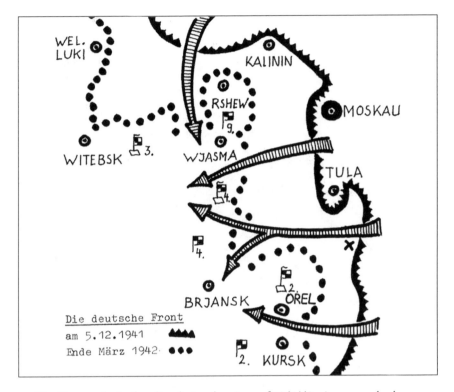

The German-Soviet frontline during the winter of 1941/42. A cross marks the area below Tula where the author fought

the USA, in the Pacific, would prevent Japan becoming an ally of Germany. Their support with their Kwantung Army would have to be withdrawn from the Russian borders. Russia now had the use of 150 divisions and 44 brigades in readiness along the 3,000 kilometre eastern border. They were fully equipped for a Russian winter. They consisted of highly experienced Siberian and Mongolian soldiers who were considered to be Russia's élite. We were to experience how good they were. All of that tipped the scales against us taking Moscow at that time.

Before the question was settled, we had a local attack from a 'Red' fighter, literally diving at us out of the high heavens. It welcomed us with a high-explosive bomb. Landing fifteen feet away, it blew half of the tar-covered roof off the railway station in which we had newly made our quarters. The side walls fell away, and no one had heard it coming. The shock was greater than the damage, with only a few of the men being slightly wounded. Our journey was by no means at an end.

The next day we were transported by lorries. We moved over roads thick with snow, and were attached to a battalion of a motorised SS Infantry Brigade. The long column of vehicles drove through the bleak landscape of

Drawing by the author showing his front-line position in January 1942

the white steppes in the direction of the Front. The 'road' was marked on both sides by wooden posts, with rough bundles of straw nailed to them.

Despite having woollen gloves, our hands were prone in those temperatures to a serious degree of frostbite. We had to conscientiously keep hands and fingers moving, beating our hands against our chests to avoid circulation arrest. In such temperatures frostbite would undoubtedly have been the result. The same exercise applied to our feet too. So we stamped continually on the floor of the lorry, for our leather boots, sufficient in warm Carinthia, were here totally inadequate. There were also no facilities for other bodily needs. There were no considerate stops made for 'calls of nature'. They had to be performed underway, with the use of a cargo-hatch and the friendly help of our chums.

We were very happy when the vehicle had to stop because of snowdrifts. We warmed up by shovelling snow once more. When the motors were turned off, we heard the roar of guns in the distance and knew then that we were not so far away from the Front. In December, in Russia, the light fades at around three in the afternoon, and we could see the far off lightning of tracers flashing against the grey sky.

Unexpectedly, some groups had to continue on foot. 'Marching' with full packs degenerated into simple torture in the deep snow. Now and again, a column of tanks would pass and we were readily given a lift. Although sitting exposed in the bitter wind and being uncomfortable, it was better than going on foot. We had not gone far before we had to spring from the tank into deep snow, as a small plane circled above us. We waved at first, thinking that it was one of ours, until we saw the red star on its rump and it started to dive in the direction of our column. The tank, a PzKpfw IV, zig-zagged at full speed in order to avoid the plane, which was firing at it with everything it had. Although boasting 30 to 50mm thick plating, the plane succeeded in bringing the tank to a halt, having damaged its most vulnerable parts, the track and track-wheels. We, as unprotected infantry, had been vulnerable too, but had been spared.

After the attack the column moved on once again. Once more, the men climbed on the moving tanks. At least most of them did. Somehow my friend Robby and I didn't manage it. We were left behind with the damaged tank and its crew of five. The crew set about repairing their tank, which under normal circumstances was a quick and practised exercise and without problems. But under those conditions it was an inhuman expectation, the ice-cold track parts literally sticking to the men's stiff fingers. We knew that we could do nothing to help. However, we did not like the idea of being separated from the rest of the battalion, and worried that we would not catch up with them. Perhaps they were in the next village? With that hope, we made the decision to go it alone, on foot. The decision was not a good one.

We 'marched' kilometre after kilometre without seeing a single house. It was now dark. We were also dog-tired. Eventually a misty shape was to be seen in the distance, to one side of the road. It had to be houses! Like a desert island in an eternal white sea, a low farm building, framed by naked trees, appeared. There was smoke wafting into the dark sky from its chimney-pot. It was in a small village. The smoke indicated people, but were they friend or foe?

We froze and sweated, at the same time, at the prospect of the only choice that we had. We must go into the village, for we could not have survived a night under open skies. We released the safety-catches of our weapons and, step-by-step, we slowly entered the unknown village with our hearts in our mouths. We had to make pauses because of the deep snow, but with ears strained and the eyes of Argus, we breathlessly reconnoitred the whole village. It had obviously come under fire at some time, for we found burned-out houses of which only the stone chimney-breasts were standing in the ruins. There was no movement in the village. It was all so still and so deathly quiet. Any tracks to be found had long been covered by wind-blown snow. So we returned, and very carefully approached the cottage with the smoking chimney.

'Hands up! *Rucki werch!*' The simple wooden door, with an old horse-blanket to keep out the draughts, was not locked. To our relief, only a Russian farmer's family huddled in the corner of the room, anxious and looking questioningly at us. With gestures we quickly found out that Russian soldiers had been in the village, only hours beforehand, a patrol of Cossacks on horseback.

One has to realise that the Russian front was interspersed with single villages, miles apart from one another. It was not so clear-cut as one might imagine, and the villagers had a lot to endure. The villages had changed hands many times, between German soldiers and the Soviets. There had been casualties among the civilians, and we were to learn that our hosts were the only ones left in the village. Many had been killed, some had fled, and every able-bodied man left alive had been forcibly taken away by the Red Army.

After it was accepted by our hosts that we two *Germanskis* did not mean them any harm, they relaxed a little. We too thawed out, that meant our stiffly frozen uniforms and leather boots. The mother of the family, the *Matka*, cooked potatoes in their skins for us, which we ate with raw and half-frozen onions. In return, we presented them with bars of chocolate from our iron-rations, for they were friendly people. We shared the warm, smoky and petroleum-lit Russian home, not only with the family, but also, to our horror, with fleas! We stayed until daybreak, alternating guard duty in those hours.

The darkness firstly was the friend of partisans, and secondly the snow was the friend of the Cossacks, making them and their horses a silent enemy. We went to the door during the night to take a look now and again, but all was peaceful outside. Single stars twinkled in the sky above the endless snow-clad earth which gradually turned to a neon-red, over the thatch of the house, in the direction of the Front.

We left in the early hours, warm once more and reasonably rested, but not knowing where we had stayed. Perhaps it had been in Krasnaya or Korosvinska, or even Senskaya, for all the villages were called the same. In the snow they were not distinguishable one from the other. We wandered in no-man's land for the whole of the next day and night, spending a few hours in another village, which was totally deserted. The houses were empty, but our common sense told us that the enemy could just as well use them for shelter against the bitter cold. So we spent a few hours in a burnt-out stall, on damp straw.

In this desert of snow, the only compass at our disposal was the sound from the Front, for there were no signposts. We made our way as best we could in the deep snow, our 'march' for want of a better word, being only 'reasonable'. We were hungry and thirsty, which was noticeable in our slow performance. In return for our iron rations, which we had given to our hosts, we were given sunflower seeds by them as we left. That was now our only nourishment, which we washed down with melted snow. With our last strength, and believing that we were seeing a mirage, we reached a road. To our relief we stumbled on a German military bus. It lay rather slanted to one side of the road and the door was frozen, so that we could not open it. We scratched the frosty snow from the windows and looked inside. We saw German soldiers sitting in the seats, wrapped in blankets. All had their collars turned up to their ears, some sitting upright. Others had curled themselves together for warmth. Of the driver there was no sign. Had he sought help and not returned? Was he also lost in the snow? All had a somewhat strange, yellow pallor and there was no sign of life. But any help that we could have given was no longer needed, for *rigor mortis* had set in. We slowly realised that all had died in their sleep.

We left the scene, the metal coffin on wheels, shaken to the core and deep in thought. Our thoughts centred on the gruesome Front. But for those in the bus had it not been a gentle death? Our 'odyssey' eventually came to an end. We were given a lift from a munitions transport of *troikas* that were driving directly to the front. We were reminded of the Petersburg sledges, as we were given places amongst the straw-clad shells on the horse-drawn sledges. They were pulled to the next village by small *Panje* ponies, but without the usual jingle of sleigh bells. The village-well was well and truly frozen over. Next to it we found an extravagant wooden signpost which gave a wealth of information, including that our battalion was just 6 kilometres away on the main line of resistance at the Front They had been in defensive positions from the moment that they had arrived.

The terrain was flat. Now and again it was broken by small woods of birches. Our first assessment of our surroundings was broken with a shrill cry of "are you both tired of life, get your heads down!" We were in the sights of the enemy. We had sauntered into open positions where two comrades held guard behind a wall of snow. Our comrades showed us the company command post. The sergeant-major was astounded at the arrival of his two lost sheep. We were already on the missing list to be sent to the regiment. The greeting on our return was a very happy one. Our chums were eager to bring us up to date with the latest news. It was disturbing to say the least. Some of the battalion's lorries had become lost in a snowstorm on the way to the Front. They had been taken prisoner by the Russians. After a counter-attack, our men, mainly the Norwegians, had been found beaten to death, and lay frozen in the river Oka. Our commander had been killed and we had many dead and wounded. Every man was desperately needed and Robert and I were detailed to reconnaissance. "Not even in battle, and you lose yourselves! Well then I can only say that you must be well rested," was the comment from our platoon leader.

A recce was ordered at midnight and until then we could snatch a couple of hours' sleep. Sleep, before our first battle? The tension of our baptism of fire however kept us very wide awake. Our assignment was to patrol a wood, lying to the east, in the sector of the 2nd Company, to see if it was free of the enemy. Punctually at midnight, twelve soldiers and a patrol-leader sprang from the foremost trenches in the direction of the enemy. The guards were informed, so that upon our return we were expected, and not fired upon by our own troops.

We were led by our corporal in the front rank, who had a machine-pistol and we followed with our rifles, at every two or three metres. It was freezing cold and a yellow-white moon shone brightly over the dark wood. No one spoke. Only the hard crunch of the frozen ground was to be heard under our boots, or the unavoidable snap of a twig or a branch or two, as we reached the wood. So far, so good! However, once or twice we fell into shell-holes that we hadn't seen, for the woods were often the target, from both Germans and Russians. The night appeared to have many eyes. Our imagination told us that there was a 'Red Army man' behind every tree and bush. Despite the bitter cold, we sweated under our white 'cammos' as we pressed deeper into the wood. Every time the moon disappeared behind a cloud, a flare rose in the sky from the east, turning night into day and we instantly thought "we've been seen"! But as the magnesium light faded, the night appeared once more like a blanket over the wood.

We started to believe that the wood was free of the enemy, when suddenly a Russian machine-gun started to clatter into the night and we hit the ground, as red neon flares snaked over our heads. In panic, I tried to burrow into the stone-hard frozen ground and couldn't. In that moment I no longer felt the bitter cold. I did however feel a dull thud against my intestines which released a frosty cold net over my skin. Was that already the end for me? Just as the war had begun? The next volley of shots brought a scream of pain from our platoon leader, who had been shot in the spine. That seemed to release our panic-stricken paralysis. In the blink of an eye, the men pulled themselves together and showed what they had learned and what they were made of. Either in lying or kneeling positions, and half hidden by the trees, we returned the enemy's fire which came from every nook and cranny. We had probably run into a Russian platoon who had the same assignment, i.e. to confirm that the wood was free of the enemy.

I was given the order from the patrol leader's second-in-command to fetch help for the wounded corporal. Like a hunted deer, I ran back to where we had entered the wood. In my haste I tripped over a fallen tree. In picking myself up, I looked into two lifeless eyes. It was not a fallen tree but a fallen Russian soldier. His eyes wide open, he stared from a yellow face into heaven, like a frosty ghost in the moonlight.

I arrived totally out of breath at the foremost trenches and nearly forgot the passwords. I reported to our company command post. Two medics then accompanied me to the wounded corporal, who between times had lost consciousness. We tied our comrade on to a Finnish sledge, i.e. a slightly formed sledge without runners, and transported him as quickly as we could to the battery's first-aid station. However, he died from his injuries that same night.

The inferno of our baptism of fire was constant, so constant that we became somewhat more composed each and every time. That did not mean to say that it did not bring new sorrow, each and every time. The question that I asked, and many others too when they were honest enough to admit it, was "will I pass with flying colours?" The question was now pointless, invalid, for the war was an examination, each and every day.

The words from General Guderian, the *Panzer* General, were to "get on with the job and don't mess around!" His words no longer applied. For those who found themselves in the central sector of the Eastern Front did not have the luxury to "mess around". The battle for Moscow was lost, for us as well as those who were situated between the Orel and the Don. One could say that the victory had frozen to death.

Those in power in the Kremlin now shared the opinion that the German Army would suffer the same fate as Napoleon and his troops, in face of the severity of nature's elements, which they themselves had never experienced. Although the view over the snow-covered steppe was without end, the German soldier of course, only saw what was happening in his own sector. We, in December of 1941, did not know that German soldiers in that sector would have to fight for their very existence.

Relevant military knowledge concerning the conditions of the fighting soldier in Russia was non-existent. We ourselves could draw from no similar experience or imagination from any such country. It stretched without end into a mist and was occupied by a race of people whose name told us nothing. Only two experiences were at hand from the past and from history. Firstly, there was Napoleon's lost victory in Russia and secondly, Russia's own performance in the First World War. Both wars confirmed the reality of fighting in winter using huge concentrations of men.

Also in masses, came the fresh Siberian and Mongolian regiments who stormed our thinly-defended lines. Dressed in thickly wadded jackets, with fur collars and insulated boots, they crawled to our foremost trenches in the night. For us the war was reduced to fighting from one village to another. There were no possibilities of cover by day or by night. To dig-in would have been pure decimation, in that winter, for us very poorly-equipped troops.

The defensive actions of December 1941 followed an unusual direction of waves and curves. One of our company officers showed us on a map where we were to be found. It was at the furthest point in the east and we believed him. We heard names from him such as Yelez, Yefremov, Russki-Brod and Voronezh, but whether they lay to the east or west of our left or right flank, only he knew.

Our regular winter clothing had still not arrived, so any blankets or furs that we could lay our hands on were temporarily used to keep us warm. Everyone wore every piece of clothing that he possessed underneath his summer coat. But not even such well-used and worn-out uniform gave us enough warmth. The longer we had to lie on the deeply-frozen ground, the quicker the frostbite nibbled at our limbs. When our wounded could not be attended to quickly, the sooner they froze to death. We took that impossible situation into our own hands and organised *Valinskis*, the Russian insulated felt boot, the felt being as thick as carpet. Our Finnish brothers-in-arms could only shake their heads at our hob-nailed leather boots that were always frozen hard and told us that we might " just as well run around in the snow in your socks." So at the rear of the front-line, the German soldier made himself shoes from straw. We didn't even have fur headgear, and a thin balaclava was all we wore underneath our cold, steel helmets.

In Germany, fur articles and other suitable equipment were requested. The call was answered by the people, who made sacrifices of useful and practical articles, in the belief that they would help the 'boys at the front' when delivered. Unfortunately very little of it was, although there were mountains of articles in the collection centres. That 'little' proved to be just a drop in the ocean.

After continuous combat, the regiments on the front were reduced to a third in numbers. The frost reduced those remaining. The loss through frostbite was higher than through combat. "The total loss on the Eastern Front, up to December 1941, was 750,000 men which equalled 21.5% of the collective strength of three and a half million soldiers. Every fourth soldier was missing, wounded or fallen." Paul Carrell gave the figures in his book *Barbarossa*. At the end of that year, another 65,000 could be added because of contracted infectious diseases from lack of hygiene, resulting in typhoid fever, nearly 800 dying from it. Stomach and bowel ailments were also rife as well as severe influenza. Frostbite however topped the list. The number of frostbite cases at the end of February, totalled 100,000.

The Soviets also had very heavy losses, but in their case they had more than enough reserves. The Russian soldier, in contrast to us was a very modest soldier, which was illustrated by his daily diet. A bag hung on his belt in which were millet heads which when mixed with water made a porridge. He carried dried fish with him as iron rations. It was swilled down when eating, with high percentage vodka from his field thermos, which he drank at any other time of the day too. He rolled his cigarettes in newspaper, using very course-cut tobacco, *Machorka*, which included the stalk of the leaves. In the matter of suffering in inhuman conditions, the Russian soldier was enormously tough. When fighting, he could and did endure far more than any other western army. "The Eastern Front was a nightmare for the German soldier. The Russian enemy fought like primitive, soulless robots, their patriotism and Bolshevik ideals not to be easily destroyed like bursting soap bubbles. The Russian commanders accepted the responsibility of monstrous losses in battle without a second thought. Their soldiers fought to their last breath, often committing suicide rather than being taken prisoner. In a hopeless situation for instance, the Russian infantry adopted the practice of 17th Century grenadiers. They formed a suicidal rank, advancing in front of the enemy machine-guns, collecting together to form a new row behind the bodies of their dead, to advance repeatedly, to the last man, or last bullet from the German machine-guns".

The war with the Soviet Union, and the form with which they directed it, escalated and surpassed all cruelty and hardship experienced in any former combat since 1939. The target was the total destruction of the enemy, a capitulation without conditions, within the framework of doctrine and structures. Our naked existence was the price. Hitler described it as the biggest crusade in world history, resembling the German crusaders, who had fought the hordes of Genghis Khan in Silesia. That we could fight such an unrelenting enemy with the motto "it's you or me!" was thanks to the truncheon-hard training that we had received.

Very soon we learned that the Soviets would shoot any prisoners that they took. When thinking about falling into their hands, it gave us nightmares. They had refused to sign the Geneva Convention agreement of 1929, pertaining to certain conduct towards prisoners of war.

When the sun shone in December, which was rare, we felt the pangs of homesickness, as it disappeared in a red sky on the horizon. Many a German soldier on his patrol or standing guard in his cold and icy trench, said a quiet *adieu* to his loved-ones, in his far-off distant homeland. Burning *wanderlust* had turned to homesickness, which was no wonder, for that land, for us, was the end of the world, as civilised people.

Nearly every day, the frosty countryside was covered in a mist until about 9am. Daylight appeared only at around 11am, and at 4pm it was dark once more. So, late in the afternoon, we no longer fought to advance, but to find a warm place for the night. That would be in a blockhouse of a farm. Only then could we survive the 30 to 50 degrees below zero temperature. In those days the infantryman overcame problems that he had not practised before. In his hour of need, in order to survive the night, he had to overcome his dislike of entering a village after dark. His needs were for cover and warmth. However primitive the blockhouse was, with its clay-soil floor, it was cover, and it offered warmth from a wood-burning fireplace or oven, a *Pyetschku*. Those primitive houses, no more than large wooden huts with one large room, more often than not where the whole family slept, no longer disgusted us, as they had before the frost appeared. To us they were lifesavers, fleas or not, and in battle we tried to protect them, like our eyes! After a cold patrol or guard-duty, we no longer minded if a mouse ran over the floor. We were warm in one of those houses belonging to a 'collective' farming system. With the sour aroma of a pumpkin soup when being cooked, we knew that our blood flowed as usual and that there was still life in our joints.

The whole family slept over the oven, covered in tattered blankets. The oven being four and a half feet high was made of clay, had an alcove over the fire itself, and dominated the room. Straw was spread over the floor for our benefit which was where we slept. If a small child belonged to the family, its cradle was slung from the ceiling and so it swung over our heads. Despite conditions from the Middle Ages, and the war, one could say that it illustrated an idyllic scene, binding two peoples together.

In our thatched house, the eldest daughter, perhaps not twenty years old, suffered under our presence. Her national pride, bitterness and privation had made the fine Asian features of this lovely girl hard. Her name was Annuschka, she was a teacher and was the only one who spoke a little German. She didn't try to hide her Communist convictions but didn't shout about it either. Only when we began to speak about the misery in that Soviet paradise, did she abruptly cut short our conversation, saying that she didn't understand what we had said. She was, at one and the same time, mistrusting and curious of us, the *Germanskis*, who were of the same age. We asked ourselves if she was actually the daughter of the family or a partisan who had been planted into the family. As inexperienced as we were, we would not have noticed had it been the case. What we did notice was, that under her patched and wadded jacket, she had a lovely figure and our difficult Annuschka let us know. She had beautiful dark hair, which we saw when she didn't have her white headscarf on her head, and she stole soulful, longing glances at us, with a brief smile. At least that is what we imagined.

Our hosts always profited when our daily rations reached us, if they reached us. It was all too seldom however. In such weather conditions the supplies always came to a standstill, for various reasons. Columns of lorries could only be pulled behind tracked vehicles over roads that were like ice-rinks. Our warm meals came from the battalion's field kitchen. Usually a stew, it was carried on the back, in a double-sided canister, or by sledge pulled by *Panje* ponies to the front-line. In some cases, it was a long way, isolated and dangerous and many a Russian soldier was provided with our meal, the carriers having been shot up on the way. Our daily ration was much better than when we were in training. It consisted of 650 grams of bread, 45 grams butter, or other fat, 120 grams of cheese, 120 grams of fresh meat, 200 grams jam or artificial honey, 10 grams chicory coffee and six Juno cigarettes, which we could so seldom enjoy.

There are three very descriptive words connected to war, which need no supporting vocabulary when being used, such as expulsion, evacuation and refugees. All are connected to the apocalypse of the Twentieth Century, for the poorest of huts is a home. To have that taken away, belongs to the hardest of fates that anyone has to endure. For soldiers like us who had become nomads of the Steppe, separated from the outside world and with seldom a chance to make a telephone call, our quarters had become no less than provisional shelters.

In the next village, but some way off, all the inhabitants had fled. It had become a small garrison for us, as a line of defence, 24 hours a day. In order to reach it, we had an hour-long march, hindered by an icy snowstorm from the north and metre high wind-blown drifts. Underway we rendered first-aid to one another by rubbing the left side of each other's face with snow. Only so could we avoid the threatening frostbite when yellow patches appeared as the first symptoms on the skin.

We did our best to make our new quarters into a home. In the one allocated to us, an optimist had written, "Humour is when one laughs in the face of all odds", in the soot on the ceiling. In the warmth of the hut and as I lay on my bed of straw, I used to gaze at it and tried to take heart from this indirect advice, although none of us had forgotten how to laugh. There was always a clown to make a loose joke or two. We had two of those happy souls with us, in the form of two Danish brothers, twins, from Copenhagen, the same age as myself, 18 years old. With their white-blond hair and pink baby cheeks, they represented the typical prototype of the Germanic volunteer. The type appeared as the young and typical, dynamic soldier of the new Europe in the magazine *Signal* and were good, sporty soldiers, whom we could not understand when speaking at their normal speed. When speaking German, we puzzled at their lisping, swinging, vocabulary mingled with a Danish accent and we nicknamed them *sür-su*. We only had to open the door of the hut for a second or two and with their aversion to a cold draught they chorused *Tür-zu* but which rang in the air as *sür-su*, i.e. 'shut the door!'

We were therefore concerned and upset, when hearing that their trench at the end of the village was deserted one morning, when the relieving guards approached it, and there was no sign of the blonde brothers. We never saw them again. We had to assume that during their night of guard duty, they had fallen foul of Soviet soldiers using a snow storm to silently approach their trench, overpower them and take them away, which very often happened.

On dark nights the guards of the front-line sent flares over the front terrain, flares on small parachutes. In order to let the Russians know that we were in readiness, we also shot a volley or two from our machine-guns. In doing that we, at the same time, sent away many a hungry wolf as it approached our trenches. Whole packs would come too close for comfort. On nights with a full moon, we were able to see enemy positions. That same moon which shone on friend and foe alike, from Leningrad to the Black Sea, also shone we knew, on our loved ones at home.

On one of those sunny days in December, we were suddenly surprised by a cheeky Russian 'double-decker' or biplane aircraft circling above our heads. We ran outside, only half-dressed, to take a look at it. The cheekiness of the pilot flying so low over the roofs meant that he must have known that we did not possess anti-aircraft guns. We shot at him with our pistols and rifles like crazy, which did nothing to scare the pilot, clear to see in his leather cap and goggles. He calmly made a bow over the village before disappearing to the east. It did not end there however, for he returned during the night. That time he stretched his arm overboard and dropped two bombs on us, without doing any harm. But we were to be pestered continually by those Russian 'double-deckers', or 'sewing machines', as we called them, for the 'Ivans' loved to disturb our peace.

The fighting zone of our battalion included several villages. With a strength of 800 men, we should have had a defence-line of around only 1,000 metres, based on the theory that the defence-line of an infantry division of 8,000, was 10,000 metres. We had to guard much more, three or four times as much. Armed patrols kept the communication system open between the units, which was only possible after dark. In that flat no-man's land, there were only small woods of birches dotted around for cover and the enemy had a good view of the countryside. There was a telephone connection from village to village and the field-lines, open to extreme elements and enemy fire, were very often in need of repair. The men carrying out the work had to be protected. Communications had to be kept open at all times whether dangerous to life and limb or not. It was a very necessary and continual commitment for the men and their protection had to be reliable as well. Recce patrols were always in demand in connection with such work and of all the men to be used, our group was chosen. That after-dark task became routine, a dangerous commodity, for it gave our enemy a weapon to use against us. We used the same well-worn paths through two small woods, in order not to lose one another.

The routine enabled the Russians to lay mines in our path, which became a suicide mission for us, in every sense of the word. Some of the mines were laid with trip-wires and were nearly invisible in the dark. We started to lose men in that way. Two of our comrades were severely wounded. The situation became one that meant those protecting the men doing their work, also had to be protected. Combat engineers were sent ahead of us with mine-detectors. They did not have the expected success however for the mines were not detectable with our type of detectors. Before burying them the Russians encased them in wood. It then became clear to us that with tricks like that, we had to outwit the 'Ivans' also with tricks, but ones that were far better. Our regular route had been our undoing and so we had to use another. Or else we let our enemy think that we were using another, and that could only be achieved by using ski-troops. Our ski-comrades helped us pull the wool over their eyes by forming another route for us, but that was not all. The Russians were quick to follow the new route and our ski-comrades were waiting for them. They had used the new route, and at a spot where they could not be seen, had turned round, and using the tracks that they had made, returned to a spot for an ambush, which turned out to be a deadly trap for our cunning friends.

That winter in Russia provided many a possibility for sly ruses, but to our disadvantage. The Russians were on home ground and one step ahead of us. We were to experience how they turned everything to their advantage, including our worst enemy, the snow. One of the 'harmless' ruses of war was their underground work, a tunnel system that they used to reach our trenches. They were underground fighters in every sense of the word. Like moles they burrowed through the snow, to reach us. The Siberian troops were the experts, who else?

One of the meanest however, that only the Russians could think of, was the use of 'living mines' for tanks and other vehicles. They used dogs, Alsatians mostly, or the Doberman, with mines strapped to their bodies. Not only humans had to suffer in the war, but God's creatures too. More than enough of them were to be seen in the eastern campaign, for instance in Mussino, 70 kilometres north-west from Moscow, with Russian Cavalry. It was, at least, spectacular.

It happened in the early hours of the 19 November 1941, when a whole Russian regiment of cavalry with 1,000 horses, galloped in closed formation towards the modern German machine guns with shining sabres. The snow-covered low land was turned into a bloodstained battlefield between volleys from the machine-guns and the mortars, splintering, catapulting everything in its path eight metres into the air. It was suicide by slaughter. It had been the same with the Polish Uhlans two years before. The attacking Mongolian riders were also slaughtered, without one German soldier receiving a scratch.

On the fourth day of Advent in the same year, soldiers from our 3rd *Panzer* Regiment came across a monument of ice, which can only be described as such. Perhaps in a snowstorm, with no alternative shelter, soldiers from a Russian Cavalry unit, came to a halt, some dismounting to take shelter and warmth amongst their horses. One, a wounded soldier with his leg in a splint, was still mounted and with his eyes wide open, had frozen to death in the saddle. Men and horses, with their heads stretched high, had frozen where they had stood and had become a monument of ice.

We also had first-hand experiences of the plight of helpless animals, such as the thin, faithful, Cossack horse, still to be found by the side of his dead master, snowed-in, up to his stomach unable to move. How long he had patiently waited we do not know, but only his faint neighs could be heard among the sounds of war, which humans had created. We cared for those creatures when humanly possible, as best we could. Decades later, I still cannot understand how we accepted the fate of those animals as we did. Were we too busy with ourselves? Had we become unconscious and carefree so much, in the toughening-up process of our youth, or did the fate of humans overshadow the plight of the animals? Death in war was always present, that is true, but nevertheless despite becoming accustomed to its presence, it always moved us anew.

With the first wounded or the first deaths, the young volunteer was always filled with respect, for the hero's death was seldom gentle and free of pain. We could always tell from the wide-open eyes staring from a yellow-tinged face. The thought of sharing the same fate filled our minds as we saw the first dead, the first lifeless comrade. He who had been so full of life, had joked, had moaned, had told us about his home and his family so that we already knew his parents and sister, and his brothers. For him there were no mornings or evenings any more, just death. As silent witnesses, we knew that his mother would weep bitter tears, but at that moment she didn't know. We knew also that a medic in his icy shelter somewhere, or a company clerk, would remove his name from the company lists, upon receipt of his 'dog-tag' and his bloodstained pay-book. He would write the standard letter of condolence to her, which included of course, how brave he had been in the face of death and been such an upstanding example of a good comrade.

When an order to dig a grave was received, with experience, we began the procedure with hand-grenades. In that earth of concrete how do you bury your dead? We began by making three holes, the size of a hand-grenade, with an iron pole. Then we made a ring of water around it, which froze, holding the grenade in place and then ran for our lives, after pulling the pin, as the frozen clods of earth exploded into the air with a mighty force. The procedure was repeated until with the help of an ice-pick, we could enlarge the hole to a man-sized grave. We buried our comrade in it, usually at one end of a village or on the roadside. There was no other way.

For the practised soldier, the war was now hard reality and we had to master the days as they came, without acts of heroism, individual or *en masse*. When being honest, it was not how any of us had imagined it to be. It could not be compared to the romantic storybook laced with heroes, brave deeds, and their courageousness. How many of us were brave soldiers?

Before every battle we all had butterflies in our stomachs. I, apart from the fear of being taken prisoner, had a terrible fear of being shot in the head, as if being shot in the stomach or anywhere else come to that, was not just as bad? We all unconsciously, or consciously, avoided danger when we could. Does that not lie in the self-preservation within every human being? In the time of war however, it is very unfairly charged as cowardice and blanketing of guilt, which we didn't understand. Any who were foolhardy enough found a very quick grave. To be able to use a rifle is no proof courage. Unity within company and battalion resulted in a high standard of warfare. It needed less ammunition. The level-headed and disciplined soldier counted far, far more as a courageous one, for me personally. A comrade on whom I could count, who took no unnecessary risks and knew what he was doing, was worth his weight in gold, in my eyes.

We were described as an 'élite' organisation and understandably we had to behave like one. The continuous standard of conduct expected of us however, was not always very easy and cost lots of discipline. That discipline meant split-second reflexes by drilling, and split-second obedience upon receiving orders without hesitation. Instinct was not wished for and had to be eradicated. Because of our military education and ideals we could not afford to weaken, when confronted with an extreme situation in combat. We were not threatened with a court martial. The combustion, which drove us to self-sacrifice, was psychological. We told ourselves "I must do it or we are all lost". That motivation stood foremost with us in the Waffen SS.

Under Stalin, deserters from the Red Army, or cowards, were shot on the spot, without a court martial. Absence of steadfastness within the troop was a bloody punishment for all. To become a prisoner of the enemy was a disgrace, which when landing back on one's home front was punished with the death-sentence. That was not all, for family members of the said 'sinner' were then arrested and imprisoned (Stalin's secret law No. 270 16 August 1941).

"The world is a constant conspirator against the courageous", was the opinion of the American General Douglas MacArthur. He was right. In defeated Germany at that time, opportunists were using the chance to ridicule the virtue and achievement of the German soldier. His awards of honour, and decorations of distinction, were described as a Christmas-tree decoration, as tinsel. Little did the German soldier know, during the war years, and it was right to be so, that his efforts, sacrifices and his duty-bound conduct would be continually slandered, a few years after. Our slogan "My honour is my loyalty" was, for the slanderers, one of seven pledges in a book, but it was not for us.

We depended, time and time again, on the reliability of our comrades in a tough and bitter fight. That was to be the case at the end of December 1941. Perhaps it was just before Christmas. Instinctively we knew that this time could perhaps be our last, as we began to march to a larger town, to the east of us. It was of great strategic importance. The *Wehrmacht*, in face of overwhelming odds, had not been able to hold it on their own. Now we, the Waffen SS were the trouble-shooters.

An impressive number of strongly armed soldiers in white 'cammos', assembled together at around mid-day and then advanced through a bleak and empty Steppe. As the evening began to fall, we saw the first woods, like strokes from a pencil on the horizon. Then we approached the rear-guard of the *Wehrmacht*. It was a very sorry picture and perhaps the same tragic scene as when Napoleon's beaten Army had retreated from Moscow.

The dead had been brought from the Front, wrapped in blankets, stacked on a cart and now were frozen. Their boots and articles of warm clothing had been removed and distributed to those still fighting. Naked and yellow unwashed feet, feet in socks with gaping holes, and feet wrapped in filthy wrappings poked from the blankets, or the pieces of tenting used to wrap them in. They at least, no longer felt the cold. Then there were the wounded on sledges having been pulled by exhausted ponies, lying on blood-stained straw, enveloped in tattered blankets or paper sacks, anything that could give a modicum of warmth. Hardly to be seen, we heard their moans of pain, as the frost bit into their wounds and which, when left unattended, brought them an eventual death. The scene did nothing to motivate us, on the contrary. Soldiers passed us by, soldiers who had been through hell. They gave us blank, lifeless glances. They stared at us pityingly. "Cannon-fodder like us!" was probably what they thought. Their misery did nothing to enhance our hopes of a forthcoming victory. We pulled ourselves together with hangman's humour. "The Guard may die, but will never surrender", is how we encouraged one another. Now, more than ever, we had to pull ourselves and each other together.

In his book *Soldiers of Death*, the American author and historian Charles W. Sydnor said, "When and wherever a situation was at its most dangerous, and hopes of success at zero, it was the Waffen SS who saved the day with counter-attacks which weakened their opponents". "No one needs to try and tell me that when fighting in Russia, they were not damned scared", announced our patrol leader, who wore the Iron Cross 1st Class and then shouted, "Let's go".

However, high banks of iced snow hindered our path and an icy wind blew, turning our noses and ears white in seconds. The advance was therefore very slow. We had support after a while from tanks, which we mounted until shortly before our objective. By now darkness had fallen. The tanks, PzKpfw IVs, had been painted white, but nothing could camouflage the red glow from their exhausts. It was this red glow that each tank followed. Firstly, it was always a target for the enemy. Secondly, it was the end of many. Clouds of snow were churned into the air behind us and time and time again, we had to jump down to free the track from clumps of ice and snow.

Upon nearing a village on the edge of a wood, which it was clear to see had been attacked, we jumped down from the tanks. As always the terrain in front of us was flat and without cover. Now and again weak attempts to fire at us came from remnants of troops left in the village and also a flare or two lit the sky, but that was all, it was seemingly quiet.

The golden rule after dark, of noiseless movement from your own body and equipment that you carried, was now superfluous, for with the roar of the engines and squeak of the tracks, we could hardly hear the commands of our superiors. Suddenly shots whipped the air from the wood and our machine-guns systematically strewed the wood from one end to the other and was the start for an explosion of fire, the like of which I had never seen. Undisturbed, machine-gun fire clattered from the dark wood from several spots, which could be seen by the red tracers from the gun-barrels. Luckily, their tracer ammunition flew high over our heads.

The Russians possessed a weapon which put the fear of God into us, which we had nicknamed the *Ratschbumm* with a 7.62cm barrel, somewhat larger than that on a tank. It was not the size which worried us, but that one did not hear the launch of the shell. You didn't hear where it was coming from, just the explosion of it upon landing. The decibels from the salvos were now deafening. The earth raised itself up at the shock of every detonation. Biting clouds of gunpowder mixed with the yellow-brown pillar of smoke caused by the explosions rose up. We sought the shelter of the tanks time and time again, and time and time again our commanders sought to prise us away from them. We clung to them however, like frightened children clinging to mother's skirt for cover, but there was none.

It was on the contours of those huge steel objects that the Soviets concentrated their fire and it was hell. A hell of fire in a storm of steel scared us to death. We no longer felt the bitter cold, on the contrary, we sweated so much that we wanted to strip off our 'cammo' jackets. After every fire pause, we automatically moved forwards a few yards, as we had learned a hundred times before, in our drilling. The grips of the hand-grenades, stuck into our boots and belts, hindered us when running and hitting the ground. No sooner had that ground been gained than volleys of fire forced us down again, so that we were only able to crawl where deep snow was to be found.

We already had wounded, some not so badly that they could not cry for help and their cries could be heard above the noise of battle. The dead in comparison lay still and cramped in the snow. Then a small hole, a bullet hole was added to the now not so snow-white 'cammo' that covered them like a shroud. Without the protection offered by the tanks, our frontal attack had definitely floundered. The tank crews had their hands full. They turned their 7.5cm gun-barrels to the left and then to the right, their shells hitting the birch-wood in dazzling flashes. Black smoke mixed with clouds of snow, like storm clouds in the darkness. The glow from the burning houses, added to the ghostly light of that inferno.

It appeared that the Soviets did not possess any anti-tank weapons. From what we could see, only one *Panzer* IV had been hit, for it suddenly started to circle on its axle having been hit in the track. Its crew of five climbed out of the turret, springing into the snow, to crawl to the rear.

The enemy fire did not stop. The Soviets added their secret weapon, about which we had heard but we had never experienced. The Russians overestimated its worth. Alexander Werth mentioned this devastating piece of artillery in one of his books, with a quote from Marshal Yeremenko. "We tested this new weapon for the first time in Rudnya, on 1 July 1941, in the afternoon. An unusual roar shook the air with the launch of the missiles, as they shot into the heavens with red tails like comets. The deafening racket of the successive detonations and the blinding flashes impressed both ears and eyes, with the launching of 320 missiles in 26 seconds. It really surpassed all our expectations and the Germans fled in panic. Our own soldiers in the foremost front-lines also retreated with speed when in the close proximity of the striking shells".

Definitely, the 'Stalin Organ' of the Red Army, or *Katyusha* as it was also called, strongly demoralised us at first. But then we realised that the psychological effect on us was greater than the accuracy of the weapon. There was little chance of it hitting its target and strewing its shell-splinters. The enormous racket of the detonations, and its flames, although considerable, were out of proportion to the damage caused by one 132mm calibre shell. It made a hole to a depth of no more than 30–40 centimetres. The performance was 'short and sweet', which was probably due to either a shortage of ammunition, or that the Reds wanted to spare their own men. In the meantime, we had surrounded the village. A bitter house-to-house fight then began. With bayonets and weapons in our frost-encased fingers, we sprang and tripped over burnt wooden beams in the ruins of nearly every house.

They were not always empty. We coaxed the Red Army men hiding here and there, with cries of *Tovarisch, idi syuda!* i.e. "Come out comrade!" When they didn't, we threw a grenade through the small windows. In its thin metal casing it caused more dust with its detonation and air-pressure, than damage. If lucky, the 'Ivan' came out, deathly pale, with raised hands and only a splinter or two in his wadded jacket, or some slight wound.

We left the houses, to the noise of MG fire and of mortars. The wounded, the numbers of whom were extensive, were transported away to the first-aid stations. The dead lay on the road, melting into the landscape just as the empty ammunition boxes, destroyed weapons and the black craters left by bursting shells. It was a picture of macabre madness, the reality of which we no longer assessed because we had seen such death and doom so often.

Despite everything we had reached our objective. The village was now in our hands, but the enemy did not fully retreat. We were still under fire from the furthest corners of the wood and from outlying houses. Then it was my turn. I was only slightly wounded and did not notice at first. I only noticed when my left glove, green in colour, turned red with blood. Very quickly my 'cammo' jacket was fully smeared as well. A bullet or a splinter, I do not know which, had grazed my thumb, cutting it open. The pity of it was that it was not grave enough for me to have 'home rehabilitation'! It was none the less very painful, and pained me for years after, especially when being pressed, probably because a nerve had been severed.

The first-aid station I found to be a small wooden church. It had however not been used as such in a very long time. From the outside one could see it had been spared any battle damage. The damage was to be seen inside, for without respect for religion, the Communists had used it as a warehouse for their local Co-operative. It gave a very neglected appearance and once again deepened our opinions of the blunt and soulless Stalin regime. There was no longer a belfry, wooden slats hung on a nail, and the windows had been knocked out. Where any colour could be seen, it was now faded, or dry and peeling. In that ignominious house of faith, the wounded had been brought to the lap of God and they now prayed for help. One could almost believe that, for some, God was a delusion, a figment of the imagination, produced out of the very human fear of dying.

In taking the village, we now had to make ourselves comfortable in keeping it defended. We used any remaining houses with a roof and four walls that might offer protection from the bitter cold. With our losses we could not and did not think of following the enemy. We were happy to have fulfilled our mission and hoped to hold our positions for as long as possible. But sleep we could not. The enemy was not so considerate and had obviously sent for reserves, as the infantry fire had increased. Only at night did it subside a little.

Reserves we had none, either to give us support or to relieve us. Our base was too far away and they needed every 'man-jack' that they had. When we were out on our own the expectations were no less than the opposite extreme. As a close-knit unit we still gave our all. We were happy for the roof over our head, and the four walls to keep out the biting cold.

We were very happy therefore, when after a few days, we received orders from the regiment to withdraw. From information from interrogated prisoners and from our scouting patrols, they knew that the enemy was drawing nearer to us, with reserve troops followed by tanks. Not even we, with our battalion in its present condition, could hold out against those numbers. They were too overwhelming. Our decimated units would have inevitably been destroyed. It was at daybreak that we secretly prepared for our retreat.

Silently we left the village that had been so important to capture. We hoped that we would not be followed by the 'Ivans'. Our fears were unfounded. The Red Army suffered with the bitter cold just as we did. They would be happy to exchange their wooded positions in the open, for our warm quarters that we had left behind.

Instead of them, large flocks of black crows accompanied our retreat, in an entourage of worrying and rowdy numbers. Their cries mocked and laughed at us, as they flew and dived over our heads. When a birch wood appeared along the way then they would sit in the snow-laden trees, their cries ringing in the air. We, in this section of the centre of the Eastern Front, could not stop the marching Red Army now with a counter-attack. Back at our base, we let ourselves be snowed in and waited.

Christmas was nearly over and only now did we wish one another, with a lot of irony, "Merry Christmas!" Christmas Eve had come and gone and we had not noticed. In the heat of the moment, or rather the heat of the battle, it was simply forgotten. That night of Christmas Eve, that night of 'peace on earth and goodwill to all men', was spent in positions, under siege from the enemy, in night hours that seemed unending. The night was full, with nothing else but death for some, pain for others and for all, hunger and barbaric cold. At home, we could imagine with certainty that all sat under the Christmas tree. We did not. As the end of the year came, we sank deeper into that inhuman war. The fight however must go on. Was there any other choice? Could we leave Stalin to march into the heart of Europe as he intended? Not at any price!

Our quarters were right at the front of the main front-line. It was a large man-sized bunker to house twelve men. It had an exit to the trenches and was safe enough when not receiving a direct hit. Two layers of thick birch trunks lay crossways to form the roof, and thin stems held the walls together. We had an iron stove and that, together with a thick wall of snow, held a comfortable, containing warmth. The stove was not lit during the day, its smoke giving our positions away to the enemy, but straw gave enough body warmth for those not having guard duty. We heated this stove at nights and used our coats as blankets, sometimes having two, the second being from a fallen comrade.

The German soldier was subjected to a 'plague' in Russia. It was an invisible and secret weapon of the 'Ivans'! Our bunker could protect us from enemy fire, and a house from the cold, but there was nothing that could protect us from the overpowering effects of this 'plague'. Lice! This revolting little beast had attacked every soldier on the Eastern Front and didn't like the cold any more than we did. It took ground cover during the day, for we hardly felt it, but in the warmth of the bunker at night, they went on scouting patrol. The itching was literally unbearable, but it was not only that which plagued us. It was the pus oozing from bite wounds that we had scratched, and which froze skin to parts of our uniform. Sleep was impossible and so we became hunters at night. We went on a lice-hunt, for they marched cross-country over breast, spine and legs. We bagged as many as eighty of the little beasts on each man, squashing them with our thumb nails. We were always covered in minute and bloody puncture marks, evidence that they had reached their target in their battle for blood, our blood, from which they fed. Their favourite targets were body parts rich with blood and covered in hair.

It had been very noticeable, upon first sight of the Russian soldier, that his hair was not only cut short, but it was shorn. Now we knew why. For the German soldier this 'lousy' chapter of the East Front overshadowed any other experiences. They were far worse than the bugs and cockroaches. Those little beasts were rife not only in Russian houses but in the open air too. Nor did they differentiate when it came to rank, they were not fussy. No one was spared, neither a grenadier nor the General himself!

Our only treatment for this on the front line, was the 'delousing station', which was an old Russian *Banja*, i.e. a sauna. When pauses in battle allowed, we used it as often as we could. For us it was a civilised 'island' of only a few square yards, but in another world. We felt that we were in paradise. We used the opportunity to free our uniforms of our sub-tenants. Before the Russian revolution, such saunas belonged in every farmhouse and were now the remnants of an old-fashioned method of hygiene. Afterwards there was only a co-operative *Banja*, a public sauna.

Apart from physical exhaustion and deprivation, and of course not being hit by a bullet, one could be surprised at the condition of the German soldier, with our reduced rations. All could be described as 'thin', or as 'lean' when being diplomatic, even our commanders. This also applied to the civilians. Despite the war and the minimum of calories, the population were then much healthier. Much healthier than they are today. We also learned to live far more sparingly. We were thankful for the basics, even the smallest of comforts. The simplest of wishes for something to eat, to drink, and a roof over our heads, once fulfilled, we were 'whole' after every battle. It all activated our determination to live once more. A simple sauna, and the arrival of a special ration, brought about high spirits such as one cannot imagine, especially in the younger men.

When the soldiers were asked in letters from home, "Are you in good spirits?" we did not know how to answer. We would just love to have said "no"! However, so as not to cause misunderstanding and worry, we considerately used a minimum of words in answer, withholding the reality of the situation, and always said "yes"! It was not simply the fact that 'only' 2,000 kilometres lay between us, but also many months of horrendous experiences. Those were engraved on our souls, and had and did change us, the longer we survived.

Soviet propaganda for the partisan war against Germany

Our appearance, which was mirrored in each other, did nothing to impress any longer. Our uniforms were patched, were no longer the strong dark 'field-grey', but from the dust, rain, mud and snow, a sorrowful pale tone. It no longer mattered how we looked, we didn't mind how we looked, for a campaign was not a parade.

When the post-courier managed to get through, the post from home always raised our spirits very quickly. We were so thankful for post from our parents, girlfriends and friends, all having been written many weeks before. A single letter, or a small parcel, bound your home together with the Front and was a bond that could not be severed. There was so much love and human feeling in the sack full of post that was then distributed over the war-torn countryside. When one of our comrades from the country received a food parcel from home, it was shared, in a brotherly fashion, with the comrades from the city. Their families were restricted to food supplies provided by ration books. Those in the countryside were not so confined and the food parcels provided many a tasty morsel that was not to be had with coupons. In between times, anything coming from home was covered in printed bureaucratic stamps, giving information and warnings, including "Caution! flammable, especially in heath and forest areas"! This tickled our sense of humour and produced many a grin, for were we not in the middle of an inflammable area? Thereafter, in a sticky situation, one of us always warned the others, "Caution! flammable, especially in heath and forest areas", when mortars exploded around us and the bombs fell!

My post did not seem to come as regularly, for want of a better word, as the others. In fact, mine was very sporadic, although the German field-post functioned quite well. It was well after the war that it became known that Dutch postmen deliberately destroyed post that was destined for the Eastern Front, out of opposition. Perhaps they were thinking that their 'acts of heroism' helped Stalin to victory?

The extreme temperatures lamed us into being almost unfit for battle, and things did not improve with the New Year. So our two-hour sentry duty was shortened. We were relieved after every half an hour. Although the sentry point was covered in thick straw, one could suffer very easily from frostbite by standing for any length of time. It often happened. If I remember correctly, one poor chap was found dead, leaning in sleep, at the edge of the trenches. It was not allowed for you to leave your post. 'Spirits', as an alcoholic immunisation were strongly forbidden. However, the Reds froze just like we did. But they thought that their vodka made them fit to fight, not only in winter. Modest in this habit they were not. Their craving was no 'happy hour' any more, but an uninhibited drunkenness. There was no wondering about it. A whole tumbler of vodka was drunk each time, i.e. 100% pure alcohol. In the wide open spaces of Russia and Siberia, 40 kilometres is no distance, 40° is no temperature, and 40% unmentionable as a spirit.

When there was a shortage of vodka, the 'Ivans' knew how to compensate. They suctioned alcohol from the exhausts of planes, and filtered it through the filter of their gas-masks, which cleansed the liquid to a good degree. Then they mixed the rest with a syrup, thus making it a more than acceptable liqueur, which they didn't sip, but just tipped down their throats.

Over a very scratchy 'tannoy' we were subjected to Russian propaganda, as well as with leaflets, which we used as toilet-paper and to roll our cigarettes. It was a weapon used by the Soviets and part of their psychological warfare designed by their Military Directive. We heard top of the chart 'hits' of that time, *I've seen you dancing, Oh Donna Clara*. They were changed to propaganda slogans, aimed at our souls, and to coax us over to their side, such as "surrender to the victorious Red Army, and you'll return home, straight after the war." Another message was "here are girls waiting for you, and lots to eat", at which we aimed a short volley in the direction of the loudspeaker, or until it was silenced. The next day however, the scratchy tones were to be heard on another section of the front.

The reaction to such rather attractive promises was somewhat varied, especially from the hot-blooded and gullible Spanish volunteers from the 'Blue Division'. They believed what they heard. It was not to be wondered at, when remembering that they came to the Russian front and its merciless ice, from a land under the hot Iberian sun.

Not only the Russians, but the German *Wehrmacht* knew the power of printed words and promises, as a tactical and strategic means of war. The Waffen SS had three war-correspondent platoons, whose members were trained firstly as infantry. Then, upon reaching the strength of a battalion, they were posted to the Eastern Front. Later, as the Waffen SS *Standarte* 'Kurt Eggers', messages of the PK, i.e. Propaganda Company, were sent over the tannoys in perfect Russian. They produced very good results at first. The Russian soldiers deserted in hoards, and when their situation seemed hopeless, and success meant an expected high loss of men, the PK provided a bloodless alternative.

The mercilessness of this war, which attacked both sides, was something that we took as a matter of course, for we had not learned anything else. We learned that the fear that we all had at the beginning could be conquered. At some time it was, in all of us, unconsciously moulded into courage. Then we accepted a basic rule. When you were too slow to shoot and you didn't hit your target, you died. You survived when you didn't hesitate, and shot to kill. It was that simple. Gruesome, but simple. This bravery disappeared sometimes, especially when you were surprised. Unexpected surprises robbed you of assessment, particularly when masses of Russians, with screams of "Urra!" jumped out of their hiding places and surrounded you. Worse still, a pack of T34s could suddenly roll steadfastly at you from a birch wood with whirring 500PS motors, along with their indestructible confidence. Often those deadly surprises dampened even the strongest of the unshakeable.

Stalin's strong arm, the T34, surprised and fascinated the legendary *Panzer* General, General Guderian. With its low silhouette, it melted into the battle area very well. The track, which was half a metre wide, 'tramped' through the toughest bog, while the German *Panzer* IV with its 36cm, protested and stopped. The Russian tank was strong and robust but manoeuvrable. However, above all else, it moved over snow and soft ground without any problem. It was the best construction of its time. Not even the 'Panther' or the 'Tiger', which came off the production line a year later, could compete. The T34, with its 45–60cm-thick plating, and its high performance was unmatched.

Like David with his sling, we, as infantrymen, had to deal with Goliath using other methods. When in the trenches we were surprised by such opponents, we simply let them roll over us. When we emerged whole from that exercise, we then had to deal with their accompanying grenadiers. We had to try to destroy the 'giant' from behind, and in close combat. With nerves of steel, combined with mortal fear, it often worked. But often it was under very heavy losses.

All of the divisions, corps and armies of the Waffen SS were commanded by the Armed Forces. Although they were not one iota better equipped than the *Wehrmacht* units, a top performance was expected from them. They were used as trouble-shooters mostly, or as 'firemen', who extinguished the 'fire' and saved whole sectors of the Eastern Front. Enormous losses were the price. "Half-way through this war, a third of these classical Waffen SS divisions lay under Russian soil, and this organisation was burnt to cinders", to quote Heinz Höhne in his book, *Der Orden unter der Totenkopf.*

It wasn't any different for us. Some very hard weeks lay behind us, as gradually the winter began to lose its grip. The countryside was still white, but the temperature became bearable. At the end of January and beginning of February, the long-promised winter clothing arrived from home. It included fabulous fur hats, padded jackets, thermal boots and warm woollen pullovers, as well as balaclavas knitted in haste and faith, by the girls and women at home. But all of it arrived far too late.

In his diary for 23 February, General Halder, Chief-of-Staff wrote, "today was especially quiet". Perhaps it was in the HQ in East Prussia, but certainly not in our neck of the woods. It turned out to be an especially bloody day, with the Red Army attacking our lines with everything they had. It was also the day that my friend Robby Reilingh was very badly wounded. He had been messenger on that day. In the very same moment as our Sergeant fell, quietly, from a shot through the heart, a mortar exploded somewhere near me and I heard him call my name. He managed to smile weakly at me as I reached him, but quickly ignored my attempts to console him with the assurance that he would now have home-leave. It was very important to him that I promised to see his parents and family. He was in severe pain and I could do nothing for him. The whole time, mortars were exploding and machine-guns clattered around us. It was awful. He was taken out of the line of fire and laid on a straw-covered sledge. As he lay waiting behind a bank of snow, to be transported away with other wounded, I covered him with a thick blanket to keep out the cold, pulling it to his face which, in between times, had turned to yellow. I firmly believed at this point that I would see Robby again. He was taken away but not before I recognised an expression that I had seen many times before on the faces of the dying. It was the expression of disbelief, of non-acceptance of what was to come. All had worn this 'astounded' expression.

It had pained me to see him go, but all hell was being let loose and it was a question of survival. All I could do was to pray, from the bottom of my heart, that he pulled through and that we meet again. Later, we had to change our positions. We were made to rest at a first-aid station, run by the *Wehrmacht*, in some outlying huts on the roadside. There the wounded and ill waited for further transport. It was warm inside, which did us all good. "We had a chap here with the same accent as you. Are you Dutch?" I was asked by a Medical Sergeant. I was happily surprised. Was it Robby? I asked for the name, for perhaps it was him. "He's lying over there" I was told. When I looked to where he was pointing, it was through the window, and outside. "No one could have lived with the load of shrapnel that he had inside him", he told me, not unsympathetically, "and he was very brave".

I stood for a long time at Robby's freshly-dug grave, not that there was much to see of his last resting place. It was no more than a snow-covered mound by the roadside, in that unending Russia. I do not know how long I stood at his inconspicuous grave, fighting with the reality that I would not see him again. The grave was simple. The cross, which was made of birch-wood was also simple, and so was the inscription. It was basic. Only the minimum of words had been used. It said nothing but that "SS *Schutze* Robert Reilingh fell on 1 March 1942".

The German Red Cross informed his family in June, with the sober information, German Red Cross Area 15 File num. 1 Advisor (VK) Reference number 8245/42 Subject: *SS Schutze* Robert Reilingh. Reference our letter of 9 June, Professor Dr. Parade, Sun Str, Innsbrück. "The German Red Cross regrets to inform you from information received, that on 1 March 1942, at 4 o'clock, *SS Schutze* Robert Reilingh, died from wounds received, in the main First Aid Station, in Sossna. His burial place is to be found, some 200 metres east of the school in Sossna, on the Moloarchangelsk–Droskovo road. We assure you and your family of our heartfelt sympathy. *Heil Hitler!*" German Red Cross Area 15 Executive/Advisory Dept.

To this day I still have a duplicate of that letter sent to the family. Only after months, was it possible for me to fulfil Robby's last wish. On my first leave home, it was to his parents in the north of Holland that I went immediately. It was not an easy duty, to deliver Robby's last greeting to his parents and his brothers. I could not have been given a warmer welcome by his family, in their magnificent villa, not far from Groningen. Everything that they had hoarded for him, including precious things which were seldom to be found at that time, were shared with me.

I was their guest for several days. I had to repeat over and over again our experiences together. In those few days the first great love of my life was to develop with Robby's sister. It was a mutual attraction from the beginning, and continued in the form of letters, and a short leave, now and again, that one had as a soldier.

Robby's death seemed to be the start of tragedy and suffering for his family, which had been a happy one till then. Less than a year later, his father was murdered, actually assassinated, cycling home on his bicycle. He was shot in the back, in what could have been described as 'peaceful' Holland. As the former General Consul in Liberia, this father-of-four was known for his German sympathies, and as a member of the NSB. It cost him his life. Towards the end of the war, such acts of treachery increased. Then, in turn, they resulted in reprisals against the said 'sinners' by the occupying forces.

The activities of the underground, even in the Soviet Union, was an incredible phenomenon of the war. Thousands of Russians, Ukrainians, Estonians, Latvians, Crimean-Tartars and Georgians worked voluntarily as *Hilfswillige* or *Hiwis*, for the German Military in rear-area positions. They did so to free themselves of the yoke of Communism. But there were just as many partisans working for the Soviet Union. Those bands of 'fighters', *Bandenkämpfer* as they were called, fought without mercy, on both sides. They were illegal fighters, according to the Hague's State War Commission decree in 1907, fighting without uniform, without visible sign of rank and therefore not 'recognisable'.

They stood outside every form of 'justice' or 'rights'. The farmer ploughing his fields, a female working in the kitchens of German units, the smithy, or the administrator of our quarters, could belong to that horde. A gruesome fate awaited those who fell into their hands. Torture, using methods from the Middle Ages, was on every day's agenda. It was even used for a fragment of information about future attacks, troop movements, and weaponry. Prisoners had their eyes poked out, their tongues and ears cut off. Those were not single cases, it was the system with which those lynch-mobs worked. No one escaped those barbarians alive, and those who were shot in the back of the neck were the lucky ones.

It is believed by some, it has to be said, that without such illegal activities, whether on the Eastern Front, in the Balkans or in western Europe, the reprisals of the *Wehrmacht* would never have taken place.

Today the picture is different, and not based on the reality of those times. The illegality of partisan activity is ignored and a very one-sided presentation is the norm, to the disadvantage of Germany. In court cases of later years one cannot speak of objectivity, of fairness in assessing both sides of the coin. It was deliberate and was none other than a reappraisal of the past. No one took the time or trouble to present the unadulterated truth.

The ten pledges in the pay-book of every German soldier, gave very strict guidelines over our treatment of prisoners. For instance number 3. 'It is an offence to kill prisoners who have surrendered, including partisans or spies'. 4. 'Prisoners are not to be abused or mishandled'. 6. 'Wounded prisoners are to be humanely treated'.

Until December 1941, the *Wehrmacht* in Russia occupied a territory of 65 million inhabitants and amongst them were 10,000 partisans. Those numbers grew very quickly. By the middle of 1942, 100,000 men and women were involved in underground activities against the German forces. There was not much success at first, with only half a dozen 'Security' divisions, mostly of older men who were badly equipped, but who had military control of the hinterland. Much more success was had from bands of *fremdvölkische* members from the surrounding 'lands', such as Ukraine/White Russia. The former were deserters from the Red Army, but they were supported by the 'locals' sympathising with the Germans. They possessed the same knowledge and determination as the 'partisans' and not even they could avert the problem.

To quote, "In the years from 1941 to 1943, Russian soldiers killed 500,000 enemy soldiers, including 47 German Generals, and many anti-communist Ukrainians". These figures are taken from the Russian author B.S. Telpukovski's book, *A History of the Partisan Movement*. Their weapons included knives and machine-pistols. On films there can be seen the 70-shot revolving barrel-type guns, and rifles and shotguns. Molotov cocktails, i.e. petrol-filled glass bottles with a wick, were first used in the Russian/Finnish war of 1939/40, were used by them for close combat with tanks. There was, as it happened, an excess of empty vodka bottles in Russia! Later those simple but effective bottle-bombs were filled with a mixture of phosphorus and sulphur, which produced a heat of 1300° when in flames.

Stalin knew what he was doing when he ordered partisan activities. Twelve days after Hitler's invasion, Stalin gave his orders for 'Partisan activity'. He also started his 'scorched earth' policy, whereby everything of use that could not be taken when retreating, was to be destroyed. Alexander Werth wrote, "Blow for blow was now the order of the day." The German troops never had time to make a thorough search of harmless looking villages for the leader of those bandits. They could only try to find the source and then extinguish the fires. It all drove the inhabitants into the lap of the partisans. The German Army, in their advance, had been looked upon as liberators from the yoke of Communism. They had been greeted with the traditional bread and salt, from girls wearing flowers.

Only a year later, how could it come to the situation where the partisans had such a hold over the inhabitants in the same areas? The answer was a simple one and the good relationship held only as long as the Military Directive ruled with goodwill. Russian so-called Commissars or Inspectors were used, in order to undermine and destroy any sympathy shown for the occupying forces, and to prepare the ground for partisan activity. Those 'Red' commissars replaced the 'brown', and Stalin made fun of the 'dumb' in Berlin.

The same lack of understanding stood between the Waffen SS and the Armed Forces, when it came to the interference from party officials in the redirection of the inhabitants. We soldiers saw the policy as an expression of extreme arrogance, which was to our disadvantage, and the advantage of the partisans. There were exceptions of course. Conscientious officials not only with ideals but also local understanding, tried to even out the inadequacies of the Ministry for Eastern Policy.

One of those was a genuine NS Head Administrator, who had been a general commissioner in the Crimea. This educated and upright national socialist, Alfred Frauenfeld, administered with so much level-headedness and expertise, that he could afford to travel hundreds of miles through the Steppe without any armed protection. He treated those working for him with decency and propriety. He understood the mentality, interests and needs of the inhabitants in the areas. Because of that, he himself was also treated with decency and propriety. He produced a highly efficient economy in the Crimea that was second to none. In complete contrast, one of the 'gravediggers' of the Third Reich was a man called Erich Koch, District Commissioner in Ukraine and former district commissioner in East Prussia. He directed with brutality, not the consideration and 'fingertip' feeling of his counterpart.

It is clear that Germany did not use the one-off chance that they had in the East. There were experts who with far-sightedness tried to save the situation. But their suggestions of altering the policy of the occupying forces, were only put into action as the Red Army took Budapest.

Despite the order to "hold at any price", the German *Wehrmacht* was threatened with the same fate in the winter of 1941/42, as Napoleon's army. In between times, the front was no longer intact and the Red Army held the initiative in the south. Only with extreme exertion, and against the will of Stalin's favourite general, General Zhukov, could the offensive on Moscow be averted at the end of January. The situation on the Eastern Front stabilised gradually. However, Operation 'Barbarossa' with its aims and plan of operation, from Archangelesk in the north in a straight line down to Astrakhan in the south, faded into the background. The hard winter in which the German Army found itself and which destroyed their plan, lasted four long, unending months. In March there was another terrible snowstorm, which was followed by 'the thaw'. It was then a 'bog-down' period.

"At the end of the winter, the faces of our men were old, from stress that was present every day. They had an unhealthy hue from the frost, that they would never lose. It was to be seen on both sides. The only visible difference could be seen from the uniform that they wore, or the language that was to be heard, i.e. German or Russian". This is quoted from the diary of *Leutnant* Wolfgang Paul, in his book *Erfrorener Sieg*.

We volunteers were still of the opinion that the battle of and for the whole of Europe was justified. The battle was not against the people of the Soviet Union, but for the people of the Soviet Union. It was proved when the USA decided to join the war in 1941 and showered Russia with vast amounts of American war material. Pope Pius XII described the action of the Waffen SS, who consisted of a very mixed bag of Danes, Finns, Norwegians, Dutch, Belgians, Swiss and French, as "the defence of the basis of Christian culture".

We had covered vast distances in comfortable trains and goods-wagons, in transport planes and lorries, tanks and *troikas*, and then marched on foot to the Front. As Germany's war-generation, we all shared the same fate, which welded us together and which only the fire of battle could separate. We had not found 'adventure', nor the 'laurel-leaves of victory', but lice, mud, polar-conditions and death. In indescribable huts, as many as twenty men were provisionally housed, waiting for the next order. We crouched in holes in God's earth, in 'ready' positions, before attacking the enemy. The minutes seemed like hours, before we could ambush those who felt at home in the darkness. We had restless, interrupted nights, 'sleeping', for want of a better word, a light and fitful sleep. We kept a finger on the trigger and had the smell of burning villages in our nostrils. We lit a fire when the opportunity arose and warmed ourselves around the flames. Flames which could not only kill, but save as well.

We had warmed ourselves with the warmth from exhausts, or lingered if only for minutes, in the warmth of the burning houses on our marches, not wanting to move away. Living under open skies with temperatures 30° below freezing, reduced us to the fundamentals. Later it dropped to 52° below freezing point. Napoleon, in 1812, suffered only at 25°. At every possibility, we German soldiers slipped into any coverage we could find in that God-forsaken land, be it a hole in the ground or the poorest of huts, away from nature's hostility. The Russian Steppe, with its unending horizon and vast heavens, was a 'lord' over the victorious, in the moment that we, its enemy, won a battle. It was natural that we had tension in us, as we first trod the earth of the Soviet Union, but the wretchedness of the Bolshevik world exceeded even our imagination.

Stalin's Empire was at this time, an actual 'state of dead souls'. There was a land, no, a continent at Europe's door which in the day and age of radio and films, was completely cut off from the rest of the world. This 'saga' in the history of humanity, this 'paradise', was nothing new and nothing but ice-cold propaganda. We assessed this 'state of workers and farmers', not with the eyes of scholars, but the bare facts as soldiers do, with eyes that were wide open and therefore all the more 'fundamentally'.

For example, one could search the whole of the Soviet Union for a replacement shaving-mirror when you smashed your own. But you could not find one for love nor money. To lose your pocket knife or your fountain pen was a real tragedy. This annoyance, this lack of, for us the simplest of commodities, was not appeased for months on end. We did find civilised articles, but then in senseless quantities. One of our comrades, who had been in Russia far longer than we, told us about a state-owned shop (what else?) that had not only enormous reserves of ladies' face-powder, and toothpaste in tons, but not a single toothbrush! One saw Russian girls on the streets, thickly powdered because it was the cheapest of goods. One could buy it by the pound. The shelves were bending under the weight of the toothpaste which tasted of nothing but chalk. But a toothbrush was never found. In another town, its shop had records, hundreds of the same record, with an excerpt from one of Stalin's speeches on one side and an operatic aria on the other, but a choice? There was none.

We were nearly swallowed up by this land, this Russia. Despite the changing seasons, be it with the changing leaves of autumn or the white of winter, to us the monotony of this land appeared as a deathly shade of grey. It was a land embedded in a vegetative condition. In the villages, the inhabitants appeared as children who had to be woken, their existence being colourless, uniform, simply nondescript. The men appeared to be exhausted, the women full of the worries of life. When one had a new apron or a new cap, then there were reasons for suspicion. Dictatorship ruled here in all of its Proletarian instinct, breeding jealousy, resentment and slander. It was better that one did not own something that no one else had.

One must ask what happened to the army of slave-workers, who worked for a pittance and saw nothing of the promises of Stalin's "five-year plan", which was nothing else but an Armament Plan and having no reform. They received nothing. The energy and the riches of the nation were used by power-crazed fanatics and turned into armaments for a war that was described by the Russians themselves as the biggest war of aggression in world revolution.

CHAPTER 12

In Hospital

The *Wehrmacht* slowly regained its strength after the winter. The summer of 1942 saw the start of new areas of attack that ran to plan and were successful. Sebastopol, in the Crimea, the HQ of the Black Sea Fleet was the strongest fortress in the world. It fell into our hands after a bitter fight, in which two enemy armies could have crushed one another.

Within the next month, we also pushed back the Russian Front by three hundred kilometres, taking Voronezh and Rostov. Nonetheless, Hitler's plan to destroy the Red Army collapsed. Even outside Russia's borders, Field Marshal Erwin Rommel in North Africa had taken Tobruk that summer. German submarines had risen out of the water at Long Island and their crews viewed the traffic in New York. The "Grey Wolf" had engaged in its first attack in Canadian territorial waters, in the flow of the St. Laurence river. However, the war leaned dramatically to the side of the Allies with the defeat of the 6th Army, in February 1943, at Stalingrad. The Allies however still needed another two years to force Germany to its knees.

The hospital train which I found myself that summer did not need as long as that to bring me from Orel on the Oka, to Warsaw on the river Vistula. The Russian soldier had not managed in months of bloody fighting, but that little beast, the louse, managed to put me out of action in much less. A high fever, which came and went over a period of five days, was eventually diagnosed by the troops' doctor, as Volhynian Fever. It is one of the typhus category and transmitted from bites from *Rickettsia*, a parasite that is neither bacteria nor virus, and which is found in the Ukraine.

The train painted with red crosses, travelled from the central sector of the Eastern Front, over Briansk, Smolensk, Minsk and Brest, into the territory of the General Government. When one could shut out the moans of the wounded and try to ignore the stench of pus and fresh wounds, then one could ask for nothing more. The comfortable sleeping compartment for us was like travelling tourists' first class. The converted hospital train was fitted with bunk-beds for the wounded. They were tended continually by the doctors, medical orderlies and Red Cross nurses. At nearly all of the stations and halts, the volunteer nurses of the German Red Cross appeared with large steaming coffee pots. This service covered the whole of central Europe, practically to the front. Among the nurses were women and girls from all over Europe, not only Germans, but all working just like the male volunteers.

Our military hospital lay very near the river Vistula, opposite the town of Praga. Before we could enter the hospital we had to be disinfected, body

Two photographs of *SS-Sturmmann* Hendrik Verton, 1942

and uniform. We entered a long barrack, as naked as the day we were born, forming long queues. We were a living conveyor-belt for the 'carbolic angels', the nurses who were ready to smear every hair-covered part of us with a disinfectant oil. It caused problems for those who had not seen a member of the female species in months. They were then the centre of teasing, grins, laughter and comments from their comrades, which the nurses diplomatically ignored, carrying out their duty with a faint smile on their lips.

After the stress of the front, the hospital was a real island of peace, and a piece of home. The BDM girls who visited us from time to time saw to that, either by the bedside of the wounded where they sang the happy songs of home, or in the shady garden of the hospital and also by giving useful little presents. I can remember an amusing incident, which at the time rather embarrassed me. I was holding up my hand to be given a razor as they were being distributed. One of the girls placed a bar of chocolate in my hand declaring that my 'baby-face' did not need a razor.

Despite the short and measured free time of the nurses, they showed the soldiers the town when they could, once they were on the mend or could walk. Not that there was anything of worth to see. The siege of the town in September 1939 had left its mark. There were many ruins and damaged houses to be seen, witnesses of the bitter fighting for the designated 'fortress' of Warsaw. The fate of the Polish capital certainly made an impression on us. A worse time for the people of Warsaw was to come, for in the last phase of the war, it would be destroyed by up to 85%.

After my stay in hospital, I was posted to a rehabilitation unit, richly laden with provisions for my journey to Tobelbad near Graz. I went first to Berlin for a few days' special leave, and where I got to know Germany's capital. Despite being wartime, there was more than enough entertainment to choose from, theatre, variety and the cinema, all at half-price for the military. Comrades already in Berlin who knew their way around the city, guided me in all directions. In the hope of seeing 'the Führer', we marched to the new Chancellery in Wilhelms street. But instead of seeing him, we were given a brisk salute from a double SS guard, standing to attention outside the gigantic bronze doors.

It was a world full of contrasts for us fighters returning from the Front, returning to a peaceful homeland which we had to digest. We were feted and richly spoiled, not only by private persons but by organisations too, with the maxim "our brave soldiers richly deserve our thanks". Gifts rained upon us and invitations too. Later that changed radically, the longer the war lasted.

Everyone had their problems and worries. The population had their contribution to make to the war-effort, in working longer hours. 46 hours a week in offices, and 52 hours in the factories. It was also at this time that the restaurants served 'front-line menus' on Mondays and Thursdays. That gave the population a taste of front-line cuisine, which was usually a stew, made exactly as the military cooks made it.

Tobelbad, in the green countryside of the Steiermark, reminded me of Carinthia with its forest covered mountains, and slopes covered with fruit trees, only these slopes were gentler and more varied. This idyllic countryside proved to be not only of a healing climate, but for the rehabilitating soldier an impetus for their appetites. In order to offset the hunger that we had from the sparse catering in Tobelbad, we had to find a solution. The solution was always one and the same for any of the military, and was called the 'fried potato relationship'. As it suggests, the aim of the relationship was always the same, extra food in any form. It had really nothing to do with fried potatoes!

It revolved around a sympathetic, young lady who could lay her hands on this extra food and amongst other things, could cook! My choice was a dark blonde from Strassgang and I happily marched the few kilometres to where she lodged. She was one of those enlisted for 'work-service' and who I found very sympathetic. Unfortunately, also in the same lodgings was a man who was head of the kitchen staff, but even so she brought me fruit and sometimes sausage, which she had secretly organised. On Sundays we went from Tobelbad for long walks in the mountains or idled our way through the town of Graz, until I had to return for roll-call. Most of the younger comrades had a girlfriend, not only to flirt with, but more importantly, to provide an extra 'dessert' for our hunger.

Sometimes an ensemble or two came from Vienna to entertain the troops. There were colourful improvised cabarets, and piano concerts with music from Mozart and Haydn, which were boring for us young soldiers. But the officers and non-commissioned officers took it in their stride, in order to flirt with the female artists, late into the night, for which they had to pay.

To believe that our time in Tobelbad was a sanatorium cure for body and soul would be wrong. It was a 'cure', in so far as our surroundings were in complete contrast to that of the front. Our quarters were in the large, impressive, detached villas, which the 'cure-guests' rented in peace time. But we had to work. We were kept in trim with gentle exercises, body-building, movement and sport. Then we had to go to school, where combat training would have been superfluous for us, and which we were spared. But we were given theory in terrain practice, map reading and also world politics. I must not forget the thorough cleaning of our quarters! I also remember Tobelbad for a very big and unexpected surprise. My brother Evert suddenly appeared, he too having been wounded in Russia. He had also been posted to this rehabilitation unit, and for the very first time we both belonged to the same company.

He was wounded again a year later, in north-west Kharkov, in very hard defensive action with the Wiking Division. His company commander sent the news to our parents, ending the letter with "in close affinity". Field Administration Post Code 33576. Dated 08.09.1943 (in the field).

Dear Mr and Mrs Verton,

The Company wish to inform you, that your son Evert has been slightly wounded. On 6 September 1943, in an enemy attack, he was wounded from shell splinters in his neck and thigh. After treatment from

Two Dutch brothers in the uniform of the Waffen SS: Evert and Hendrik Verton

the unit's doctor, he will be transferred into a field hospital from where he can write to you himself.

Greetings in close affinity,

Yours faithfully ... ...(Signature Unreadable) pp, SS *Leutnant*

Only today did I notice that the usual *Heil Hitler* is missing in this letter. Even the German Red Cross, in their letter of condolence to Robby's parents informing them of his death, do not forget this formal address. With this comment I wish to point out that those of the Waffen SS soldiers fighting on the front were not the "Upstanding stalwarts of the Party" as they are deliberately depicted today.

It was also in Tobelbad that I had to present myself before the whole company. There my company commander presented me with a medal for the 'offensive in the East' in the winter of 1941/42. All of those from the Eastern Front received one, those who fought in the period from 15 November 1941 to 15 April 1942. The medal had a striped band in red, white and black, red for blood, white for snow and black for death, the death of many of our fallen comrades. Perhaps it can be described as 'grim humour', but thereafter we from the Eastern Front, referred to this medal as the 'frozen meat medal'.

CHAPTER 13

A New Apprenticeship

The longer the war continued, the more resolute and brutal it became. It was clear that success or defeat depended not on how good the soldiers were, but how well their commanders guided them. What was even more important, was the worth of their weapons with which they worked. The modern war therefore demanded perfection from one another and with one another. Not only that, but a variety of highly developed weapons had to be mastered. Although every man was needed on the front, every unit was ordered to send chosen men for special courses, to bring them up-to-date with new military techniques.

I was one of those posted to Czechoslovakia on one of those courses in the autumn of 1942. In Kienschlag near Prague, I came to grips with a weapon which for its time was a small wonder and which the experts had been working on since 1935. Until then, close-combat with tanks had depended on an explosive charge, which upon detonation had produced only splinters in the plating. This new weapon was a magnetised hollow-charge. It had deposits of explosive material and a copper funnel which, in the moment that it had magnetic contact with the surface, released a high-speed detonation, producing holes through the armoured plating, and putting the tank out of action.

The course took place in the SS *Panzergrenadier* School and for this course we had to practise the usual tactics of tank close-combat used by the infantry, with Molotov/smoke cocktails and explosive charges. The charges were made from five hand-grenades, four without grips and bound around the fifth. To use such weapons one had to be fit, for instance by springing on to fast-moving captured Russian tanks which were used for these exercises. The 'roll-over' exercise was also one that we had to master. There was nothing to surpass the superhuman effort one had to make, when cowering in a hole in the ground, knowing that this giant, weighing tons, which was moving towards you with the deafening noise of its screeching track, would roll over your head. There were other exercises that needed not only a lot of pluck, even from the most daring of us, but needed almost acrobatic expertise. For instance, one had to place a T-mine, i.e. a Teller-mine or 'plate mine', also an 'S-mine' or 'disc mine', between turret and hull of a zig-zagging practice-tank. Or we had to push a hand-grenade down the muzzle of an oncoming tank.

Only later did we have a close-combat weapon at our disposal, which meant that we did not have to break our cover. Only with this could we curb the destruction caused by Soviet tanks. I mean the *Panzerfaust*, a highly developed anti-tank rocket launcher, a metre long, weighing only six pounds, and lovingly called 'Gretchen' by us. This was a sensation for the troops and the *Wehrmacht* made good propaganda from it.

Not only the parachute troops but also we of the Waffen SS were expected to operate in single-combat now. We were schooled to assess and to act, and those taking part had not only to be physically fit but mentally too. From tactical experience, soldiers from the Eastern Front were ideal, with their front-line experience of the Russian campaign. For instance they assessed with practised eyes, as soldiers should, an advance into enemy-held woods. They were not only familiar with refined tricks but used them themselves, taught by the reality of war.

Although prepared for everything to be thrown at us, nonetheless we were tense as we advanced through the training grounds, jumping with fright as a 'comrade', made from cardboard, suddenly jumped out from the door of a replica blockhouse, followed in quick succession by a volley of blanks. Our hearts raced for a few seconds when a life-size, stuffed puppet sprang unexpectedly from behind a tree and then a practice hand-grenade was aimed at us, by one of the instructors hidden in the bushes. This training programme in Prague's peaceful surroundings was well designed. It was designed to improve our chances of survival and to beat the enemy, for after all the war was not lost.

At that time there was no anti-German hostility aimed at us, as we wandered through the 'golden capital' of Czechoslovakia in our free hours. Despite the war, it held the status of a neutral land. Where war held practically every other land in Europe tightly in its grip, these people lived and worked in an oasis of freedom. Despite having 'protectorates', the land enjoyed the freedom of self-government and internal development. The men were not enlisted to fight. With the exception of the Ministry of Defence and Foreign Affairs, administration was fully in the hands of the Czechs.

I can remember that we could shop without the usual ration books and that we could eat normally in restaurants, with normal portions which elsewhere was no longer possible. Even the luxury industry bloomed here, in the region of the Moldau, as always. The Czechs were given lucrative contracts from Germany, from Reinhard Heydrich as the representative of the "Reichs protector", with the Bishops' kiss, *Pax Domini Sit Semper Vobiscum* from the Teutons.

En masse they were the most faithful of Hitler's collaborators, which even the House of Commons in Britain ascertained. "The Czechs have lost faith in themselves and have not even protested against the occupation of their land". Heydrich held a great deal of sympathy from the working-class, in particular for his social security plans. The relative peacefulness in the land did not please the western powers. Flying them out in British planes,

SS-Rottenführer Hendrik
Verton, 1943

exiled Czechs were flown into Czechoslovakia with a mission. Heydrich was murdered and in protest 30,000 Czechs assembled on the Wenzels square in Prague in 1942. This provoked 'disturbance of the peace' produced unexpected results for the Allies and because of it, the Germans made reprisals in the village of Lidice.

Blood flowed later in Prague, on 5 May 1945, as the *Wehrmacht* capitulated. Nowhere else in Europe was the revenge so great or so gruesome against helpless prisoners, the women, nursing sisters and children, as in the land of Czechoslovakia. In 1982, in the German magazine *Horzu* (edition No.45) the Czech Chess Champion Ludeck Pachmann wrote, "When there was hell on earth then it was let loose in Prague on 5 May 1945. I saw it with my own eyes"

Time went by and I found myself on yet another course, this time in Lauenburg for subordinate training. It was there that I learned of the assassination attempt on Hitler, in his HQ in East Prussia on 20 July 1944. For us in Pomerania, it was a quiet day and just like any other. It was hours later that we found ourselves under emergency conditions, and it was forbidden for us to leave the barracks. Details over this attempt were sparse, and even in the next few days the information was vague and inexact.

We soldiers were relaxed, but none the less, at a time when the Russians were gaining ground every day, we were outraged, at the thought that in the middle of total war, our Commander-in-Chief should be eradicated. The civilian population thought so too. As one who was there at the time, I did not meet anyone who regretted this unsuccessful attempt on Hitler's life. We were all the more astounded, when weeks later we learnt who the guilty parties were and that they were our own, their names belonging to the most influential and highest ranks of the Army.

It placed a new light upon unexplained 'incidents' that had been happening on both the Front line and on the home front. The extent of them ranged from acts of sabotage in the armament industry, to the delayed delivery of the winter clothing which had caused the deaths of so many of our soldiers. There was deliberate misinterpretation of orders, which also cost innumerable soldiers their lives. There was the betrayal of highly secret information from headquarters to the enemy. It was certainly no coincidence that German weapon production reached its highest productivity quotas, in the last years of the war. At about that same time the conspirators were eradicated. There was continual bombardment by the Allies. "It is not good to change horses in mid-stream", is what the famous American President Abraham Lincoln said.

Eugen Gerstenmaier, one of Germany's post-war presidents, put the errors of those conspirators into very clear, explanatory words. "What we in Germany's resistance did not understand, or did not want to, was that this war was not against Hitler, but against Germany. Only afterwards did we understand that all the efforts of those in the resistance were unsuccessful and that was also no coincidence".

"The opposition did not offer even the smallest chance of better conditions of freedom, than the National Socialists themselves, not even in the event of a successful *putsch* and a proclaimed cease-fire". Quoted from Hellmut Diwald. The opposition against Hitler himself, a third of it stemming from the aristocracy, did not come from the people themselves, but from the old conservative leadership. Their failures had caused the very emergence of a dictatorship in Germany.

When the Heads of the military were united in the opinion that Hitler should be deposed, even before the Stauffenberg assassination attempt, then the question must be raised, why this was not carried out by those in uniform, in close proximity to Hitler. They had all been allowed to have a regulation pistol on their person. It was all too late. Those same officers gave daily orders themselves to their soldiers in deployment and under risk of their lives. True, this act of opposition would have demanded the willingness to take a very big risk and needed the courage of conviction. But it would have been characteristic of resistance activity. Many, if not all, had profited under this 'Bohemian Private'. They had been promoted in rank and highly decorated, resulting from the efforts of those soldiers at the Front who had paid a very high 'price in blood '.

Only with the turn of the tide, i.e. the invasion by the Allies on French shores, in June 1944, which could no longer be halted, did those very opponents of Hitler turn to the use of bombs as a more effective means of disposing of him. Nazi propaganda denounced them and the people too, seeing them as traitors and renouncers of their oaths. It was Hitler himself who interpreted this attack as "a ratification of my commission in the name of providence." It gave him the will to carry on as before, to attain his life's work. It has certainly not been easy for post-war generations to sort the chaff from the wheat of this scenario. Who were the 'opportunists', and who were the 'idealists' prepared to make sacrifices for their ethical demands? Only the last of those requires any respect.

We wanted however to win the war. So we used the opportunity given to us to improve our education in the SS School for Non-commissioned Officers. We also got to grips with the course, and the use of the light 7.5cm infantry gun and 15cm howitzers. The drill for the heavy 15cm howitzer was hard, especially for those who had to manhandle the heavy cartridge-cases and shells with speed. I was however spared the work. I was spared this muscle exercise, as team leader. But for that I had to be perfection itself on the optical sights, with speed and perfection even at a distance of 3,500 to 4,000 metres. No mistakes were allowed, which meant no 'dud' shots. No *Fahrkarten!* i.e. a ticket back home in soldiers' slang. If even one shot missed the target, then there was an almighty dressing-down from our instructor!

CHAPTER 14

East Prussia

The victory fanfares were now seldom to be heard. The orders over the radio to 'hold your positions', and 'at all costs', became more frequent. Even in June 1944, the collapse began in the East. The central sector of the Front line that had been held by Army Group Centre collapsed. Without doubt, there then began the most forceful and horrific chapter of the war for Germany. The coming months brought the hardest months of fighting and the highest losses for the Eastern Front soldiers. For old people, women and children, it also brought unimaginable suffering and senseless death.

With the coming of autumn 1944, the Polish and Lithuanian country-side sank into mud. The battle for East Prussia had begun when six Russian armies broke through the lines of the 3rd German Army. They severed the lines of the central and northern sectors. Four days later, at Krottingen, the Russians trod German soil, for the first time. Once more our time had come. The heavy losses of non-commissioned officers, the backbone of the army, had produced many gaps in the front line and these had to be filled. Our course therefore came to an abrupt end. With our packs on our backs we were on the march again, not knowing where we were going.

As the long train, laden with pieces of heavy equipment, passed Danzig, it was clear that we were returning to the Eastern Front. We had so much wanted to finish the course and receive our certificates and promotion as non-commissioned officers. However I was promoted, and at a later date decorated for 'bravery on the Front'. I belonged to the 8th Company, *Kampfgruppe* 'Römer'. The train took us 300 kilometres eastwards, to our final destination of Lötzen in East Prussia. The journey then continued by road, to a village called Kruglanken in the middle of the Masurian Lakes district. There we were based in readiness for 'Operation Scharnhorst'.

Provisionally, I was used as a motorcycle messenger and was given a 250-BMW motorcycle, to accompany motorised convoys. I enjoyed that, racing up and down the columns, like a shepherd dog with a flock of sheep. Later on, in the depth of winter, it was no longer so pleasant when, despite balaclava and goggles, the ice-cold wind froze your face to a stiff mask.

Reconnaissance and security runs were now the order of the day, together with one other comrade and with machine-pistols slung around our necks. We were our own masters. We could plan our own routes in this fantastic countryside. It was near the front that we found two young women about to leave their empty property, an estate. We had to do our best to persuade their very old grandmother to leave with them. We did our best to explain the danger that she was in, amidst the war and the Russian soldiers. It was all to no avail. If she had to die it would be where she was. She would rather do that, than leave her home. There was nothing more to say or do. She was adamant. The two granddaughters left with us, crying bitter tears. They said 'goodbye' to their grandmother, leaving her with her cat on her lap, having provided enough food for them both. It was a heart-rending scene.

Not only there, but in other places as well, where we made our quarters, we were witness to indescribable human tragedies, particularly when in the villages, estates and farms, the inhabitants had to leave at a moment's notice, only taking what they could carry. The evacuation of the areas was the responsibility of the area administrators. They often gave the order of evacuation at the very last minute, not giving the inhabitants time to think about what they should take, and what had to be left behind. Where we could, we soldiers helped them with packing their meagre belongings on to horse-drawn carts, hand-carts, or their tractors pulling trailers. But they had other help as well. Prisoners of war, who had been sent to work on the German farms in the area, where they had been well treated, also helped the local inhabitants to pack up their possessions. The majority were Poles, and there were also some French who joined the trek of refugees, fleeing from the Red Army.

'Operation Scharnhorst' was designed to ensure amongst other things, the security of Hitler's headquarters the *Wolfsschanze*, or Wolf's Lair, and the wide circumference around it. The HQ in the Görlitz forest was made up of eight, one-storey, above-ground bunkers and some other wooden and brick-built buildings. All of the roads on the complex, the paths and the bunkers were covered in enormous 'cammo' nets as protection from aerial view by the enemy. Lying behind several barriers of barbed wire and other security barriers, the *Wolfsschanze* was the most secure of Hitler's quarters. As the Russians forced their way further west, his HQ was once more transferred to Berlin on 20 November. So that it did not fall into the hands of the Russians, the *Wolfsschanze* was blown up at the beginning of January 1945.

We, in our sector in Kruglanken, really did not have much to do and so we found time to explore the fascinating countryside of East Prussia. I have memories of black forests, the green clear water of lakes and rivers, and of the spicy, dry, cold air. There were small towns with cobbled market places and memorials of great German princes. Other memorials were to 'Old Fritz' (Frederick the Great), while quaint villages, avenues of birches, or birch-lined roads, lead to farmsteads. All were within distance of a lake, or a whole chain shimmering to the horizon. Today the recollection is still bright and clear. That land, as large as Holland, and with 2.5 million inhabitants normally, was practically empty of people at the end of 1944. The ivy-covered country seats, with their wrought-iron park gates, long drives and pillared porticoes, standing in the shadows of age-old trees, lush green meadows and pastures, or dark forest, were deserted then. Those memories will stay with me and will never fade.

The Postmaster also lived in our quarters and although there was no work for him, he stayed dutifully at his post with his daughter. That was a piece of luck for me. From the first moment we met there was a rapport between us, we understood one another. She was young, an attractive brunette and a real 'Masurian' maiden. Thanks to a very understanding company commander living in our quarters, she was allowed to accompany me on my runs, to show me the sights. Perhaps it would be better to say, 'to allow me to get to know the area'. But we were alone and could forget that there was a war, even when it was only for moments. We wandered through spruce-woods and aisles of trees bending towards one another up above, almost forming the arches of a stately cathedral. It was still and peaceful, with only very faint sounds of the front disturbing this paradise, this unspoiled countryside.

Our romance however was brief. The Postmaster and his lovely daughter had to flee like all of the others and were in the last trek of refugees to go west. There obviously was not one soldier, anywhere in the whole of the army, who did not enjoy a rendezvous with the opposite sex, whether a spontaneous flirt or a real heart-felt romance. Far be it from me to give the impression that we soldiers behaved like farmhands, were promiscuous or philanderers. We were not. We were normal, healthy, young soldiers forced together in one another's company. We longed for the company and love of a woman, exactly as the young men of our own age in peacetime. It was the situation that caused us problems, for a romance of permanency was impossible. The soldier was always on the move.

It was between December 1944 and January 1945 that the Russians started to collect around the Vistula. That river, stretching over hundreds of kilometres, was the German demarcation line. More than three million Russian soldiers, with nearly ten thousand tanks, 40,000 artillery guns, as well as 7,000 planes made up the largest army of aggression in world history. Their opponents, the defenders of the German Reich, sought to stem the steamroller effect of the Russians, with the courage of the desperate. They fought to win every available inch of ground. The will to hold ground was reinforced when information seeped through the lines of inhuman atrocities, committed against civilians by the Russians, in particular the 11th Division of Guards.

In winning back the village of Goldap, German soldiers found a picture of sheer barbarism against the human being, an apocalypse. They found women and young girls had been raped. Old people, infants and babies had been murdered. French and Polish prisoners who had not fled from the village, had been beaten to death. There are no words to describe the barbarity of the atrocities in the many cases committed by the Red Army, one being the case of Nemmersdorf.

A column of exhausted refugees made a stop in Nemmersdorf in the early morning hours. It was to be their death sentence. Their hand- and horse-drawn carts filled the width of the main road. Amongst the noise of stamping hooves, one could suddenly hear the screech of tank tracks. A column of Russian tanks emerged from the veil of morning mist and the steel giants rolled over the refugees, the screaming women, children and old men. The Russians could not hold Nemmersdorf, and the German 4th Army under General Friedrich Hossbach took the village. They were eyewitnesses to the unforgettable evidence of barbarity to its inhabitants. Along with Goldap, Nemmersdorf is one of the names from the Second World War that will never be forgotten. The men found 72 corpses, including infants and babies in nappies. The bodies of women and children were found hanging from hay-carts and barn doors.

The hate against Germans was brought to boiling point by extensive propaganda, until it was pathological. The disease became an epidemic. "Kill the Germans!" With that, all of the Ten Commandments fused into one, for the Soviets. The Russian author Ilya Ehrenburg was first and foremost of the propagandists when it came to hate campaigns. "When you kill one German, then make it two. There is nothing so pleasurable as German corpses!"

The Russian newspaper *Krasnaya Sveda* was more reserved and commented,

> One has to admit that the German resistance in East Prussia is so strong and steadfast, that it exceeds any previous performance. The battles are extremely bloody and they offer resistance that is fanatical. They are untiring in counter-attack and in defending every inch of ground.

Radio London, which at first had no idea, were also astounded and said that "the fight for East Prussia is extraordinarily tough and is obviously a contest of wills. The Germans fight bitterly for Prussia's holy ground". The German soldier knew, far better than Radio London, why and for what they risked their lives. In villages that they had retaken, they had first-hand experience of the monster against which they were fighting. They needed no propaganda, no historical example in order to give, to the last, all that they could and did offer. Nevertheless, Prussia fell to the Russians. That lost paradise had always been top of the list as booty for foreign imperialists. It is only the stork that returns home to East Prussia from its migration, or the wild geese, in their wedge-like flight, giving a false but lenient illusion that all is right with the world. But that land will never be the same again.

CHAPTER 15

Silesia

There was a natural hurdle between Stalin's mighty advance to the eastern borders of the German Reich and Berlin. It was the river Oder. The giant Russian offensive was one that threatened Silesia and the target was Breslau, Silesia's metropolis in the southern sector and a key position for the Red Army. It was stated at that time "Europe's fate will be decided at the Oder". Therefore strongly concentrated defensive measures were decided upon for that theatre of war, and we too were sent there.

Suddenly, the *Kampfgruppe* was sent on a long train journey, from East Prussia to Pomerania. It lasted a few days. We were newly equipped, had packed, and were sorted into new units. Then express trains took us from our old barracks, in the School for Subordinate Commanders, in Lauenburg, direct to the Oder. Without knowledge of strategic plans, we all wondered why the *Kampfgruppe*'s destinations were so very often changed. Even as we were underway, we would find ourselves relocated to places where originally we were not meant to go, but then became urgently needed. "The wheels had to roll to victory!"

As the convoy of trains finally reached the rolling Silesian countryside, snowflakes had fallen, framing the carriage windows, for winter had arrived in Silesia, in the middle of December. We arrived in the evening and wondered at the peaceful, undisturbed atmosphere and obvious daily routine in this, for us, unknown city of Breslau, for it held no signs of war. Cars and trams still fully lit, drove through glittering snow. A queue of people stood patiently outside a cinema, with its coloured posters. Children were skating on the town's frozen moat. The trains still ran to their scheduled times from the main railway station in the town, and from Freiburg to the west.

Next to Dresden, Breslau was the only large city, until the end of 1944, that had not been bombed by the Allies. This important east German city grew during the war, from a population of 630,000 to nearly a million, with the storing of its industry's war material, which had been transferred from the west. Both the government departments and the officials of the Ministries of Finance and for Foreign Affairs, were moved after heavy bombing raids on Berlin, to this eastern province. Breslau, as well as surrounding small towns and villages, was also the home of evacuees from heavily raided areas such as the Rhine and the Ruhr. It was the air-raid shelter of the nation, for thousands who had been bombed out of their homes.

It was time for us to find our barracks. They turned out to be in the 'School of Infantry Replacement Training Battalions', in Deutsch-Lissa, 8

116

As *Wachhabender* (commandant) at the NCO School in Lauenburg, Pomerania in 1944
(front row, far left)

kilometres west of Breslau. The three-storey, stone complex had been extended, with wooden-built houses for the regular army. It was of all places
in one of those that I was quartered. It was no use wishing for our lovely
warm quarters that we had left behind. We were, after all, outside during
the day and were only in this ice-encrusted barrack to sleep. After we had
given it a thorough clean, it was heated in the evenings after duty, by using a
large, ugly, iron stove, until it glowed. It only left enough space in the middle of the room, so that the straw-sacks for our bunk-beds never caught fire.

Every day we exercised outdoors, with the infantry howitzers and mortars. Our numbers had grown and totalled a full battalion, with men from
Pomerania and East Prussia, plus many from other units. Most had Front
experience, but there were others who had just finished their training and
were waiting for their baptism of fire. Some couldn't wait for 'a piece of action', and others only said so to hide their fear. From our own 11th Company, we were now 120 men and grew into a close and faithful clique.

Unexpectedly, as we were exercising at the daily terrain training, a messenger reported that we must all return to camp straight away. There we had
to assemble on the parade ground, in the snow. The assembled battalion
was then informed, in few words but of military tone, the reason for our
hasty return. We were then given our marching orders, but not before we
were reminded that "every man must fulfil his oath to his flag and do his
duty to protect his fatherland from the storm of the Bolsheviks". Iron rations, live ammunition and extra daily rations were issued to us. Personal
items, considered to be superfluous, were stored in the attic of the barracks.
The post office suddenly filled with telegrams and hurriedly written letters
to family and friends back home. For some, they would be their last letters.

Others would eventually return home. We were sent off to the Breslau garrison, on the same day, as an independent regiment, SS Regiment Besslein, to 'combat ready' positions.

It was from southern Poland that the Russian Marshall Zhukov approached Breslau, with a strong and superior force. Despite ferocious German defensive actions, his advance could not be stopped. Marshall Koniev was also advancing, just as strong and supported by uncountable tanks, having crossed the Oder at Baranov. Both used bridgeheads to cross the river, which had been no hindrance, neither hoped for nor expected.

Stalin, fully aware of the problems on the Western Front, with the Ardennes offensive, asked the Allies if he could anticipate his own plans by eight days. He had dropped reconnaissance troops by parachute, in small groups, behind our lines. They were equipped with powerful radio sets, with the receiving range of two to three hundred kilometres. He knew precisely every move that we made. Our coded information, on fortification, strength of units, troop movement and, in particular, the combat areas of the Waffen SS who were feared by the Russians, was used against us for their plan of attack, by their military chief of staff. Information was also received from his undercover network of Russian workers in Breslau. They, amongst other things, befriended the refugees for the slightest information which would be of help, and that could also be passed on to our enemies.

With Breslau having been declared a 'fortress city' in the summer of 1944, it was therefore not surprising that the whole of the population was still there at the beginning of January 1945. As a junction for traffic, Breslau, which was in the heart of Silesia, was an open city and only wishful thinking could make it the classical fortress that it had once been. It was now protected by only a few lightly-built bunkers on the left bank of the Oder. Unfortunately, its military worth was vastly exaggerated.

The 'fortification order' from Berlin, had not been taken seriously enough by the region's *Gauleiter*, who did very little for the defence of the town. The *Gauleiter*, Karl Hanke, did order anti-tank ditches to be made. But those were put near the former German/Polish border, along with other defensive installations, as part of 'Operation Barthold'. All of it was too far away, and as it proved later, of absolutely no use in hindering the advance of the Russians.

Despite directives of evacuation for the city having been long since received, the plans to evacuate its citizens to safety, over a period of days, using hundreds of trains, were not put into operation until the town was already encircled. On 20 and 21 January, the echo of loudspeakers was to be heard on the streets, not only in the centre of the town, but on the outskirts too, advising the women and children to make their way to Oppenau and Kanth, but on foot.

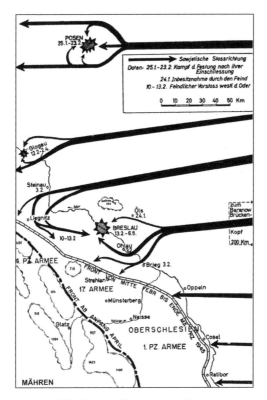

The Soviet offensive into Silesia

Kanth for instance, lay twenty-five kilometres away from Breslau to the west. It was difficult enough to reach under normal circumstances, but by then it was plain murder, especially for women with small children. Temperatures of minus 20–30 degrees were nothing out of the ordinary in Silesia, or to have the Oder frozen over until March. In the previous two weeks over two feet of snow had fallen, always accompanied by bitter hoar-frost, and it lay on the roads. Many women did not even try to leave Breslau under those conditions, but many thousands did. They packed food and drink, wrapped themselves and their children in wool blankets over thick coats, and tied scarves over their heads. They packed their children in prams, small carts or sledges, and taking the older ones by the hand, they left the town. For them it was a fearful Odyssey, an inferno of ice and snow.

The women managed only the first few miles. Although the countryside was bathed in weak but cold winter sunshine, at mid-day the thermometer read no more than between 16–20 degrees below freezing. A wind began to howl, a cutting icy wind coming from the east. With incredible determination they tempted fate under unimaginable odds. They were to fail, despite their motherly instinct driving them further and further, to the

The author's drawing, made in 1946, showing close combat between the Red Army and members of the 11th Company, SS Regiment Besslein at Peiskerwitz, January 1945.

point of exhaustion. They could no longer push the prams against the wind and even the sledges could not be pulled through knee-deep snow. So the mothers carried the children in their arms. The milk froze in the bottles, and some mothers faced the storm to breast-feed. The bitter wind knew no compassion.

The babies and infants were the first sacrifices. No blankets, no cushions could have given them the body-warmth of life. So they died, 'sleeping' in their mothers' arms. They were carried miles in this belief, many mothers not wanting to accept that their baby had died. The iron will of some of the mothers broke with that bitter realisation. They were to be seen shovelling away the snow with their hands, to make a grave for the little one. Some of those too busy battling against the wind, did not see mothers lying beside their babies delivering them both into the hands of 'mother nature'. Only later did others see those dark mounds covered in glittering snow, but did not possess the strength to clear their path of the dead or dying. No one counted those from Breslau. The statistics on those who died on that trek have never been recorded. Many were refugees who had sought shelter in the countryside, not knowing that they would meet their death much earlier than those they had left behind in the city.

The Russians had advanced to the Oder and very near to our new location of Kirschberg. The *Wehrmacht* and Waffen SS units, under the leadership of *Rittmeister* Speckmann, could not deter their forging of a two kilometre-wide bridgehead on the western side of the river. Despite bitter fighting the Russians widened the bridgehead, until they had reached the forest area south of Peiskerwitz. As the Regiment's reserve, we had been waiting for orders, just three kilometres from the front line. We had seen how quickly the Russians had increased this bridgehead, with all of the military strength that they possessed. The heavens over Peiskerwitz glowed. From fire and flames, and from the continuous tumult of exploding shells, one could assess the enormous firepower used by both sides. During the moments of a pause in the duel of artillery, red flares provocatively lit the sky heralding the next barrage.

The wounded were brought to us to wait for ambulance transport to field hospitals, and there were those separated from their units who also found their way to us. All told us of the desperate battle on the banks of the river, and that part of our battalion was trapped. They were engaged in close combat in the rubble of the houses. A messenger arrived reporting the hopeless situation in Peiskerwitz, resulting in our combat order. As a company of 120 men, we were be used as shock troops. We were expected to go in, clean up and not only rescue our comrades from the main sector of the front, but push the 'Ivans' back over to the other side of the Oder.

It was on the afternoon of 28 January that we left Kirschberg, equipped with the usual firearms, light machine-guns, and very many hand-grenades and *Panzerfäuste*. We marched cross-country through Wilxen, in the direction of the Trautensee estate. We joked with one another, to relieve a little of the tension that had built up with waiting. Now the waiting was over and we made progress.

The clang of rifle-butts hitting our bayonet-sheaths and the crunch of our boots in the snow, mixed more and more with the noise of battle from the front. Very soon we met the first of the wounded on foot. There was a look of shock on their grey faces. They had staring eyes, blood-smeared uniforms and signs of provisional first aid. Some moaned in pain with every step that they took as they passed us. We, the 11th Company, had nothing more to say or to joke about.

After a short rest in the grounds of the estate, the company hurriedly crossed over open ground, in a line of skirmishers, to the edge of the Peiskerwitz woods. By keeping our heads down, and with long intervals between each man, we raced over the open ground. Miraculously we all reached the protection of the woods. However, our relief was soon shattered, as the Russians discovered us. All hell was then let loose. In seconds, we seemed to be in the middle of a fireball. Artillery spewed at us from all directions, from light and heavy emplacements in the area of the banks of the

Oder, who were firing without consideration of their own men in the woods. Many Russian infantry were hidden behind trees and bushes, and all joined in the assault on our detachment.

Apparently unafraid, our company leader *Obersturmführer*, later *Standartenführer* Zizmann, urged his men on with a hand-grenade in his left hand and a sub-machine-gun in his right. My group had the order to stay right behind this calm and experienced officer, who somehow gave us the self-confidence that we needed. We strode forward with fixed bayonets. The enemy too was grim and determined, they were ready for hand-to-hand combat. Lively rifle-fire flew around us from snipers who had waited, hidden in the trees, to fire on us as soon as we were in range. Some were hanging in the trees, apparently dead, but we could not know if they were or not. We had to be damned careful!

Forest fighting was always dangerous, particularly for those entering, not knowing where the enemy lay. The racket from the firing was intense – mortars, uninterrupted firing from the infantry, to say nothing of whistling bullets, as they 'pranged' against the trees like messengers of death, and re-bounded through the air.

As if they had done nothing else all their lives, our grenadiers crept through the snow-covered wood, to every leaf that gave cover, winning ground, yard by yard. It was now important to keep together and not let the Reds strengthen their defensive line. With a doggedness that surprised the Russians, the 11th Company gradually began to push them back, shooting from behind trees, from kneeling positions or, as they moved forwards, from the hip. We advanced deeper and deeper into the wood. We saw the Reds running in panic, leaving ammunition and equipment behind them, including a very antiquated water-cooled machine gun on wooden wheels. There were the odd one or two ready for close-combat with fixed bayonet, but their retreat continued, until they reached the edge of the wood on the far side. Then they stopped.

Very soon the proportions of the Red Army were visible and we knew that we were at a numerical disadvantage. The Reds had called up fresh re-serves, reformed, and were defending their positions in houses and barns, most of which had been set alight. Despite their numbers, this made them very easy targets and we picked them off, as they hopped from house to house in the flickering light of the flames. It also applied to us, as we moved away from the flames and choking smoke. We ourselves then became a sac-rifice of the 'Ivans', and the losses of the 11th Company, in dead, missing and wounded were very heavy. With the dawn however, we had driven the Russians back to the banks of the Oder. The remnants of *Kampfgruppe* Speckmann, who had been fighting for days in Peiskerwitz and were now totally scattered, could be relieved.

The Reds still had to be pushed back to the other side of the river. That could only be done after we had stormed the river's near-side banks, and held them until reinforcements arrived. Part of our detachments had to lie in readiness, in the terrain between the edge of the woods and the bank, waiting for a new order. Scattered shelling kept us pinned down, lying in deep snow, until we no longer felt that biting cold. But, in between the bombardment, cries and moans were to be heard from those who had been hit and wounded. There were also shouts of *Vpiröd! Bysstro, bysstro!* i.e. "forwards, quicker, quicker!" Presumably some of the political commissioners in the Red Army were a little nervous. Between orders, those with the tempo of a snail were encouraged to quicken their pace, with a shot or two from a pistol.

As our company commander at last gave us our order to attack, he moved forwards a couple of steps, then turned and came back as no one was following him. Few had heard the order and others had hesitated. We knew what was waiting for us over the rise and somehow our limbs had been frozen. We felt our hearts pulsating in our throats and a cold sweat creeping over the back of our necks, but it was not for the first time, and the order came again. *Obersturmführer* Zizmann shouted at the top of his voice, and the order was followed with a scream of "Hurra!" We rose as one man, to advance as best we could in fresh knee-deep snow. We fired like wild men, without aim, and with only yards separating us from the enemy.

Close-combat lasted only a short time. Some of our men, without orders, returned to their former positions. Both sides sank in the snow as they climbed over their dead comrades in order to escape. *Obersturmführer* Zizmann knew that this action was plain slaughter and so he gave us the order to dig-in. In frozen ground, with our short-handled spades and under artillery fire, the fallen had to lie where they were. The wounded who could crawl to our positions did so. Others were dragged back under extreme difficulty by our medics, to be given first-aid. We had obviously surprised the Reds who did not risk a counter-attack. It would have meant disaster for us, but they could not know that, thank God!

With the information that shock troops were attacking the left flank, we retreated into the foremost houses of a village. From my squad of twelve men, only six remained. I chose a small farmhouse which had a cellar, and a barn which had been badly burnt. The cellar provided a place to sleep for two men at a time, while the remaining four kept guard at the windows, the glass of which was non-existent. Not that sleep was possible in the next couple of days and nights, for the Soviets tried, time and time again, to storm our positions. They gave us no peace. It was in such conditions that we could only send messengers to neighbouring groups at night, to receive information as to our situation and because our ammo and rations were very low.

It was during the third night in this farmhouse that an unexpected delivery, of ammo and rations, came in the form of my faithful friend Georg

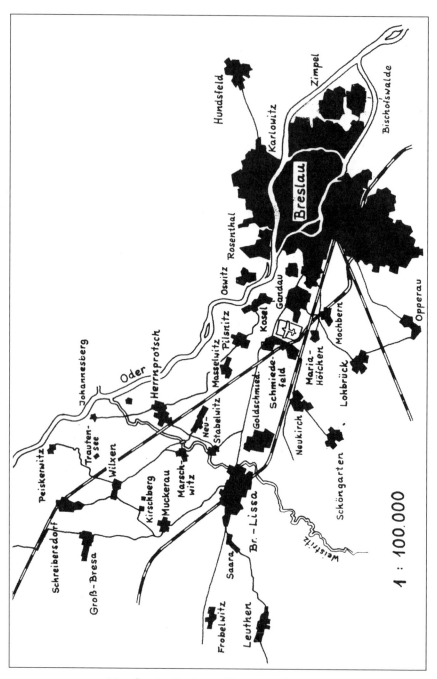

Map showing Breslau and its surrounding area

Haas, who was the company's accountant. He had not forgotten us. He reached us with his provisions on a sledge drawn by a sweating *Panje* pony. He had found us, guided by the flames from the houses and the noise of the front. He was not to be deterred. Having himself been wounded in 1942, he was accompanied by a comrade who had also been wounded. They had come cross-country over snow-covered fields to find us.

We also had a very long wait for support from our own artillery. However, heavy shells were being sent over our heads, in the direction of the enemy, by an 8.8cm gun battery from the Reich Labour Service (*Reichsarbeitsdienst*, or RAD) who were positioned very close to us. The gunners and all the very young privates did a great job. Enormous fountains of earth erupted skywards. Trees too were tossed upward, having been torn out of the earth by their roots. Every shot had hit its target. The boys had very little ammunition. They used what they had sparingly and only in small amounts, making every shot hit home. Not so far away from us was a high, narrow transformer house in which an enemy artillery spotter had made himself at home. But it did not last long before those lads found him. They blasted him and the house in the direction of Heaven.

In order to bring some excitement of another nature into our daily routine, fate decided that I was a good candidate. Unwillingly, but it really wasn't my fault! We were forced to make permanent lavatory conditions in the back yard of our temporary 'fortress' because ours had been shot to pieces. In the form of a cesspit, it was a ditch with 'thunder' beams placed over it and well out of view of the enemy. As a soldier with front-line experience, one's ears attune to the whistling tones of an oncoming shell and can estimate when you are in the line of fire or if the projectile will land in another direction. This saved my life, one day, as I was in the yard. It 'perfumed' my life for the next few days however, for I had to dive into the cesspit and I did not come out smelling of violets. I unfortunately did not possess an extra uniform at that time, much to the annoyance of my chums, who avoided me like the plague. It was only some time later, with the melting of the snow, that I could discard my white snow 'cammo' so that this unwilling air pollutant was once more an acceptable member within his circle.

The features of the landscape had altered overnight. The untouched white snow of the battlefield was now a dirty grey carpet, a morass of soft earth. The wet snow made crawling and hitting the ground a wet and messy business, but a wet stomach was far better than one with a bullet-hole in it. We had to crawl around the farmhouse yard in it too, during the day, for the Reds were not giving us any peace. A grey light, blocking out the weak winter sun, hung over the smoking ruins of Peiskerwitz, where our fallen comrades still lay in their half-frozen field-grey uniforms. We, with red-rimmed eyes and totally exhausted, kept watch from the glassless windows in our small farmhouse. Frozen from the cold moist air we dozed unwillingly, not having the will to stop ourselves. The young unshaven faces of my chums were thin now and angular, and our uniforms gave us no warmth. Outside was grey, only grey, and in the grey of the evening, one could not determine where the earth ended, and where the heavens began. It matched our fighting-spirit.

Our comrade, Szibulla, who came from Upper Silesia, understood a little of both Polish and Russian, and he kept us up-to-date with the movements of the Reds, for they were to be heard, loud and clear. When he heard something that meant they were on the move, or we had a combat order, then we were suddenly very wide awake. Mostly it was the bad language from our counterparts which he translated and which we did not want to hear such as "F ... your mother", or tantalising attempts to win us over to their side, "Come to us comrades".

Then we had real cause for alarm as we heard the faint squeak of a tank-track coming from the riverbanks, which became suddenly louder and louder as well as the loud 'brumm' of its motor. A recce detachment confirmed that it was a heavy Stalin tank that could worsen our situation badly, for apart from *Panzerfäuste*, we had no other anti-tank weapons. It was *Scharführer* Harry Kähler, a very experienced 'front-man', who solved the problem for us, taking the responsibility on to his own shoulders. Under cover of fire from my squad, he emerged from cover only thirty metres away sending two shots broadside into the giant from his *Panzerfäuste*. The roar of the detonation produced a crescendo in which our own weapons could not be heard. Thick black smoke soared through the turret as it opened, followed by tongues of flame. Then a succession of earsplitting explosions emerged from the 46-tonner, as its ammunition exploded. It was a daredevil mission that could have ended in the death of our chum from the south-east of Germany. But like David and his sling, his pluck paid off. *Scharführer* Kähler was presented with the Iron Cross 1st Class for his bravery, on that same day, and our fighting spirit was sent soaring. Yes, I must admit that we were proud to have stopped the westwards advance of the Reds on the Oder, whose numbers and material were superior to that of our own forces.

At the same time as we, the 11th were holding strongpoints, another part of our Regiment narrowed and eliminated another bridgehead near Peiskerwitz. The *Wehrmacht* General Hans von Ahlfen and General Hermann Niehoff, commanders of *Festung* or 'Fortress' Breslau wrote about those incidents. "The elimination of bridgeheads around Peiskerwitz was successfully conducted by the best organised Regiment of the garrison, Waffen SS Regiment Besslein, on 8 February. Many attempts before this had failed. The bravery shown by the troops and the necessary support they gave, stems from a tried and tested pattern of combined skill and tactics in the line of fire. The Peiskerwitz success had and still has a symbolic meaning. The whole garrison, not only Regiment Besslein, found faith in them-

One of the many propaganda posters put up in Breslau

selves, one another and their subordinate officers, and we could not have survived without them."

Two days before we were to be relieved, we had found ourselves in a critical situation stemming from a bitter attack on us from the Reds. My squad found itself separated from the rest of the Company as they moved out. Before we knew where we were, the trap closed in around us and we knew that we were left to our own devices, having missed the withdrawal. We had no other choice but to fight to the last bullet. In order to give the impression to the enemy that we numbered more than we actually did, we hopped from house to house, window to window and other positions, firing as we went, in the hope that we could hold out until we were relieved. We didn't even think about being taken prisoner, of receiving a bullet in the back of the neck, or, even worse, submitting without a fight. We knew that the revenge of those outwitted Russians, having been cheated of success, would have been terrible.

The Company did not forget us however. This time it was another known daredevil, of the same calibre as Kähler. It was our platoon leader Erwin Domke from East Prussia, who came to our aid. He was not going to leave us in the lurch. With a handful of men, this highly-decorated subordinate officer, managed to free us at dawn on the second day. He surprised the sleeping Red Army men with *Panzerfäuste*, hand-grenades and small arms. Under protection of their fire we could retreat. We lost one of our younger men, a machine-gunner whom we had to leave. But we were able to take Szibulla with us. He had been wounded in the thigh at the last minute. We willingly handed over the position to our relieving troop, without further losses to the 11th Company.

Numbering over a hundred men, we had stormed and held this position for eleven days. We left it without many words, exhausted and sad at the thought of having to leave our fallen comrades behind us. Peiskerwitz had been their fate. Only a few had been spared the hell of it all. We slowly made our way along the country roads, and met many of the company's wounded at the first-aid station in Trautensee. They included one soldier who, since seeing him last, had turned grey overnight. Separated from his unit and totally alone, he had hidden in the loft of a barn as a band of Russian soldiers made it their quarters. He lay there for the next three days. He had to lie almost motionless for those three days, in the fear of being discovered by them, and in fear of what they would do to him. He watched their totally intoxicated antics through the slits of the loft's wooden flooring. He had to listen to their singing. The Red soldiers enjoyed themselves for those three days, ignorant in their stupor, of his existence. Finally, they moved on. He was so thankful that they had not set the barn alight, thankful and grey.

We stood once more on the parade ground in Kirschberg, the Regimental headquarters, where twelve days before, we had started our march to Peiskerwitz. Apathetic and freezing with the cold, we let the following proceedings wash over us. We stood with deathly-grey faces, forced to accept how many had not returned with us. The names had no ring to them as they were read out on that occasion. Many, very many, did not answer "here" to their names on being called out, for here they were not. The voice answering with "wounded", "missing", or "fallen in combat", was exactly as lifeless as we felt, for from a proud company of 120 men, only 26 were "here"!

It was on 15 February 1945 that an announcement was to be heard on the radio, with information that the Red Army had been beaten in Lower Silesia. As in Breslau, there had been bitter fighting from our attacking troops. Many were decorated for this feat, with the Iron Cross, or the Infantry Assault Badge. Our company commander shook our hands, without uttering a single word. We were then released to go to our beds, where totally exhausted, we slept solidly for the next 48 hours.

Sometime later we were to be found once more in our old barracks of Deutsch-Lissa, having been brought back to full strength, with new men from all arms of the services. We were kitted out with only the best of equipment and arms, as well as a new platoon commander, Leo Habr. This *SS-Scharführer* was well-known, an experienced front-line fighter, and one with whom I formed a good relationship, as his second-in-command. This amicable native of the Ostmark left the day-to-day duties to me, but in combat he was an example to us all. Our old company leader Zizmann had been promoted to and had been given the command of the 11th. Together with the new men, we were all posted to Johannisberg, to defensive positions on the western banks of the Oder and only a few kilometres from Peiskerwitz.

From our recent experience, and in our naïvety, we were convinced that we could hold the Red Army here too. Having done it once, then we could do it again. What did not occur to us was that then, and now, we had no knowledge of the strategic plans of the campaign as a whole. Because of that, our convictions were to prove to be very, very wrong.

The pattern was the same as before, and we were given quarters in the deserted houses to be found near our defences. There we found to our joy that the larders were full of food. We helped ourselves and for once we altered the tone of our cuisine, which was such a change to the meals from the military 'gulash-cannon', or mobile field kitchen.

My platoon-leader and I took a short walk to acquaint ourselves with the surrounding area and found that a biplane had taken a nose-dive into one of the fields. We inspected this 'sewing-machine' which had caused us so many pestering moments in the past, and then we found the pilot. Whether he had been flung from the plane or had crawled out of it we couldn't tell, but we found this red-haired Russian a few metres away from his biplane, dead in the snow. We buried him the next day. As German soldiers, so to speak, we gave the pilot a soldier's grave, complete with a wooden cross which we made from branches of trees. In doing so, we gave him more than we could for our own soldiers at times, but at that moment we had the time. When the roles were reversed, would this have happened with one of ours? We hoped so!

We could still hear the noise of combat coming from around Peiskerwitz, but in our own sector the enemy was surprisingly quiet. In fact it was a little too quiet on the other side of the riverbank. Red flares gave their nightly performance and lit the heavens. Now and again we heard the faint sound of motors, but the war did not seem to want to have anything to do with us. The longer that situation lasted, the more suspicious we became. Was something brewing that we didn't know about? Was it to be a nasty surprise? An order came from our company command-post, to send a recce detachment from our right-hand side of the sector, to the other side of the river. Strength of troops, weapons and positions, and perhaps a prisoner for interrogation were needed. I volunteered, together with our platoon-leader, Leo Habr who came from Bavaria. We were both curious. Apart from that, a boat-trip at night was a welcome change to guard-duty in the trenches.

There was a *Volkssturm* battalion some kilometres away from us, positioned in the lowlands of the Oder. They were to provide us with a boat. It was also to be our starting point. The battalion's commanding officer was an older man, a major, who was not enamoured with our task when we reported to him. "One should not challenge the enemy unnecessarily," was his critical comment. But we needed his support and we argued that the information would also be of use to his sector too. He had no choice but to give us his support and as it was not quite dark enough, we enjoyed a drink in the command post. We left some time later, leaving behind our pay-books, 'dog-tags' and private belongings, for obvious reasons. Among the grey-haired *Volkssturmmänner* who manhandled the rowing-boat to the shore, was a young HJ lad of perhaps no more than fifteen years who wanted to come with us. The planks of the rowing-boat, which was old, seemed to be somewhat porous, but it would certainly bring us three over to the other side of the stream and back. We were rather sceptical as we left the *Volkssturm* and so were they, as they wished us "good luck with the return". They themselves returned very quickly to the cover of the command post, perhaps thinking that someone might make the suggestion of sending some of them too!

Although there was thin ice on the shores of the riverbank, the river flowed to our benefit rather sluggishly, so that we did not have to strain on the oars. So we rowed as silently as possible in the quiet of the night, until the boat hit sand. It was the shore on the easterly side of the river. Armed with hand-grenades and pistols, we slowly and tensely made our way through overgrown shrubs and trees, making signs to one another as we went. Flares lit the night sky now and again. Then we froze to statues until it was dark once more. We had advanced quite a way and there was no sign of the enemy. Not knowing how far we had moved away from the riverbank, we became a little uneasy. The darkness seemed to envelop us, as if it would swallow us up and we would not escape.

"We cannot walk to Warsaw, in the hope of seeing the 'Ivans'," whispered Habr, breaking the spell. Our mission seemed to be at an end, but almost at the same time, he saw a glimmer and it was back to sign language. It turned out to be the red, flickering glow of a camp-fire. We watched, having crawled on our stomachs for a closer look. From the look of things, a small band of very unconcerned Russian soldiers were enjoying themselves, laughing loudly and enjoying themselves as only Russian soldiers could. But we could not understand what they were saying. I lay there and thought "if only we had Szibulla with us". His knowledge of the Russian language would have helped us so much in that situation, but we didn't. It was clear to us that the sector was very thinly manned indeed and now having what we came for, we could depart. Could we take a prisoner? We decided against this order under the circumstances, and left those very happy men of war. Besides that, there were more of them!

We had fulfilled our mission, and happy that Habr had said that we could return to the boat, our march back was much quicker. Very soon, we saw a band of shimmering water and so that the *Volkssturm* men were warned of our return, Habr lit a cigarette in mid-stream. Alighting from the boat, they all slapped us on the back when we told them how far away the enemy were and how peaceful too. The major seemed to have been relieved from a nightmare and then invited us for a 'moist' night-cap, in his command post.

Incidentally, the *Volkssturm* was officially initiated into active service with the *Wehrmacht* on 25 September 1944. All men between the ages of 16 and 60 years of age, competent in the use of firearms, would be active in the defence of German territories. The enthusiasm of the young was huge. Sometimes that enthusiasm had to be curbed so that it did not develop into careless, boisterous, high spirits. Many of the 'infant' soldiers proved themselves with heroic acts, but on the whole the military performance of the *Volkssturm* was minimal.

I must point out that a continuous front-line did not exist along the Oder. Very many soldiers were left to their own devices, became lost, and fought in the bleak and wretched winter countryside without adequate supplies. They had to fight against an enemy that was superior in numbers and material. Very often a single tank, or a group of them, would suddenly appear from the north-west sector, and in the rear of troops holding defensive positions. The attacked units never had a chance. They were destroyed like seeds between two millstones.

Just as in East Prussia, the raging, merciless fury of the Russians was also felt in the areas that they conquered in Silesia. Even the dead were not spared their fury. The 19th *Panzer* Division in Blüchersruh, south-west of Breslau, found a skull just 'lying around' in the street. It had been removed from the tomb of Marshall Blücher also known as Marshall *Vorwärts*, the freedom-fighter from 1813–15. Not even he could rest in peace.

The fight on the Oder was one of continuous movement of troops. With the threat that Russian tanks could break through our front-line, the 11th was moved to Frobelwitz and the winter returned, in all its spitefulness. The Leuthen-Frobelwitz road leading to the north is a very straight country road. We had sentry duty along this road, in a snowstorm. Placed at an interval of 50 metres, we stood alone and deserted as the wind whipped the snow around us. It created a white screen that obstructed our view. We could not see one another. If a tank had appeared then it would have been too late. We tried with half-closed eyes against the biting wind, to find our next comrade, either to the right or the left of us. But we couldn't. So we tried oral contact, calling to one another. But the cry of the wind swallowed our calls. Our hands froze around our rifles and the storm really raged.

We held our positions that afternoon, through into the evening and the night, without being relieved. Some of us stood there and asked ourselves if we were the only ones, perhaps the last 'Sentries for Europe' who were left. I was reminded of the winter of 1941/42 whilst standing there. I remembered the snowstorm raging unhindered over the flat and endless Russian Steppe. There was however a very big difference. The enemy was still the same, but now his advance was on German soil. We held our posts, all of us. Only with dawn the next morning, did a messenger arrive with our marching orders.

The village of Leuthen, which lies south of Frobelwitz was our next position. It was practically deserted. Those who had remained in the village were women and children, who looked at us through cellar windows as we arrived. We were not expected and were not welcome. They had all hoped that the war would spare their tiny village, which was of really no importance. We took up our positions behind stonewalls, and pyramids of harvested turnips and parsnips. Although we understood the fear in their eyes, for them, our presence also meant the presence of Russian soldiers. We tried our best to warn them of the danger that they were in, as women, if the village were seized by the Russians. But our reasons were ignored by those few who even talked to us, and many didn't. We were to leave and then they would be left in peace, was the way that they interpreted the situation. Such ignorance caused some of the men to wish them to the devil. One couldn't really blame them, for this was the first time that we were not welcomed by our own, in our own land.

A little time later a Russian lorry drove leisurely past the village and came under fire from us. The driver and his companion were killed after a short fight and the lorry burst into flames having been hit in the motor. Before being fully enveloped, we were able to see that it was laden with feather beds, furniture and other household articles, ready to be sent back 'home' to Russia. It had been stolen from German farmhouses in the area, the 'liberation' had begun, with German goods and chattels, which were certainly luxury articles for them.

At midday, the low-lying sun cast a faint red glow over the snow. Through our field-glasses we saw Russian tanks advancing towards the village with their infantry on board. Their progress was indeed slow, perhaps because they mistrusted the peaceful impression the village gave. Suddenly, fire spewed from a gun-barrel and the first shell exploded in the village. Then the tanks stopped in their tracks, staying at a respectful distance. The infantry alighted in order to seek protection behind the white-painted tanks.

Once more we were in a position which offered very little protection, for Leuthen lay like an island, in the middle of flat terrain, in a farming area. There was also little or no protection for reserves on their approach to the village, if we called for them. It was so small it really was not worth defending for any length of time. A direct hit on one of those pyramids of turnips would flatten you too, if you were hiding behind one of them. It was then that we saw white bed-linen on the west side of the village being waved by the women surrendering. The situation altered dramatically. We received the order, with some bitterness, to retreat. We reformed, just a couple of kilometres away and dug-in separately on the road to Saara, which was not an ideal place to dig-in either. We would have preferred to have sought protection on the edge of the wood but the infantry were there. So we found ourselves in no-man's land but between the line of fire from the infantry and that of the enemy. To say that we were uneasy would be an understatement.

All was quiet until the next morning because the Russians were busy looting the houses in Leuthen. That was confirmed by one of our recce detachments who had made their way under cover of darkness to the village. Upon their return they told of the cries for help from the women and children, who were easy prey for the Russian soldiers. They were now paying for their obstinacy, unfortunately. We were rudely awakened at dawn, with an ice-cold greeting from the Russians, as was to be expected, as a shell exploded somewhere behind us in the woods. We were now wide awake. More followed, hitting the road and the fields in front of us at the same time. The higher the sun rose on that day in late February, the more intense the barrage became. Heavy artillery began to plough the terrain, and we had no other choice but to cower in our dug-outs and let it roar over our heads. We were helpless.

We closed our eyes tightly against the flashes of detonating shells, but had no remedy for the decibels bursting our ear-drums or the clouds of choking gun-powder causing us to cough and splutter. Our dug-outs rose and fell and shook with every explosion. The timpani began as steel splinters, sods of earth, sand and stones hit our steel helmets, with the barrage coming from the Russians. In the pauses between the impacting rounds our infantry returned their fire and we had to duck once more against the blast of whistling shells whipping around our ears, although they did their best to fire over our heads. I dared to take a quick peep from my dug-out to find that the terrain had now another face. It was almost ghostly, as banks of smoke hung over a landscape of craters. My neighbouring comrade to my left lay lifeless in his dug-out, which was no longer a dug-out but a crater. He had received a direct hit. On that occasion there were no wounded, only the dead. To my right lay a legless comrade, who had perhaps tried to leave his dug-out, unable to hold out in such hell. The price was losing his legs and his life. He no longer moved. In doubt, I called out to others who may be living. Almost in slow motion, one after another steel helmet rose out of the ground. The faces of my young comrades had eyes wide open in fright. They were hardly able to speak.

We then had a pause in the firing. It was still, it was sinister, and not a good sign. We knew from experience that our infantry would attack immediately. Already they were to be seen, about a battalion in strength. We saw the soldiers in *Sturmangriff*, in assault formation and widely spaced from one another. The dark figures in contrast to the white landscape, came nearer and nearer, and became larger and larger. For once, the Russians considered their own men and did not fire. We showed ourselves too and left our holes in the earth. We had swallowed the first 'potion' the Reds had served, but we were not going to sell ourselves so cheaply. We were ready, come what may.

With targeted firing from our machine-guns and machine-pistols, we fired directly into the screaming masses of oncoming Red infantry, including ponies pulling the carriages of anti-tank guns. They halted now and again to allow the 'Urra'-screaming gunners to fire a salvo or two in our direction. Our officers in the foremost lines fired tracers, aiding us to concentrate our fire in the right direction. Although our own bitter attack may have delayed the impetus of the enemy's attack, in the end there were too many of them. We were outnumbered and the situation was hopeless. A few of our comrades still lay in their dug-outs and used their last ammunition. In front of us we had the attacking enemy, behind us flat terrain giving no protection, and all of two hundred metres before we hit the woods. We had no choice. The prospects were grim. We had to fight to the end, and it appeared on this occasion that that would be the case.

Death was so near that I do not believe we fought as perfectly trained soldiers in that situation. A careless instinct took command, guiding us almost in a trance. I certainly was no longer aware of what I was doing, but I remember that my life replayed before my eyes with great speed. Because of that, it took some time before I heard the calling from the edge of the wood. Company and platoon leaders were signalling towards a stream, running in a straight line through the fields to the wood. Together with others, I used the last of my strength to spring into the ice-cold water, with machine-gun fire whipping around our ears. Although splinters and fragments landed in the water and only light wounds were received, under such freezing conditions it meant the end for many of us.

We reached the wood and the protection that it gave. We were soaked, and with chattering teeth. We saw the 'Ivans' spring into our dug-outs. In looking back at our dead comrades lying on the road who we had to leave behind, the scene blended into the battlefields of Leuthen in December of 1757. Troops of Fredrick the Great, numbering 34,000, had reached Silesia to fight the invading Austrians. They were outnumbered by 2 to 1 with 70,000, and won. 188 years later German nationals, together with volunteers from westerly lands, in a futile attempt, tried to do the same against an Asiatic power threatening not only Silesia, but the whole of Europe.

We received orders to move to Saara and make new positions there. We found it to be deserted, except for two very old ladies, sisters, wrapped in woollen blankets in one of the farmhouses. We found them when looking for something to eat. Like many others, they did not want to leave their home. Equipped with more than enough food, they were going to acquiesce to their fate, whatever it was to be. An odd cow roamed around the village, giving a bellow now and again and the cats greeted us with a purr and cuddled around our boots, hungry, just like us.

Our next stop was once more the garrison town of Deutsch-Lissa. The companies of the battalions collected together on the parade ground of the barrack complex to receive new orders. We had very little time, for the Russians were at the door. They had advanced very quickly. We had just enough time to change our still clammy uniforms, as Russian tanks roared over the parade ground. Together with the infantry we managed to delay their advance with well-aimed firing, but only for a while. Continuous defensive tactics could not stop them. So we retreated once more, through the back door, to the outskirts of the town and the river. There was a stone bridge over the river Weistritz.

It was the only river crossing in the direction of Breslau and was of strategic importance. Situated on the eastern riverbank it led to the main road, which the Russians must use. I was given the order to occupy with my group a two-storey house to the right of the bridge in the southern terrain. They were terraced houses parallel to the river, the gardens of which were now overgrown and which stretched down an incline, to the riverbank. We took up positions at the back of the houses, digging in just a few feet away from the cellar door. I put six men to digging trenches, others attended to the machine-guns and others made themselves comfortable and familiar with the contents of the cellar pantry. It was full of conserves for the winter, and we helped ourselves. We had profited over the last few weeks from such housewifely customs, adding to our meagre provisions with fruits, pickled meats including chicken meat and many other commodities including eggs, a feast for us.

Our combat engineers prepared to blow the bridge as soon as the last of the German troops crossed it. Because we were in close proximity, we promptly took cover in the cellar. Suddenly the explosion was deafening. The dark cellar suddenly became a hall of light and the floor shook. The candles flickered so violently that they were almost extinguished. We held our breath as it rained chunks of brick and roof tiles. We heard it all hitting the house, as well as the sound of splintering glass. The cellar then filled with clouds of dust particles and the biting stench of gunpowder. It was so intense that it robbed you of your breath. We nearly choked. Our lungs full, we all started to cough and splutter as we rubbed the dust from our eyes.

We left the cellar and went outside. It looked as if a hurricane had hit the houses. None had roof tiles anymore. They lay on the cobbles, strewn together with glass splinters and other rubble. A large part of the bridge had disappeared, the large blocks sinking into the river. But other parts remained. They would all be used in a rebuild. The Russians were experts. They began to rebuild the bridge the same night.

The whole time, of course, they worked under fire from our infantry, and paid a very high price for their bridge. They worked away with death-defying stubbornness. Many Russian engineers fell screaming into the dark waters of the Weistritz, having been hit as they worked to repair the bridge. The loss in men for the Russians must have been enormous. But they only had themselves to blame, for they had begun the work without prior safeguards. Naturally we had everything under fire that was in close proximity to the approach of the bridge. However, I have to admit that an efficient defence was not possible. We then had a surprise 'cease-fire' order from a *Leutnant* of the combat engineers. He was giving continual progress reports to the *Festung* commander. "Let the 'Ivans' alone to build their bridge", he told us. That was bewildering to say the least. He was going to have the pleasure of destroying the bridge, when finished, with his Goliath tank. That was news to us, and yes, it was a tank, of a sort, but not in the usual sense of the word.

This tank was no more than 67cm high and had a length of 160cm. It could carry however 75 kilos of high explosives and was remote-controlled. It was a mini-tank and not sensitive to infantry fire. It was a piece of equipment developed to save lives in situations where large obstructions, be it bridges or other obstacles, needed a solution, other than manpower. Radio-controlled by radio waves or a wire connection, it could strike from a distance of 600 to 1,000 metres and was controlled by specially trained soldiers. We couldn't wait to see what this wonder-weapon could pull out of the hat! They were indeed 'wonder-weapons', for there were three. With the eyes of a engineer and the instinct of a hunter, the *Leutnant* observed the progress of the rebuilding. As soon as the bridge flooring was laid with planks, the Goliaths, at all of 20 kilometres an hour, drove into position.

It was six o'clock in the morning on 18 February. With one almighty thunderous crash, the Goliaths spewed their 225 kilos of explosives at the bridge. The thick black cloud over the bridge slowly disappeared to reveal the devastation our little 'giants' had caused. Two spans of the bridge and a pillar lay in pieces in the Weistritz. It was all over in the blink of a Russian eye. We had only one wounded engineer.

That action however, only gave us a short pause. A little further along the riverbank from the bridge or what remained of it, 24 Russian soldiers had crossed the river in a rubber boat. They had landed on our side, unnoticed by our neighbours on the left flank. Our friend Domke, who had freed us from Peiskerwitz, then formed an assault detachment. In engaging in close combat with those Russians, he lost his life. In a dawn mist and in clouds of dust from hand-grenades, plus a little nervousness from one of his own men, he received a bullet through the heart, from the said soldier. Domke was posthumously awarded the German Cross in Gold.

In order to ward off surprise attacks of this nature in future, we organised 'listening posts'. Near the river in no-man's land, one man kept guard in a dug-out. Armed with pistol and hand-grenade, his duty was to report, without a fight, and give the alarm the moment that he recognised enemy movement. The guards were relieved at hourly intervals and were accompanied by the commander, so that he could inspect the situation at the same time. On a nightly inspection I lost my way through thick shrubs. The well-camouflaged guard could not be found. I ordered the relieving guard to lie low and wait. In absolute darkness, I made my way through the gardens to find myself at the water's edge. I turned round to go back.

Suddenly a blinding flash hit me, a detonation threw me to the ground and my pistol flew out of my hand. Dazed, I felt myself from top to toe in order to see that I was still in one piece. On hands and knees I felt around for my pistol and called the passwords several times, before I received an answer. The guard who had thought that I was a Russian soldier, then answered. He was dismayed when finding that I was not Russian. I had splinters from his hand-grenade in my thigh. With blood staining my trousers, I limped back to our positions, hanging on to my two companions. I was given a tetanus injection. Then I slept for some hours in the cellar, with a provisional dressing on my wounds. Despite this I had to stay put, the criteria being that I had not broken a bone and could walk, albeit in a lot of pain, for every man was needed.

The guard, a Hungarian-German, would not admit that he had slept on duty. He had thrown the grenade in panic on being woken, without asking for the passwords. He had certainly slept at his post. I did not accuse him of doing it on purpose, for he was shaken to the core at what had happened. After all, I had escaped without serious consequences, but I still had parts of his hand-grenade in my thigh. He felt very guilty over the whole affair. Thereafter he 'spoiled' me with bottled eggs and pickled pork that he organised from the pantries of the other houses. We then received our marching orders.

We left the river. As we marched, we reviewed the situation of being constantly in combat for the previous few weeks, without a break. Our combat in flat terrain was bound together with high losses in men. The constant changing of positions had delayed the advance of the Russians to the Silesian capital, Breslau. While we were busy with such delaying tactics, other units were able to organise defensive measures. But only just in time, at least, so we were told.

The march for me became unbearable with the splinters boring into my flesh. I had a stick and the support of two comrades who never left my side. They supported me in every way they could. We reached Schmiedefeld in the early morning hours. It lay to the west of Gandau aerodrome. It could not then be very far to Breslau.

We secured our positions between the greenhouses of nurseries, dug our trenches and set up machine-gun positions. My squad settled into a newly-built house on a new housing estate. The pantry was very well stocked. But no sooner had we cooked a warm meal for ourselves on a coal-heated cooker, and were looking forward to a couple of hours' sleep, than the guards gave the alarm. Thick dark smoke was to be seen over Neukirch and we were bitter that the 'Ivans' were so close on our heels and could not give us a moment's peace. It was only a couple of hours later that their shells started to hit us. The shattered greenhouses and their broken glass lay all around. Some of my men cut themselves very badly when hitting the ground amongst the shards of glass. Around the same evening the Russian advanced units reached our positions, trying to break through our lines in various places. Each and every time we drove them back. I lost one of my men, my best machine-gunner, in the bitter fighting. He had that day prophesied his own death. His prophesy became reality when he died from a bullet in the stomach. We also lost Leo Habr in the dawn hours. It pained us that we could not recover his body, for the Russians were too far advanced into the grounds of the nursery.

A sudden depression enveloped us, for Leo Habr was very popular with the men and was a good officer and comrade. He had possessed a typical Viennese charm, was a successful soldier and we had thought that he was invulnerable. His dry humour had turned the last experience with him, that dangerous boat-trip, to one almost of pleasure. I then was to replace him and take over his platoon. We could only hold Schmiedefeld for another few hours. Then we saw dark smoke from fires hanging over the Maria-Höfchen estate to the south, in the direction of Mochbern. The enemy was standing at the doors of the city. From the lowland around the town, their next target was the aerodrome in Gandau, to the west of Breslau. That aerodrome was very important as the supply link to the city's garrison. But it was some weeks before they could take it. We were under pressure from the continual attacks and so we retreated to the outskirts of Breslau and into the grounds of the aircraft and motor manufacturer FAMO. That manufacturer was the successor of the famous Linke-Hofmann factory. It had a worldwide reputation and took over the armament programme during the war. Between the highly qualified staff, of whom there were 8,000, and the fighting troops, a very trusted and almost dedicated association formed. The extremely large factory premises provided more than enough protection from enemy shrapnel and infantry.

The houses around were already evacuated, apart from a few people who, in hope, had left it to the very last minute before leaving. Now the last of them packed the most precious of their belongings. They locked their doors, as if that last action was going to save their valued home from further damage.

CHAPTER 16

Festung Breslau

After weeks of varied fighting to the north-west of Breslau, our SS Regiment Besslein was moved back to the outskirts of the city. There we were to learn that the 6th Soviet Army had completed their encirclement on 15 February 1945, and with that my private fears became reality.

Seven well-equipped divisions then stood on a front that surrounded Breslau, with another six as reserves. In total 150,000 Russian soldiers waited to besiege the Silesian capital. They were experienced 'Red' fighters who had not been defeated in many a battle on their way to the west. On top of that, they had support from numerous aircraft.

Altogether the Armed Forces, i.e. the Waffen SS, *Volkssturm* and Hitler Youth, had a third of their expected strength. There were 50,000 men and an odd assortment of members of the Navy and Air Force, mostly with no fighting experience. With that lack of experience, plus the disproportionately older age of the *Volkssturm*, an assignment for them, on the front-line, was out of the question. A death-defying battle began with only 200 artillery pieces, 7 tanks and 8 assault guns, in an unequal fight against an appalling opponent. In that situation we had to fight for five extra men, get dug-in without sleep, and always keep changing our positions from one place to another. Meanwhile nearly 240,000 citizens, mostly the elderly, and mothers with children, waited expectantly for better or worse.

Instead of attacking from the east, the Red Army attacked from the south. Supported by Stalin tanks, they managed to advance 2–3 kilometres into the southern villa district of the city. The *Hitlerjugend* fought by our side on that tough assignment. For some it was their first fight, and many of those very brave young men lost their lives. After three weeks of street fighting, that lovely district, with its villas, parks, gardens and lakes, was reduced to dust and rubble.

The mercilessness of the fighting was recorded by Russian war correspondent W.J. Malinin. On 24 February 1945 he described it as follows: "Every house bears the mark of the bitter fighting. The streets, in which one or two of the larger houses have been deliberately demolished by the 'Hitlerites', are barricaded with stones and gun emplacements to obstruct our path. Every barricade is defended with machine-guns and with mortars. Our Soviet soldiers must find new routes for our infantry. Our engineers have to blow holes into the walls of other houses through which our artillery can push their guns in order to advance. Our soldiers have to fight from floor to floor in the remaining houses. Yesterday, Sergeant Ivannikov with

The author (right) with comrades in *Festung* Breslau

his men fought in one house for an hour and a half. In it the 'Hitlerites' had destroyed the stairs. His men attacked with anti-tank rifles, through a hole in the first floor. They killed five of the sixteen men above, who were dropping grenades on them. The remainder surrendered. 1st Lieutenant Odinkov managed to clear four blocks of houses inside two days, killing 300 Hitlerites. The 27th birthday of the founding of the Red Army was very well honoured indeed".

The expectation was that the Russians would attack from the north and east. In the last few days of January, the order had been given to evacuate thousands of the inhabitants who had wandered into empty houses in the southern part of the city. As the danger from the south was recognised, two-thirds of the evacuees were then evacuated once again. For that purpose, trams that were still running were commandeered to go within a few miles of the front. It was a psychological therapy which calmed the population. The theory was that when the trams were still running, then the situation couldn't be too bad. It was a sign of normal life, even when the enemy lurked on the edge of the city. We were dependent on the radio and official announcements from the NSDAP in the form of the Silesian daily newspaper, the *Schlesischen Tageszeitung*. It was known as the 'megaphone' of the Armed Forces. This front-line newspaper appeared daily with advice, information, colourful propaganda, commentary and appeals for stamina, right up to the last days before the capitulation. After the bombing on the 1st of April, the last tram ground to a halt with the collapse of the overhead cables. Having lost their use in carrying passengers, they were then used as anti-tank obstacles. They were parked in double rows, to block the whole width of the road, in order to stop enemy vehicles. During the fighting, many enemy tanks were destroyed at such barricades by *Panzerfäuste* and anti-tank guns. Very early on, paving stones had been torn up by willing men, women and youths. They barricaded empty windows, leaving just an embrasure for the weapons of our infantry. The sturdily-built homes housed many a machine-gun nest, and the bitter fight for Breslau became tougher with each day.The population gave us 100% support. The slogan painted on nearly every door, "Every house a fortress", was no propaganda in Breslau, but a meaningful military measure. From those provisional embrasures we were able to keep the Russians at bay, very successfully, and for long periods of time. A great compensation for the German soldier in Breslau, was the fully furnished quarters in which he found himself, that were left behind by the fleeing inhabitants. Even when the pauses in the firing were short, the luxury of falling into a made-up bed was thankfully appreciated.

I was also able to enjoy the luxury of a 'white' bed when our military doctor ordered bed-rest for me. I had a couple of days in the Military Hospital, which had been erected in the evacuated Institute for the Blind. Pus oozed from the wound after the metal splinters had been removed from my leg, and I wallowed in the care of the friendly Red Cross nurses.

From where the Institute for the Blind was situated on West Park it was not far away to where the company supply unit was to be found. Upon being released from hospital after the third day, I limped my way to the Pöpelwitz housing estate to report for duty once more. The 11th Company military clerks were housed in Malapanese Street in a very large house with many floors. Also there was my friend Georg Haas, the company accountant, who was overjoyed at my appearance. There were no doubts as to where my bed was going to be! That was in 'his' flat, in 'his' house.

When he was going about his duties during the day, I helped him by preparing the Notification of Death letters that were waiting for signature by the company leader. The letters of communication, to the families of the dead, did not tell the truth of the conditions of death. Of course, that was out of consideration for the bereaved. Our unspoken law was always to retrieve the bodies of our comrades for burial. It caused us great sorrow when circumstances did not allow this to be done. Very often, as I have described, it would have meant suicide for us to have attempted this, in situations that we could not alter. We could, however, with these notifications of death sent to parents and family, imply that it did. Every one of my fallen comrades, and I knew them all, were respectfully given 'a hero's death'. The parents, mother, or wife, should and would never know of the long hours in no-man's land that he had spent in pain, and dying alone. Our message of death had to be as painless as we could make it, and so we deceived and

Artillery rounds strike a building in Breslau

veiled the truth, in doing this duty. It was the worst of any that one had to perform in one's life.

Fate can often be followed from a photo-album. I had this chance while in quarters with Georg. I was much moved, as I looked through a thick raffia-covered album that I had found. Each photo had been neatly and accurately inscribed, so that I could imagine the scenes behind the photos. I followed the fate of that young family and, although unknown to me, I knew all about them.

There were photos from a happy childhood. There were wedding photos. 'He' standing proudly in his Air Force uniform as a Technical Sergeant, in his No. 1s naturally. 'She' as the pretty bride dressed in white, wore her hair in a large roll on the back of her neck, in the fashion of that time. Of course, those pictures were followed by those of their children, two sons who had been photographed on the Holtei Hill, perhaps on a day's outing. There were many, including some of their last holiday, where they were seen in a tree-lined avenue on their bicycles. Fredrick the Great had those trees planted. But the growing conditions, plus the raw east winds of Silesia, were not ideal and all had bent trunks. The very last which had been glued into the album, was a cutting from a newspaper, edged in black. The article was decorated with a black cross, which announced 'Fallen for Germany'.

Where was this lady of the house, this war-widow and her children, who had left her house as if she had gone shopping and would be returning soon? Had she, had they survived? It was spick and span and everything was in its place. It was clean and tidy, so we as guests in her home, tried to keep it that way, knowing full well that it would soon be a sacrifice of the war, as would the album, the record of their lives, that she had had to leave behind.

Among her possessions in the lounge was a gramophone, which we happily used, listening to modern hits and martial music. To put this machine into gear after a glass of dry red wine, which Georg had procured from somewhere in the city, was sometimes a problem though. We did not always have the opportunity. The occasions were rare and of short duration, for even in the supply unit the alarm had to be audible. There was also a radio, an extremely good set with a long-range receiving capacity. It was made in elegant black Bakelite, at which we sat to hear the news which was always richly descriptive. We could pick up foreign radio stations too, and did, although that was forbidden.

Sometimes our very human curiosity got the better of us, and among other radio stations we would listen to Radio Moscow. It was transmitted in the German language and prophesied doom and gloom with phrases such as, "Fright eats away the soul!" and other well-known Russian sayings. On every hour, and punctually at midnight, a monotone feminine voice would begin to dramatically proclaim the death of a German soldier. The mixture of 'hot-air' and poisonous 'black propaganda' made no impression at all on us soldiers. But how was it received by the not-so-robust members of the public who also listened in?

Continual movement of the besieging forces demanded constant movement from us within. We had to change our positions time and time again. On our marches to new positions, we were stopped by many of the residents from the quieter areas, who asked about the current situation on the front-line. Everyone was frightened, in particular the women. The two main questions from everyone, were "how long can we hold out?" and "Will you be receiving help from outside?" We did not know, and could only answer with some vague knowledge based upon rumours. The rumours were that the Commander-in-Chief of Army Group Centre, General Ferdinand Schörner, with several divisions from the Strehlen and Zobten areas, wanted to try to reach Breslau. That was true, but throughout the period of the siege, there was no sign of them.

Alongside this hope of outside help, the military leadership within the fortress looked at possibilities of escape. A Breslau-born professor was very useful in that way. He produced parchment scrolls from 1767, showing a system of underground tunnels beneath the city. The entrance was to be found below the City Hall, and ran parallel to Schweidnitzer Street, deep under the Church of St. Dorothy, to the city walls. The engineers then went to work and found the tunnel which, as could only be expected after all those years, was in poor condition. To restore even a couple of kilometres would take months. That does not mean that they did not try, they did! The short distance they restored was very useful. They were able to erect an artillery observation post going under the Russian lines, for the direction of firing and observation of enemy movements.

The inhabitants had much to suffer, which they did with patience. Their stoicism would have pleased the old Greek teachers. Their philosophy taught that it is wise to remain indifferent to the vicissitudes of fortune, or as in this case, the vicissitudes of fate. The troops faced that every day.

Helplessness, worry, the loss of homes, together with the ultimate fear of being conquered by the Russians, and fear among women especially, brought about many hundreds of suicides. This we knew, and we tried to calm people, telling them that they could count on us. After the war, Paul Piekert, priest of St Mauritius, reported that the extent of the despair of the Breslau inhabitants had resulted in 100 to 120 suicides every day. This was confirmed by Ernest Hornig, the priest of Silesia's best known church, in his book *Breslau 1945*. He wrote that in total, a known 3,000 took their own lives in the 84 days that Breslau was besieged, and that many more have never been recorded.

Breslau's only remaining line of communication was the Gandau aerodrome. Food was in plenty and no soldier or civilian went hungry in all the months of the siege. It was the ammunition that was very low and our 'hungry weapons' that had to be fed! Deliveries were made by our reliable and proven *Tante* Ju–52 transport machines. They took the lightly wounded out on the return journeys. Those men were to be treated outside the encirclement, so that they were fit for combat once more. The badly wounded who could not be healed so quickly, had to stay in the hospital in the city. It was not only ammunition, many tons of it being flown in up to 19 February, but also supplies of medication, first aid supplies, bandages etc, and also our post which came by air. The loss of the trusted planes was very heavy. The fleet of planes under the command of General *Ritter* von Greim lost 160 of their machines. At night, the soldiers as well as the civilians would follow the flight paths of the providers in the searchlights of the night skies. The droning of their engines and the timpani of Russian anti-aircraft guns added to the awful and, at the same time, breathtaking spectacle taking place in the heavens. Frequently we saw our planes in flames, falling from the skies, with their helpless passengers on board.

General Hermann Niehoff was rather critical of his flight to Breslau on 2 March. He was replacing the *Festung* commander General Hans von Ahlfen. He found himself in an unusual situation, flying into a city where the only wish of nearly 250,000 men and women was to be flown out. He described his flight, which to say the least was spectacular, in an article for the magazine *Der Welt am Samstag*. In the edition of 15 January 1956 he wrote as follows:

> We were flying on a northerly course to Breslau, which was only 46 kilometres away. I knew it could be a fateful one for me and perhaps one which

A pause from the fighting, *Festung* Breslau, 1945. A drawing by the author.

could lead to my grave. The dark night skies gave protection for the moment. Then a sea of flames was to be seen which grew bigger as we approached Breslau! The protection of the darkness was suddenly rudely shattered with the burst of anti-aircraft fire. Then the searching fingers of searchlights lit the sky, just one or two at first. They increased in numbers, bumping into one another, in their haste to find us. They were blinding but not enough that I did not see the fright in the white faces of my chauffeur and my batman who grimly and silently viewed the scene below. There was a hurricane of shells bursting all around us, their noise adding to that of our engines. Like white mice, the flight of the tracers appeared to be directed at me, as I looked out of the window. They were concentrating at penetrating my heart, and this vivid impression accompanied me thereafter. It was an impression that I could not lose, even years after, as a prisoner of war.

Suddenly a very agitated pilot told us that we would have to turn around and return to base. Our engines had been hit and slowly the view disappeared behind and to the right of us. Gradually we left it all behind. The sea of flames disappeared. We landed not long after where we had begun our journey. The pilot wordlessly showed us where we had been hit at the rear of the plane and in the engines. Then he relaxed and his humour returned, for his mission had come to an end. Mine however had not.

A second attempt to fly General Niehoff into Breslau also failed. The second time it was because the controls of the Junkers were completely frozen. The third was successful, and it was through the efforts of a Technical Sergeant and *Feldwebel*. He had a trick up his sleeve, according to General Niehoff, and "simply oozed self-confidence!" The *Feldwebel* delivered the General with a daredevil flight, but safe and sound, into the inferno of Breslau. His technique was to spiral the Junkers high into the atmosphere, as high as "the old crate" would allow, and then turn the engine off! The Junkers would then noiselessly spiral to earth unnoticed, to just above the roofs of the houses. Daredevil indeed! However, after that experience, and landing safely at the aerodrome, the General then came under fire. He had to crawl on all fours, guided to safety by an ordnance officer with a torch.

It did not take long for this General to win the trust of troops and inhabitants. He was never to be found in his command post, an old ice-storage cellar that had damp walls, because he was always inspecting the current situation. He firstly made a reconnoitre of Breslau, making an underground house-to-house inspection. He squeezed through holes made in the cellar walls of the houses, providing access from one to the other. Up top, on the street, he had to run under fire in order to inspect the troops. Every unit in his command came under his critical eye. As the position of the front-line altered, his command post was changed to the building that housed the State and University Library on Sand Island, very close to Sand Church. He could then be found in the deepest cellars, thought to be the safest in Breslau.

In contrast, the rather young *Gauleiter* Karl Hanke, resided in a bunker of another quality, with many comforts. It was also assessed to be extremely secure. It had a number of offices, including a telephone centre, a communications room, a kitchen, canteen, shower rooms, and other rooms that were sectioned off with dividing curtains. He would sit in his 'presidium', a very large office or committee-room, surrounded by oil paintings, carpets and antique furniture, and using an oversized desk. In those surroundings he must have felt very comfortable indeed, and into which I stumbled quite unintentionally one day.

It was, if I remember correctly, in the middle or end of March that we had to change our positions because of very heavy artillery fire. We were seeking a safer place. Underground we could not know where we were, or where the long flight of stone steps which we took, would lead us. While investigating we suddenly found ourselves in a smoke-filled room. It was a fully furnished cellar. There were many people, both civilians and members of the military, and others wearing the brown Party uniforms. They were enjoying a feast at a very large table laden with food and drink, all of the finest quality. We, with our sudden appearance, had caught them unawares and put them in a very embarrassing position that could be clearly seen. Their guilty consciences demanded that we were invited to join them. We were duly showered with compliments on our performance, and helped with exaggerated gestures to the dishes. It was as if we were guests of honour, and not unshaven, unwashed and tattered 'front-swine' fresh from the main line of resistance, with 'potato-mashers' stuck into our boots!

We, as small fry, really could not complain about our Front-menu but this was another category. It was another world about which we could only dream, and somewhat grotesque at that. Up above there was all hell let loose. Deep under the centre of the burning city there was this almost Mephistophelian feast. We were sitting at this table! We were also overjoyed some time later, when bottles of 'good cognac and wine' were placed in our haversacks, with a hefty slap on the shoulder, to celebrate the 'final victory' and a victorious end of the war!

Today perhaps it is not so understandable that we were not disgusted at the Nazi 'Golden Pheasants' morals. That was a term very often used after the war and not understood by us at the time. But it did not 'disgust' us then. Perhaps we were too phlegmatic? I am no longer sure if in fact *Gauleiter* Hanke was present. If so, then he would have made himself very noticeable with his continual slogans. Throughout the siege, he was not very well liked by the inhabitants because of his over-exaggerated self-righteousness, when confronted with what he assessed as defeatist attitudes.

There was another encounter with a high-ranking Nazi official that was not so sociable. It happened because of complete carelessness with a weapon. There was thoughtlessness, because of impatience, and it all ended in tragedy. We were about to take over new quarters in the Zimpel district. The responsible district officer accompanied us to garages that had corrugated iron doors. In attempting to open one that had stuck, he attacked the door with the butt of a fully loaded machine-pistol, without its safety catch on. It exploded, as expected. Our sergeant-major received the full load in his intestines and within seconds was dead on the spot. We pounced on the man, taking his weapon away from him, shouting and cursing at him. That should not have happened, not to our sergeant-major. He was a man loved by his men, who fulfilled his duty as 'mother of the company' and who, above all else, had come through the whole of the Russian campaign without a scratch. His death was a very bitter affair for us, very bitter indeed.

It was only a matter of time we knew, before Gandau was taken over by the advancing Russians. Hitler also knew. He kept his eye on the situation in Breslau and personally gave directions. One was that another provisional landing-strip be made in the centre of the city. For this plan, all of the houses between the Kaiser and Fürsten bridges in the proximity of the Schneitzniger Park, had to be demolished. Tramlines, telephone poles, iron girders, as well as the mountains of rubble from the houses on the Schneitzniger Stern had to be transported away. It also included everything from the mighty Luther and Canisius churches. That meant that all of it had to be removed by hand. Part of it could be used for barricades, but the rest had to be removed. Thousands of women and youths were conscripted for the work. They toiled by day and by night to fulfil that project.

And the Russians? They were very quick to find out what was going on in the middle of Breslau, in the Kaiserstrasse. The project was therefore the target of attack from ground-attack aircraft, which spat machine-gun fire and dropped fragmentation bombs on to the civilian labour-force, leaving a bloody trail behind them. The death toll was enormous, increasing daily during the month of March. That project was to be the main cause of death for the Breslau inhabitants, being estimated by the priest Ernst Hornig at 10,000!

The Russian advance on Gandau, and the continual bombardment during March, meant that it could only be days before they took the aerodrome. We knew that, but it did not take place until early in April. Until then, the faithful Junkers had carried out their duty in the supply of everything that the fortress had needed. It was on 4 April that the supply-line was finally severed. It was a day of heavy bombardment from the air, and heavy artillery fire from the ground, until finally Soviet tanks rolled into the aerodrome and took possession. The defence of the air traffic, incoming with supplies, and outgoing with the wounded, had been protected for as long as was humanly possible. It had been the largest and most worrying task of the fortress Commander-in-Chief, who wrote in his diary on 24 March 1945:

> The supply-line for Breslau has become extremely difficult to protect because of increasingly heavy anti-aircraft guns and searchlights. On 15 March, from a total of 55 machines that had tried to land, only half of the machines managed to do so. Despite this, 150 of our wounded were flown out, most of the machines being able to take 20 of the wounded per flight. Inside three days, 150 planes were able to drop ammunition overboard, small arms and mail for the troops using *Versorgungsbomben*.

Versorgungsbomben were not bombs at all, but supply-canisters attached to parachutes. They fell to a large extent behind enemy lines, into marshland and on to the roofs of the houses. Then it really was not worth breaking your neck in order to recover them. We did however recover some, complete with parachute, for the red, soft silk was readily worn by the lads as a scarf tucked into their shirts. The anger, the disappointment, and the frustration were great when we opened them one after the other. There were 50 altogether, each holding two *Panzerfäuste*. Firstly we found that the detonators had failed. Secondly, the *Panzerfäuste* held no explosive substances! We could not imagine why. We just could not understand. The disbelief turned to anger at such shoddy work. We could not believe that it was simply human error. Was it then deliberate? Was it then sabotage? Were secret saboteurs at work in the homeland? As a result, pilots doing their best to bring us much-needed weapons were losing their lives, in waves, in the line of duty, on extremely dangerous sorties.

When we found ourselves in that emergency situation our frustrated minds brought invention to the fore. After all, why did we have the FAMO engineers at hand. From the original employees totalling 8,000, there were then only 680 left in Breslau. They consisted of workers, technicians and engineers and they were there for our problems. They gave us their technical know-how and their time. Working both by day and by night, they replaced what was missing. I must stress that they worked miracles. All made a supreme effort to give us what we needed. For instance we had more than enough new machine-guns, but all without their locking units. The FAMO men constructed this complicated lever-arm from just an illustrated spare-parts catalogue, just as a locksmith would do. Despite bombardments and coming under artillery fire, the men worked 'like the devil' in the partly-destroyed factory. They not only restored small arms, but even tanks as well. The finest achievement of all was the armoured train that they produced in fourteen days and nights of hard work.

From an old chassis, they reconstructed a 'rolling fortress within the fortress' which was strengthened with steel plating and armed with 2cm and 8.8cm anti-aircraft guns. It chugged its way right into the middle of the Russian lines. From pure fright this iron Trojan recouped many a lost position for us. Soviet magazine-fed rifles were re-designed to use German ammunition. Because we needed tracer pistols, the FAMO men produced them newly made, from an old existing model that we had given them. The Russians had no equivalent of the FAMO men and were left with the useless newly delivered weapons dropped by our parachutes.

For the defence of a particular railway embankment, a pyramid-shaped shelter was produced from steel tank plating, as a machine-gun nest for a rifle squad. It proved to be very efficient indeed. Their work was interrupted more than once because of damage to workshops. Provisional ones had to be erected elsewhere. The epilogue to the super-human efforts of those men, for whom nothing was impossible, was sadly, that 13% of the remaining employees died as a result of enemy attacks.

Another example of stamina from the inhabitants, was shown by a group of skilled workers at an old factory in the Wilhelmsruh part of the city. They produced grenades with the most primitive of materials. Explosive material from Russian 'duds', plus steel splinters, were used to fill 8.8cm anti-aircraft cartridges. The men were then producing as many as 200 to 300 per day. Due to their efforts, we caused heavy losses for the Russians, even when 15% of the hastily produced grenades were also 'duds'! The soldiers on the front also had ideas, stemming from the new experience of house-to-house fighting. They needed new fighting tactics in an overwhelming experience for which they had had no training. One of those ideas came from the hazards of collecting fresh supplies of ammunition and rations. We had to cross a large and dangerous junction which caused us to lose many men to snipers.

The Russians just waited for us to make a move. We scratched our heads for ways to fool them and came up with the idea of hanging washing lines, with carpets, runners and curtains etc, to obstruct their view. The camouflage washing-line worked so well that we made more of such screens, in every imaginable direction, to draw attention away from our runs. We felt safe enough to hang banners with the message, "The SS Regiment Besslein fights here to greet the 'Ivans'!" That pledge was adhered to by the Regiment.

During streetfighting we didn't need to worry about the enemy artillery, for the distances between the two sides was such that neither wanted to endanger their own. Small arms and grenades decided the style of fighting. We had to get used to house-to-house fighting. One could not mention the theoretical training at the Close-combat School in Prague or Klagenfurt. That bore no relationship to the practical experience in Breslau. In the Steppes of Russia, large armies fought over large distances and there were clear physical lines and fronts. Apart from partisans and a few enemy air raids, everyone knew where the front was, and from there only, came the danger.

However, in Fortress Breslau it was very different. Here our enemy hid in unexpected places, perhaps next door, on the other side of the street, or in the house behind you. Sometimes we could feel that he was there, very close to us, but did not know where. With time we developed a sixth sense about him, and even his weapons, just as we had done in the Steppes. We could determine not only the range but even the calibre of his bullets that whizzed around our heads. Then, I could have written a booklet on the seismographic sense that I, that all of us, developed with the day-to-day routine, despite the turmoil in the city. In the maze of uncountable streets and squares, alleys and corners, we had to change our tactics. We were forced to, for the Russians had many a trick up their sleeves that were not so honourable, that were in fact downright cowardly. With time, our tactics were exchanged for sniping, and ambush was the order of the day. However, for us, creeping up on our enemy was made easier, for the cover in the ruins and cellars was better than the Russian Steppes had ever given us. None the less this street warfare was calculated, malicious and brutal. A glaring example of misconduct from the Reds, was the striking misuse of Red Cross armbands, breaking the laws of both the Hague and the Geneva Conventions.

One day three 'unarmed' Russians wearing those armbands, carried a stretcher to within yards of us. We honoured the code of stopping firing whilst they recovered their dead and wounded. That to us was sacred! As they came nearer to the house-frontage, they threw hand-grenades that had been hidden under the blankets on the stretcher. As we could not react as quickly, they were able to disappear to the other side of the street, unharmed.

It was the worst form of soldiering that we had experienced, an unfair and unscrupulous method of war and one which we had never used, however hard or bitter the conditions became. But after that, we changed our tactics too, returning to ancient but ethical ones, in which we became specialists. To be fair, I must add that this incident was the only one of its kind that I heard about in Breslau.

In the desperate situation in which we found ourselves, we could not carry on a war without also improvising. If we wanted to come through it in one piece and beat the enemy, we had to use their underhand methods. Sometimes, no-man's land was no wider than a street that could give us some sort of protection. Our engineers scratched their heads, for the laying of mines in the normal manner could not be considered, as every move that they made was observed by the Reds. It was the soldiers who suggested that the mines be laid as booby-traps in 'bricks'. There was more than enough material from bricks lying around in powder form which was then used to paint the reconstructed wooden boxes as 'bricks' in which the mines had been packed. After the reconstruction the 'bricks' could not be distinguished from the real ones. Under cover of darkness, they were pushed into position with long rods, from cellar windows or ground floor balconies. The Russians never noticed and our engineers had ensured that their combat area was as safe as they could make it.

After information was received from the main line of resistance, of the retreat of our soldiers from certain areas, the engineers were very quick to lay explosive material in the houses in the foremost lines. We worked closely with the engineers, relying on the damage caused to the houses and those who had managed to reach them. After a short time, many Russian soldiers had done so. As soon as the engineers, whose positions lay 200 metres behind, detonated explosives, then we sprang into the still-smoking or burning house, to hunt down the Russians still dizzy from shock and surprise. Sometimes a five-storey house had been demolished, flames reaching its roof-beams. Sometimes we had to wait and sleep in a house in which an unexploded bomb lay. In that situation nerves of jelly were of no use to us. Despite our ingenious ideas, the Russians were far superior in their 'underhand' strategy of war. Their ingenuity had already been obvious to us in the winter campaign in Russia, where we had had to learn to adapt. We were still learning in Breslau.

Naturally enough, weak links formed in our front-line, even in the 'take from Peter to give to Paul' action within the troops. There were occasions where units could not be given any help and were left to their own devices, ingenuity and superhuman effort saving the day. One of those weak links was in Augustastrasse. The Russians knew this and were determined to break through at that point. We were also in Augustastrasse. Budka in the next house to us had a very hard time of it when, in the very large building of the Regional Institution for Insurance, coke stored there was set alight. A fight for their lives started for Budka and his men. Fighting bare-chested, a team of helpers showered cold water over them, so that they could continue to fight in an increasing heat of between fifty and sixty degrees. They were forced to change shifts at half-hourly intervals. The men upon being re-lieved, went immediately to the entrances of the building. There they were handed supplies of mineral water from the Selters Mineral Water factory nearby, and gasped for 'fresh air'. This superhuman effort paid off. The Russians did not break through, for Budka had known that relief from re-serves was not possible and to retreat would have given the Reds exactly what they wanted.

Another unforgettable encounter took place in an old and very large school. Another lesson had to be learnt from the Reds, in the use of small arms. The scene was a changing one. It took place in the corridors and then on the staircase of this large building. We were to be found on the top-most floors and the enemy in the cellar, where we eventually penetrated to in total darkness. It was so dark, that we could not see a hand in front of our faces, so communication from one to another was verbal. Only so could we deter-mine how close we were to the Reds. We were in fact actually as close as the length of the unexpected use of a flamethrower, i.e. 30 metres. Such indoor use of flamethrowers was very rare. We could not anticipate it, and some of the men suffered terrible burns at such a close range. It was pure hell. But we eradicated the fire-fiend with a *Panzerfaust*.

As mentioned before, it was not only the military who made sacrifices, or who became sacrifices, as General Niehoff came to experience. He was approached by a young Breslau-born woman who made a very dangerous suggestion. It could not be hidden within the fortress that we had a 'prob-lem-child'. It was a small one, but nonetheless one that was our own fault. It need not have arisen if we had done our work properly. A wooden bridge over a small river had been left intact on our retreat, much to the delight of the Russians as bridges are always of strategic importance. This 'little bridge' enabled Russian supplies to be brought, as and when needed, and as ex-pected, was strongly defended. After asking for help from the 17th Army outside the fortress, it was still intact, two air-raids having both been unsuc-cessful because of very strong anti-aircraft fire.

Ursula, nineteen years old, a telephone operator in the Breslau tele-phone exchange and a BDM *Gruppenführer*, knew all of this. She appeared in the Command Post of General Niehoff, offering her services in destroy-ing this bridge with explosives. The offer moved General Niehoff, for what more could prove the desire of this 'Silesian' to defend her home city? It would however have been totally irresponsible of him in allowing it. So he told her that her work in the telephone exchange was also vital and that was where she should return. It was just four days later that General Niehoff learned that the bridge had been destroyed, only charred wooden remnants for posts being all that could be seen emerging from the water. Ursula? Had she not taken "no" for an answer? It was to prove so. Research revealed that she had found an explosives expert and with feminine wiles had convinced him that she could learn everything that could be learned about this material and its uses. She learnt quickly, in days, what usually took engineers weeks, if not months. She was not alone in her work, for two other BDM girls accompanied Ursula on her mission to the western front-line. They swam under a drifting paddleboat using the flow of the river to bring them to the bridge. It lay immediately behind enemy lines, and there they completed their mission.

Whether she, whether they, lived to see the success of their mission is not known. Nothing more is known about Ursula and her friends. Did they die in the explosion? Were they killed by guards when trying to return to the city? Even today nothing more is known and their fate that cannot be pursued. Their sacrifice must however, never be forgotten.

Other women and teenage girls within the fortress, also gave 'over and above their call of duty', especially in the now-overfilled First Aid posts, and military and civilian hospitals. Nurses and auxiliaries worked day and night under the worst of conditions, showing civil courage and garnering achievements beyond human expectation. It was an incredible talent and invention when literally hundreds of people, including patients from sanatoriums, mental institutions etc, had to be evacuated from these sometimes burning buildings and under fire from the artillery.

In bunkers, three above ground and four underground, and the ten hospitals in Breslau, an eighteen-hour operation programme was the order of the day. The flow of casualties was unending. I had cause to visit one of the above ground-bunkers, in the search for a friend of mine, who had been wounded when we were fighting in Augustastrasse and whom I found after a long search. I found him eventually in the round, concrete and steel six-storey bunker at Striegauer Platz, which I could only describe as a catacomb of death. Originally it was to be used as an air-raid shelter for the inhabitants, but the building, which was without windows, had been used for the wounded since the siege began and housed as many as 1,500 patients. It was always full and the doctors and nurses always gave dedicated care in that mausoleum.

Entry into this bastion was through two steel, fireproof doors, designed of course for the protection from fire. Because of that, one was confronted with firstly a wall of darkness, upon passing through the doors. Secondly, one was immediately met with foul air, the stench of pus, blood and ether, mixed with a pungent sweetness, reminding one of the battlefields. A narrow staircase wound its way upstairs around the round building. The electric light was sparse, very sparse. Leading from the passages were concrete cells, for want of a better word, housing three patients lying on collapsible beds, almost in darkness, for the only light came from the passages. The delirium of dying men emerged from the ghostly darkness, together with the cries of pain or the faint murmur of "Comrade, comrade". The suffering of mankind rang in their voices. It came from the remnants of men, who had 'run the gauntlet'. They had received the military 'punishment' of that destructive war.

I wanted to escape from that horrifying place, but I found my friend in his wretchedness, lying on bare boards, bandaging protruding from underneath his open jacket. There was a light in his eyes as he saw me and silently he gave me his hand. I did my best to console him, telling him that he would pull through. But three days later he died from his wounds. If that was not enough, I saw with my own eyes the facilities available for the dead, in that situation and place of death, which were far, far less than offered in a catacomb. The corpses were piled one on top of the other, on the ground floor near the stairs that I had to pass. My friend, with his broken 'dog-tag', was finally to be put on top of that pile of corpses.

There were many rumours about that bunker at Striegauer Platz, some becoming a legend. They stemmed from German soldiers not wanting to surrender it, but abandoning the burning bunker in the end. My friend and assistant field-doctor from those times, Markwart Michler, who was an eyewitness and with whom I have been friends since we were both prisoners of war of the Russians, told me however, that a planned evacuation of the bunker took place at the end of April and the bunker was left to the Russians.

I visited Breslau in 1972 and apart from obvious shell holes in the structure, I could not determine any other form of damage and certainly no burn marks. That still mighty concrete bastion was naturally sealed against inquisitive eyes and stretched itself to heaven as usual twenty-seven years later. Twenty-seven years after, the Polish authorities had not thought it necessary to clear the rubble of war away from its portal where it still lay.

Life in the besieged city was full of contrast. Here one fought and died, there one lived and loved. The front was not recognisable as anything but a communications zone, and there was practically nothing to determine soldier from civilian, for we had become a conspiratorial community. The war was everywhere, but even that slept, if only for a short while, like a beast of prey, bloated from the blood of its sacrifice. It was then somewhat peaceful and the soldier-lad dreamed for a couple of hours of the love of a lovely girl, for it helped him to forget the nightmare of war.

Everyone in the fortress, be it soldier or civilian, now greeted one another with an ironic "Stay healthy!" this irony interpreting the ever present mind-set which did not hold much optimism of surviving. When however, the few opportunities presented themselves, then they used them to the full, with wine, song and girls, with the motto "Enjoy the war, as freedom will be hell on earth"!

We were frustrated young men. We had seen nothing of the world. We had not sown our wild oats. We had not lived or loved. What had we had from life? Was our final chapter to be death, or to freeze in the wilds of Siberia? To ignore a 'tantalising situation' is a question of moral determination, is it not? To enjoy this 'tantalising situation' while in the midst of it, one needed to adapt, to make the best of life under the slogan, "Live today, for tomorrow you die!" And we did! People must understand, that with the enormous exertions that we had to make in that besieged city, in war-time, inhibitions that we would have had to overcome in normal times, were at a minimum and quickly thrown aside.

A new order was received and executed, in the middle of March. All women and girls, from the ages of 16 to 35 years of age, were conscripted into the Labour Service, to help the military, some in uniform helping the *Wehrmacht*. Naturally enough this brought us into closer contact with the feminine species. Many of the girls were employed in the ordnance units and were mostly very young assistants of supplies. Some were engaged as helpers in the kitchens, others as auxiliary nurses, who were lovingly called 'carbolic-mice' by the men. Despite their age, these girls became mothers for confessions, comforters of the soul, and bracketed as 'soldier-brides'. It was very easily understood, by everyone, when such young girls, alone and away from their familiar surroundings, sought the company of the soldiers. In sharing the same fate as we did in that inferno, the 'fortress Lolitas' were dancing on the top of this volcano with us. It is therefore no wonder that they sought, and found, more than willing guardians and protectors, in order to survive the 'fate of Breslau'.

As a man of the cloth, the priest Ernst Hornig saw the situation differently. He criticised it as "depraved, a definite lowering of moral standards and inhibitions" and described "Orgies, whereby women and alcohol were the main priorities, and the overflowing cup of lust led to intoxication".

Of course it was a contradiction and a paradox. Soldiers were engaged in bloody house-to-house fighting and people were enduring unbearable pain and suffering in Breslau's hospitals. At the same time, perhaps just a couple of buildings away, comrades danced a 'ring o' roses'. It was however a very big exception to the rule and not to be over exaggerated, for after that 'honeymoon in hell' the said soldiers found themselves in the middle of a merciless battle, just a few minutes later. They could, and many often did, lose their lives. Willingness and discipline suffered the least of all under those conditions, for such virtues were too deeply rooted. Although strongly forbidden by the rules within the fortress, a short visit by lady-friends was allowed, even in the foremost lines of the front. The 'hard-necked' and love-hungry among the girls, donned long military coats as camouflage, daring to visit the chosen warrior at his post. It was dangerous not only because of the iron-polluted air, but also the danger of attack, and of course of being discovered on the spot. The comrades did not care and looked in the other direction. It must be said in looking back, that the soldier lost his life before his innocence. The reality of fighting within Breslau's fortress was far from 'love and lust' as described by the priest Hornig, but of fighting and dying.

An affair, and my feelings for a female worker from the East, developed into a spectacular story, and one that could have had a fatal end. In the same manner that foreign volunteers fought in Germany's army, foreign volunteers worked in civilian positions as nurses. For example, some came from the north and west European countries, as well as forced female labour from eastern Europe. It was a pure coincidence that I learned that both Flemish and Dutch nurses were working in the Spital, on the west side of the city. Overjoyed at being able to use my mother tongue, I found not only them, but also the beautiful Tanya, a Russian girl working in the kitchen. She came from somewhere around Smolensk and was very sympathetic. She had been a student and spoke very good German. In our 'fire-pauses' I visited her, drawn very much by her beauty, and the strange aura that she radiated. She had high cheek-bones denoting her Slavic origin. I can remember very well how her dark curly hair peeped from the white headscarf that she wore. Despite her simple clothes, for me she was the absolute Venus. I warmed in particular to her sympathetic interest in the fate of my comrades at the front. When I told her of the fate of some of my friends in that merciless war, the resonance was of utter pity and sorrow.

I could not, and did not want to believe that her absence one day was because she had been arrested as an enemy spy. Tanya a Russian agent? My friends advised me very strongly not to intervene on her behalf and luckily I followed their advice. Unwillingly I realised, and later it was to be very clear to me, how dangerous such a *tête-à-tête* could be, for she was in truth a Russian agent. My behaviour was based on the presence of soldiers from Ukraine fighting alongside us. I wrongly assumed that she was of the same opinion as they. Before she had begun to work in the Spital, her mission had been to inform her Red Army comrades of the supply routes and movements of German troops. It was done from her hiding place under the eaves of a deserted house in Striegauer Platz, for the Russian artillery. She was not to be compared with Mata Hari from the First World War, but was more the perfect actress. I own up to being a romantic and clearly naive admirer, and became one of many of her 'sacrificial candidates'.

We had been warned so many times! Many times in our training period we were warned about sabotage and spies, as in Reibert's "Service Laws of the Armed Forces". We were particularly warned about the wiles of the feminine species. I had fallen, 'hook, line and sinker', into that trap. Only now is the enormity of the potential results of that situation quite clear. Cleary Tanya was very interested in the situation in our fighting zone, and had shown false sympathy for the fate of my friends. I found some consolation in the fact that I, as a subordinate, could not and did not give her any important strategic information, thank God! Despite an enormous disappointment in Tanya's character, I had to admire her courage and her dedication to her Bolshevik convictions. It could have led to her execution, as the International Rights of Law permitted. But it pained me too. It did not turn out that way, however. Fate decided to show Tanya some mercy, at least provisionally.

Long after the war, I was informed by one of the women who had also worked in the Spital, that she had seen Tanya, in the uniform of a Lieutenant of the Red Army, driving in an open horse-drawn coach through the city, decorated with medals. I would have loved to have had the chance to ask her how she had escaped, or was freed, for that was a real wonder. The throw of the dice from 'lady luck' had given her the 'six' that she needed. Never had a German soldier such a peaceful, happy and also naive relationship, with a member of the enemy, and a Russian agent at that.

There are times when the truth is not as believable as fantasy or fiction, but is none the less the truth, such as the following. Our soldiers bumped into their well-armed Russian counterparts on a wander through the cellars, looking for wine. It was to be found in well-stocked but deserted cellars. They bumped into a group of Russian soldiers with the same idea. The 'Ivans' and the 'Fritzes' it would appear, had the same fine nose for the bottle, and both had the same needs.

Although armed, there was a stand-off. Perhaps the Russians, already in a light state of stupor, decided that reasonableness under the motto, 'well, you find what you want, and we'll do the same!' was the best course of action. For that is exactly what they did. Is there anything more curious than that? It is said that Roman warriors fought with a short, sharp sword in their right hand and a bottle of 'juice from the grape' in the other.

The 'good stuff' was not the only necessity sought after in the cellars of Breslau, shelter was sought, too. It was in those cellars that both the civilians and the military found protection, when not on duty. The ceilings had been strongly supported with wooden or steel posts, to prevent collapse. The advantage of the man-made passages through the cellars, connecting whole streets with one another, was that one could escape when trapped in a house. It was carried out at the beginning of the siege and was the escape route for both the inhabitants and the soldiers, during the air raids. There was, at the same time, an orienteering problem down below. You had to know where you were and how to get to your destination. Otherwise you very quickly found yourself behind enemy lines, bumping into the 'Ivans'. The problem was quickly recognised and the routes provisionally walled-up, or under armed guard.

Along the front-line, the cellars of the houses were emptied of their contents. Everything landed in the garden or the back yard, but the big, fat rats, in whose territory we were encroaching, stayed. The doors of their quarters were the drains into the underworld and their numbers were not small. There were literally hundreds, which is why one had to sleep, when sleep was possible, with one's blanket over one's head. Chairs had been commandeered for the cellars from the deserted or damaged flats and houses. So we were hunched together in the pantries or coke-rooms, or where space allowed, pale faces giving a ghostly appearance in the flickering candlelight. There was seldom conversation, as it disturbed those who dozed while sitting in a chair. We were in a continual state of listening, with at least one ear cocked as an antenna. Our weapons had been cleaned in the lull and were at the ready, for the 'enemy' must not surprise us.

When peaceful in our zone, then we always heard the spasmodic rat-tat-tat of Russian machine-guns and mortar fire somewhere else. When we were the target, we knew that we had to go into action immediately after the firing ceased, into close combat. With that habit one could have slept for a couple of hours, in theory, but we never relied on this, it being the unspoken advice of our inner guardian. When exhaustion overcame us, which was often, and we slept, then it was always only enough for a short dream or two. Our dreams were never about the gruesome war, for our unconscious saw to it that we had a recovery period from it. We dreamed about the exciting and the peaceful. With death breathing down the back of my neck, I dreamed about my trouble-free childhood playing in green meadows, in the polder. My brothers, sisters and parents, and all of Zierikzee, came to life when I was dreaming. It was only after the war and my time as a prisoner of war was over, that my dreams then plagued me. They became nightmares about the war and followed me in my sleep for many, many years after.

In comparison with our brothers-in-arms on the front line, who were never in danger of aerial bombardment or very heavy artillery fire, we were regularly under shell fire from the Russians. "When the 'Ivan' spits", began the verbal apprenticeship of newcomers from the 'old hands' of the Eastern Front, or "when it bangs over there, then count to twenty, for it's a twenty-gun salute!" Then we had to 'watch out'. If you were surprised by a sudden swish in the air, then hit the ground 'pronto', for that could be your end. "If that hits you, it is not only you but everything and everyone around!" The conversation was about the Russian 'Big Bertha' whose shells had a very sensitive detonator. The shells detonated on a hair's-width contact with the earth, without making a crater but reducing everything to splinters as they raced, flat over the ground. Everything and everyone without adequate protection, was grated into splinters, within a radius of 50 metres. A weapon with a steep trajectory, it was ideal in reaching much wider targets behind the defensive lines and field positions. Although we had this weapon too, it was of course the German version.

When the alarm went, we sprang up instantly, using the already rubble-covered steps, to join the combat above. In the pauses, the positions were only protected by a one-man guard and a machine-gunner. When well and truly lost in rubble-reduced Breslau, and one heard that whistling projectile, then one had to duck to avoid it. Your luck had run out when you were a part of a direct hit. In the mountain of rubble within the fortress, we felt that we had returned to that of the Middle Ages with battlements and embrasures. We were surrounded by an overpowering enemy outside its walls.

The reliability of our comrades within our battalion was still very strong, despite heavy losses. That was something at which Tanya had wondered, on meeting my comrades, into whose eyes she looked, to find them still full of optimism. It must have been clear to her, why all of the assaults of her Red Army friends had failed till then. The crown of laurel leaves was for them as 'victors', but it remained out of reach. The field-grey uniforms were perhaps tattered and patched, but the spirit of their owners inside was not. Their faces had not shown her any fear of this merciless siege. She could not ignore the fact that these *Germanskis* had been able to withstand the stranglehold on Breslau for so long. The spy from the east had perhaps felt some apprehension, that despite the dull silver runes on their collars, such men could still survive a storm or two.

The fortress had now been under siege for some weeks and not fallen to the enemy. It was not only the German newspapers that reported the high losses of the Russians and "the fanatic fighting of the brave defenders of Breslau", but also neutral foreign newspapers regularly reported on 'the tough defence of Silesia'. In the Stockholm News of 22 March 1945, they said the following, "One cannot really imagine how the defenders can supply themselves with food, water, and ammunition. During the whole of the war, there has been no other example to compare with this dramatic and fantastic battle of wills, where the bitter defiance of death is second to none. *Pravda* echoed the report of "stiff resistance in Breslau". They had paid "a high and bitter price for a success that could only be called at that stage, minimal. The toll in men was unimaginable."

We made the assaults of the Russians harder with every day that went by and they began to make tactical mistakes that were to our advantage. Even General Niehoff began to scratch his head, wondering at his Russian counterpart. In his account, printed in on 5 February 1956, he stated that he had never understood why Major General Vladimir Gluzdovski had always attacked from the south. When it had been seen that a supposed combined attack from both the west and the north was planned, he had so easily broken the belt of defence around Breslau. The Russian radio messages were never disguised. They were heard, translated and therefore delivered a mass of information for the military leadership in the city, which was also to our advantage.

We could also ascertain many a mistake from enemy behaviour, an attack from them never being a surprise. For instance, we always knew of an assault when they were seen to collect together on the front-line, were loud in their actions, and hasty in their chaotic organisation in the combat zone. The moment that we heard the 'neighs' of their shaggy steppe ponies, always to be found in front of their anti-tank guns, we knew what was about to happen. From our experience on the Oder, 'forewarned is forearmed'. That one advantage evened up the many disadvantages in which we found ourselves.

CHAPTER 17

The Last Battle

We were approaching Easter and the cold winter weather had disappeared. The layer of white powdery snow, which had covered the rubble of the city, was now a horrible sooty black. The besieged city had been unusually quiet for the last couple of days. It was as if newly wakened 'Mother Nature' had called 'Halt!' to the madness of the war. It was welcome, but portents hung in the air. Was it the lull before the storm? The Red Army had been forced to alter their opinion that they could take Breslau in 'passing through' on their way to Berlin. It had taken far too long and had engaged the whole of their army for weeks. The situation simply had to change. The atmosphere in the palace of the Crown Prince of Oels, the headquarters of the Russian Commander-in-Chief, could be cut with a knife. Stalin was calling for 'Attrition' and ordered an immediate 'end' to Breslau. That name had become 'a red rag to a bull' and Marshall Koniev was made responsible for a 'decisive battle'.

Once more we were to hear those scratchy loudspeakers spewing verbal poison over the population, promising heavy air raids over the Easter period. Rumours circulated that Breslau was to be the Easter present for the Russian high command. The inhabitants were very uneasy. Our intelli-

The author (far right) with two comrades in Breslau, April 1945

161

gence and reconnaissance reported heavy massing of troops to the west, giving the German General Staff a very clear picture of what was about to happen and fulfilling General Niehoff's worst fears.

The front to the west was under the command of Lieutenant-Colonel Mohr and his battalion. They had watched the massing of Russian troops for days. Two parachute battalions were hastily called up, as reserves behind the threatened front-line. They were to be a reception committee in case of an eventual breakthrough at that point. They had to stop the enemy advance to the centre of the city.

It was deathly quiet on Easter Saturday. It was still and filled with tension, until 6 o'clock in the evening when the bombardment came. On the stroke of six, the Russians heralded their intentions with a bombardment, the like of which General Niehoff had only experienced at Verdun in the First World War, and then during the Second World War at the Baranov bridgehead. I think that I can speak for everyone, when I say that none of us, but none, from the commanders down to the privates, will ever forget that Easter in Breslau, where we were kept on our toes and in battledress for forty-eight hours. The Soviet artillery regiments pulverised buildings one after the other, with their 28cm shells. At the same time, squadrons of planes showered their bombs over the already-burning city. A glimmer of hope came, but lasted only seconds. We saw German bombers, clearly, with the swastika on their tails. But they too threw a carpet of bombs on us. They were captured war-booty, along with fully-loaded goods trains packed with our bombs. Ash and soot rained down on everything that lived, and of course we were not alone in that experience.

The inhabitants of other large German cities had seen whole residential areas disappear in fire, night after night. But for the people of Breslau it was a 'hurricane'. There were heavy bombardments from the air, and on the ground, heavy artillery, mortars and 'Stalin organs', all firing at once. Our one sense of forewarning had been taken away from us. With so much deafening noise, our ears could not be attuned to the movements of the enemy's close combat detachments. It was impossible. We could not assess how far they had advanced into the city. Any minute a trigger-happy 'Ivan' could jump out at us from the cellars. They came in numbers of 'ten to one'. We had 'companies' consisting of only 25 men. Our Regiment had been reduced by 70%. At West Park and the Institute for the Blind, close combat detachments were at their strongest and were supported by snipers. Our machine-guns showered the attackers without mercy and some who had been hit fell only metres away from us. We threw our last hand-grenades at them, to receive a hail of Soviet grenades as payment in kind. At the harbour a strong group of Red Guards drove a dozen or more German soldiers into the harbour basin. With the courage

A drawing by the author, made shortly after the end of the war, showing a scene from the fighting in Breslau, during April 1945

of the desperate, we gradually moved to where the paratroopers were grouped around the Institute for the Blind, fighting off the approaching Soviet infantry. The pounding of machine-guns was without pause, drowning out the raw cries of "Urrah!" We received the order to counter-attack. I was convinced that the inferno was one that I would not survive. Our platoon leader was the first to fall. We had no other choice but to slowly retreat under enemy superiority. We stumbled over mountains of stone as, metre by metre, we retreated in clouds of biting smoke. Surprisingly, the Soviets did not attempt to follow, the single bullets whipping around our helmets being scattered, did no harm.

Once more we survived. I was whole. I had escaped a final trip to hell once more. Only then did I see that there was no longer a stone standing anywhere amongst the surrounding houses, which in that part of the city, had been spared until now. I looked at skeletons of houses with blazing roofs and beams. I could hear the crackle of flames. From somewhere I heard the ghostly banging of a shop door swinging to and fro in a plateau of soot and ash. Standing with amazing grace, in the middle of that desolation, was a beautiful tree, covered in spring blossom. It was a sight that one rarely saw so early in the year.

A black mushroom-shaped pall of smoke hung over Breslau. It could be seen as far away as Zobten, the mountain to the south-west of the city. Anyone who saw it, and the burning torch of the city, from the darkness to the borders of the Sudeten mountains, could be forgiven for thinking that the city had met its end. It hadn't, not quite.

It seemed as if the night into Easter Sunday did not want to end. Dawn should have broken, but it couldn't, for black smoke blanketed the earth, obstructing its path. Early that morning, again on the stroke of six, another firestorm of shellfire was to be heard and lasted for six hours. It was a repeat performance of the day before. Another spring day, when it rained death out of the sky from Soviet bombers that systematically bombed what was left of the residential areas, square metre by square metre. In between, one heard the exploding rounds of the artillery also in that area, combined with the rapid whining of the 'Stalin Organ', erasing Breslau from the face of the earth.

One tram, still able to run to the very last minute, from the ring-road to Richthofen Platz, was blown to smithereens. Of all days, it was on Holy Easter Sunday that the Church of Marie on Sand island received a direct hit, the first of the Breslau churches. That was followed by a hit on the Cathedral. It dominated the city with its twin towers that burned like giant candles.

It was around midday that the Soviets ploughed the earth around our positions, and Russian tanks stood in front of the command post of that sector's commander. By a miracle we kept them at bay, for the time being, in the worst of the fighting. They had warned us via their 'flying leaflets' and scratchy tannoy that they would try to force a capitulation of Silesia's capital.

Easter Monday was also to be a black Monday in the history of Breslau. Air raids started at eight o'clock in the morning and carried on throughout the day, without a pause. Like a forest-fire, flames spread, enveloping the cultural buildings of historical and architectural importance. All of them were destroyed. In Neumarkt there was not one house left standing. The Museum of Art was reduced to a pile of stones. In the Botanical Garden in Lichterloh, not only the conifers gave fuel to the fire, but an ammunition bunker too. Everywhere one looked it burned, making it impossible to stay outside in that inferno for any length of time. Like the blossoming tree, and in spite of the wrath of those Russian invaders, Breslau's symbol and crest, the City Hall, still stood unmarked. Built in the late Gothic period with resplendent oriel bay windows, it seemed to say "stand fast"! For Breslau was always a German centre. It will always remain German, even when foreign races live within its walls.

This Breslau, late on Easter Monday, was a tragic sight. It was nothing but a ruin. The beautiful river promenade on the banks of the Oder was a maze of trenches. Everywhere one looked, from Gneisenplatz to Lehmann, was a ruin, a ghost of its former self, including the completely burnt-out

Hendrik Verton (right) and *Rechnungsführer* Georg Haas, 11. *Kompanie*, Regt Besslein,
pose with a Bugatti racing car in Breslau, 1945

Grammar School. The lovely facade of the Oberland Courthouse had
wounds from heavy artillery shells, the Seminar of the University too. The
Church of Elizabeth had grazes from shrapnel in the stonework of its
Baroque facade, but still stood tall. A bomb had gutted the inside of the
Bartholomew Church, whose graveyard housed the many graves of female
members of various institutions. The Exhibitions Halls were also devastated. The "Hundred-Years Hall", with its giant dome, still stood almost
undamaged. It was the largest in the whole of Germany. Within its walls,
10,000 people could be accommodated.

There was an intense and unbearable odour in the air. It came from
damaged sewers and drains, and mixed with the stench of decomposing
bodies. There was no one who could help, neither workmen to repair the
sewers, nor undertakers to bury the thousands of dead. So the dead remained on the streets. The hospitals, full to overflowing, had wounded lying on stretchers, anywhere there was space, even in the cellars and bunkers.
On Dome Island, uncountable wounded lay on stretchers in the open,
under fire.

When we were relieved from our positions at the Institute for the Blind,
I made my way from the line of battle and wandered into a cellar. It was
filled with civilians, the old, and mothers with their children tightly pressed
against them, as if in the thunder and lightning of a storm. All were
hunched together, fear engraved into their faces as they sat on ledges around
the cellar walls. The cellar was in a large block of rented flats, and as usual
supported with wooden posts. There was an older man, who was the

air-raid warden. He was in the uniform of the German Railways. I was in the uniform of one of the 'front-swine' which awoke a sense of trust and protection in them. I was therefore bombarded with questions. My uniform was not at its best! It was dirty, crumpled and covered in soot and ash, and I was not able to hide the fact that I had just come from the combat-zone. It was natural that I was asked, "how near are the Russians?"

The house swayed and the cellar floor rose and fell under the blast of each explosion. The noise was deafening. After a while we all looked like ghosts, dusted in white distemper from walls and ceiling, like an unwanted shroud. There was no electricity. The only candle giving us light was extinguished time and time again from the air pressure from exploding bombs, as they fell nearer and nearer.

I was the only soldier in the cellar and I had to hide my feelings. Enduring an air raid in such a confined space was not something that I was used to. Such a bombardment as this, even in the main line of resistance was something that I had never experienced. At least when outside, one was armed, and active. Here in this cellar I was not, and so I tried to hide my fear. I made myself useful, as a waiter, handing each one a piece of the traditional crumble and poppy-seed cakes that the women had baked, ready for the Easter celebrations. This action produced weak smiles from starched and stony faces, but didn't reach the frightened and staring eyes of their distraught owners. I wanted to leave that suffocating place but couldn't for the crescendo of the falling, whistling bombs was continuous. There was hardly a pause in which I could escape. Spontaneously, loud praying began. "Holy Mary, Mother of God." Then someone lost his nerve and shouted "Hold your tongues!" The cellar was full of chalk and loosened mortar dust. Mixed with the biting stench of explosives wafting through the cellar ventilators, it was suffocating.

I realised that there seemed to be a lessening in the raid. But still there were a number of low-flying Soviet planes with trigger-happy machine-gunners. I wanted to leave and return to my unit. At last I dared to take a look and saw a dying city, in unending agony, waiting for the next bombardment. It must have been pure unadulterated lust on the part of the Soviet pilots, to fly over the defenceless city as if they owned the sky above Breslau. There was no fighter-bomber resistance, nor any anti-aircraft fire. How long it had all lasted, no one really knew. But it was twilight enhanced with the light from flames.

I made my way back to my unit, with the very strong impression that Breslau was one giant glowing smithy. It was only possible for me to walk in the middle of the road. The houses were licked with flames on both sides of the road. It became a zig-zig obstacle course for me. Then a house suddenly collapsed. The road and I were enveloped in a giant cloud of dust and flying stones which reached to the other side of the street.

Some hours later, a church bell, high in its belfry, was heard to ring out the Easter message over Breslau. But it was not rung by bell-ringers. The sheer waves of heat, from the burning city below, gently nudged the bell into movement. It was no 'happy Easter' message, but a death-toll.

The storm of fire would not die, for it was fanned through every glassless window like a giant bellows. The waves of heat blew sparks and glowing particles of wood high into the air, where they nested on the roofs, to create a new fire. There seemed to be no end to Marshall Koniev's 'decisive battle', for during the night, we heard that familiar and unmistakable sound of engines belonging to 'sewing-machines'. Who could forget those Russian biplanes? They too had the treat of flying over the broken city of Breslau and making sure that it didn't rise from its knees. They fired tracer ammunition into the already burning buildings.

There was an eerie peacefulness over the city next day, 3 April. The polluted air stank of burning buildings. Gentle rain began to fall. After experiencing the demon in modern explosive techniques, one realised what a God-sent peacefulness was, and how determined nature could be. Here and there, undamaged tulips and hyacinths poked their heads through the rain-washed earth, heralding the spring. They bloomed alongside yellow forsythia, now black, having been burnt to charcoal. At dawn, soldiers and civilians alike, armed with shovels and an assortment of rakes etc, went to work, feverishly looking for the dead and the living under the rubble. The corpses were wrapped in sheets, curtains, even brown packing-paper, without ceremony or consideration of male or female, officer or private. But some were wrapped in flags, for tenting was too costly. What of the usual gun salute? The explosions of time-bombs had to suffice for that.

Crowds of inhabitants who had survived the Easter inferno, went about looking for a new shelter over their heads. Some were overjoyed when, standing in front of a pile of rubble which had been the former home of friends or family, they found a scribbled message in chalk on the stones to say they were alive, and where they could be found.

We were asking ourselves why the Russian high command had used this tactic of attack on Breslau? The answer was easy. It was an example to the Western Allies. The desired result being that when Russian infantry and tanks could not succeed, 'carpet' or 'blanket' bombing could! Breslau had to be razed from the surface of the earth. It had to be another Stalingrad! The Red Army had sealed Breslau's escape routes. There was no escape for man nor mouse, and that was the way they wanted it. Attrition, to the last man.

The Russians had reached parts of the centre of the city. But not even with Siberian guards and the enormous numbers of Mongolian sub-machinegun squads could they break the last German defenders. The decisive battle was still not over. General Niehoff reported later that two battalions of the Waffen SS Regiment Besslein had caused the enemy heavy losses, with their excellent performance, and above all their endurance, during that Easter attack. Their commanders were named, being Captains Roge and Zizmann, the same Zizmann for whom I was messenger at the beginning of the fighting. He was wounded during that Easter attack.

The threatened and unavoidable end of the capital was not destined to take place just yet, for through a stroke of 'luck', a rather daring Russian officer pushed his 'luck' a little too far. He and his tank were captured. One could suppose that the Russian was under orders, just as we were, never to have his combat orders or his map of operations on his person, which could be of help to the enemy or show the secret co-ordination grid-map. This one did, however. As was to be expected the Russians based all their operations on this grid, consisting of numbers and letters of the alphabet. The garrison's staff could never previously have deciphered messages such as "the attack is to be directed in the direction of F6", or the operations commander report that "the spearhead has reached lines H3 to B5". Confirmation came in seconds by quick reference to this map of the Russian commanders themselves – but for our radio-operators who were listening in, without a copy it was a puzzle.

Now our radio-operators and commanders listened in too. They now knew at the same time as their counterparts, of the moves being made. They could take countermeasures and with more than enough time. It was the biggest piece of 'luck' that fate could have given us, in our time of need.

Naturally enough, we too used code names for our military operations. They were constantly changed, for we also knew that our radio messages were overheard. We used botanical names, or career, job or profession titles. The sergeant-major was the 'painter' and our Regimental commander 'Mr 22'. The noble residential areas of Breslau equipped us with more than enough exotic and tropical names, or fantasy-based material, not to mention the familiarity of the city's buildings. The city hall was now the gas-works, the kindergarten the crematorium, or vice-versa. The wounded were called *mulatten* and the dead, *Indianer*. The growing numbers of both, mentioned in reports from the front, became more difficult for those working in official departments who wanted to veil the official fighting strength. I was told by one of them, that they adopted the motto, "Even when we lose the war itself, we will have won it on paper!"

The prophesy that "when the Oder flows with blood then the end of Breslau is near" was one well known to every 'Breslauer,' having learned it in their schooldays. The river already tainted, flowed with the blood of many. Marshall Koniev still had to wait before he could withdraw his troops from Breslau. He waited for the rest of April and into May.

In his headquarters, General Gluzdovski had not reckoned on the endurance of the soldiers or the civilians in the besieged city, not even after the mercilessness of the Easter bombing raids. As if the Soviets wanted to give us time to consider our plight, for the next few days all was unusually quiet. Unbeknown to us there was also another very grave reason on the Russian side. After the Easter attack, the forces of both the 6th Soviet Army and the 1st Ukrainian Front were so depleted, and the remnants so exhausted, that they were unable to recover from their enormous losses.

In spite of this, our command could not even afford a well-earned rest, for there was a great deal still to do, to think about and to organise. As well as our own losses in soldiers and civilians, there was an extreme shortage of ammunition, so extreme that our artillery were ordered to use their ammunition only in emergency situations. Our legendary FAMO armoured train could only occasionally be used for the same reason.

Not everyone possessed the same threshold for pain or stress, and many of our own changed sides. They deserted. Those deserters exposed the whereabouts of General Niehoff's HQ, at Liebichshöhe. It was instantly under continuous bombardment from artillery and bombs. It was engulfed in smoke as if from a slumbering but puffing volcano, which could be seen from a couple of miles away. Even the move of his HQ to the cellars of the State University Library, on 14 April, was known to the Russians twenty-four hours later. There were with certainty other 'Tanyas' at work, who were to be found within the walls of the fortress. They infiltrated resistance groups as well, to form small cells of opposition, and kindle the flame of mutiny among the soldiers, or even to plan the assassination of Niehoff. Therefore, when the suspects were found and arrested, their fate was an instant court martial.

We had the bitter experience of Germans fighting against Germans in Breslau. That former comrades could fight against their own, and with Russian weapons, was in sharp contrast to the sacrifices made by those not in uniform. As late as 2 May, 80 men of the 'National Committee for Free Germany', in German uniform, crept into western Breslau. Their task ended before it had begun, although they did overwhelm the guards of a battalion command post. Their undoing was coming face to face with Waffen SS who recognised their ruse. A former *Leutnant*, *Leutnant* Veith, and his deserter accomplices were arrested and shot. Even a group of former Ukrainian Waffen SS tried their luck, but fled.

After the war, those gullible German *hiwis* for the Red Army were to receive a short sharp lesson about the Communist character. Radio Moscow reported in a broadcast firstly that the Free Germany Committee had been dissolved, and secondly that the desertion of both Paulus and Seydlitz had been nothing else but 'war propaganda' to discredit them. For those who had deserted in following the example of the two 'gentlemen,' who had been the epitome of the German soldier for so many men, it brought about the realisation that their sacrifice had been totally worthless.

Who were Paulus and Seydlitz and what was the Committee for a Free Germany? Friedrich Paulus began his career in an infantry regiment. He was an officer of the General Staff in 1918, and captain within various staff and other units until 1931. In 1935 he was Chief of Staff of the 16th Army Corps, Chief of General Staff in 1939 and General and Commander-in-Chief of the 6th Army in the winter crisis of 1941/42. He was captured by the Russians in January 1943. His army career was brilliant until the siege of Stalingrad, which appeared to be his undoing, for various reasons, one being that this situation was one with which he could not cope. He as Field Marshal joined the already existing Committee for a Free Germany whilst in captivity in the camp for officers, in Lunjewo. One must ask why?

Only after his death were the memoirs of Walther von Seydlitz-Kurzbach, known as the 'Stalingrad General' published. To this day there is a divided school of thought about this man. Was he a traitor, or a patriot who had 'changed horses in mid-stream' to become a resistance-fighter in order to save his own skin? He, like Friedrich Paulus, also had a brilliant military career and was the 54th soldier to receive the Knight's Cross with Oak-leaves from Hitler. He had fought in France. In February 1942, on orders from Hitler, he released 100,000 German soldiers with four divisions and a mountain infantry brigade from the besieged city of Demyansk. He was captured by the Russians in late February 1943. He spent the next four months in a special camp in Krasnagorsk on the outskirts of Moscow, for reasons only known to the Russians. The Generals were separated and given quarters of their own. At the end of June they were transferred to Voikovo.

On the initiative of the Russian government and German emigrants, the 'Committee for a Free Germany' was formed as a propaganda machine on 12 and 13 July 1943. Seydlitz learned of those events from fellow prisoners who could read the Russian newspaper *Isvestiya*. Reports were read daily about the latest military disasters on the front. Meetings were organised for the Generals to attend. A delegation of officers and men had, at the end of the day, persuaded 12 officers, 13 subordinates and 13 emigrants to be members. The Committee was at first ignored by the German Generals. So on 19 August Seydlitz, together with Generals Korfes and Wulz, was transferred to the same camp as Paulus, which was now overflowing with prisoners, mainly those who had fought in Stalingrad. There were around 70 prisoners in all, officers from General down to Lieutenant.

Was it co-incidence? Was Stalingrad the basis of their association? Perhaps it was in combination with the realisation, at almost the same time as the 'Committee for a Free Germany' was founded, that without the prominent names of the highest ranks of German prisoners, there would be very little success for the Russian government in their propaganda campaign.

The seeds of that action had not fallen on totally barren ground. Those accustomed to commanding, and who came from aristocratic houses, had military forebears and backgrounds, were also accustomed to being part of the ruling forces. Seydlitz was one such. Perhaps there were noble intentions from those who knew that the end of the war was near, and that Germany would lose. Perhaps others wanted to end the misery of thousands. It was suggested that they form their own Association of Officers, the *Bundes Deutscher Offiziere*, the BDO. But that was not without some protest from the original delegation.

It was founded on 11/12 September. Seydlitz declared that he was prepared to take over the Presidency. The aim of the Association would be to win as many as possible still-loyal soldiers away from Hitler. In other words they would incite desertion. On that day a committee was voted in. 95 officers signed a petition demanding the resignation of Hitler and the German government. During his internment, Paulus was prepared to send a birthday card to Stalin, on his 70th birthday, to thank him, on behalf of the German prisoners, for the good treatment they received. It annoyed Seydlitz who ignored both of those suggestions, saying that Paulus could not know of individual fates and could not therefore speak for the POWs that he did not know. Perhaps with that affront, he prepared his own death sentence. On 23 May Paulus left the camp and Seydlitz never saw him again. For his sins, Seydlitz was accused and tried for war crimes by the Russians and condemned to death. He was already 62 years of age. This was then changed to 25 years' imprisonment, upon which Seydlitz demanded to be shot, on the spot. To this the Russians replied, "only the SS do that."

In September 1955 and after the visit of Adenauer to Moscow, Seydlitz was released on 4 October. He found himself in the camp for released Russian prisoners of war in Friedland, where his wife was waiting. They had four daughters. Under pressure from former Nazis, she divorced him some time later. He was ostracised by his former friends and comrades. He stayed silent over his behaviour until his death in the 1970s. Then his memoirs, which he had long since written, were released for publication.

The ancestor of Walther von Seydlitz was none other than Frederick the Great, whose name was a symbol for Prussian soldiery. Seydlitz declared that in his oath he had wasted his faithfulness and his obedience on a 'criminal', i.e. Hitler. He became firmly convinced of that after the battle of Stalingrad. Stalingrad was, and still is a name full of meaning, not only to the German and Russian veterans who fought there, but also for every student and would-be student of the Second World War.

In contrast to those German traitors, there were also the stoic and the patriotic, who even as Russian prisoners of war, found ways to support their brothers-in-arms. In our need and shortage of ammunition, we feverishly collected together Russian 'duds' for adaptation. We found a puzzle. Many were not filled with the necessary explosive material, but with sand. It remained a puzzle for some time, until one day a scrap of paper was to be found in the sand with a scribbled message, "more than this, comrade, we could not achieve". It was then clear that German prisoners of war must be working in a munitions factory and it was their way of deactivating the bombs and shells that they made! Somewhere in those unending 'steppes of Russia', were heroes, practically powerless, but who quietly worked away for Germany's cause and were prepared to lay down their lives, in such dangerous acts, for their still-fighting comrades.

The psychological terror and persuasion from the Reds now began in strength, urging desertion with rewards. The usual was offered. Feasts for the stomach and girls for one's pleasure. Both however were still in plenty within the fortress in Breslau, even then. The Reds even went to the expense of printing extra leaflets for the Waffen SS in which they guaranteed the lives of those members of the Besslein Regiment, after being taken prisoner!

Once more, rumours circulated around Breslau about 'wonder weapons' such as the V2 and V3, new planes flying faster than the speed of sound, turbo-jets which rendered Allied bomber flights into scrap metal. It was said that only a few weeks were needed until their usage was possible. Could we hold on until then? It was simply a case that we had to hold on until then, i.e. until the enemy would receive a very nasty surprise.

The small flame of hope that we had, grew with the death of Franklin D. Roosevelt on 12 April. The news spread that there were disagreements in the Allies' camp. That ill-fated 'alliance' it seemed was about to crumble after all, for we had even heard that the British and Americans were about to march together against the Bolsheviks. Added to that, we were elated to know that moves to free us were about to take place. There was a tangible possibility of relief from outside, in the form of Field Marshal Ferdinand Schörner, who knew about the saga within the fortress walls.

However, his plan to release a large portion from his army group to come to our relief did not materialise, despite permissions, plans and radio messages bouncing to and fro. All too often, 'General Chaos' had taken command, but the successes from him were few and far between. So our release from Breslau remained a rumour. We still held on to our hope of a 'miracle'.

We had survived the worst attack on the city, which had not ended in capitulation. We may have taken a beating, but were still in the ring and on our feet. What more would the Reds do? They could still lose many a tooth by biting on the bone called Breslau, the ultimate target being the defence of Silesia's city until it had earned the name of 'unconquerable'. In the last few weeks, every soldier had interpreted for himself the term, 'fighting to the last man'. That expression had its roots in Stalingrad, but Stalingrad was not the only example in the previous few months. General Otto Lasch, had also fought almost to his 'last man' in East Prussia, in Königsberg, capitulating only on 9 April. Despite defeat, those actions had deterred the strongest of Russian troops on their advance to the west. Perhaps, unbeknown to us, it had saved the lives of thousands of refugees on the move. We would do the same, come what may.

We lay like a lonely island in the middle of the Russian flood. Each new day ran its course in the fortress, as it had done yesterday and the day before. Daily, thousands suffered physically in military and civilian hospitals. Endless sacrifices were made by the civilians in that bloody warfare. By day and by night, hour upon hour was spent in the cellars, by the old, the women, the children and the sick.

It was 20 April, Hitler's birthday. As was usual, we received a birthday present from the *Führer* in the form of a bottle of wine which was presented to us by a NSFO i.e. *Nationalsozialistischer Führungs Offizier*, responsible for Party propaganda. Even under those circumstances tradition was not forgotten, although the duty of that officer could not have been comfortable for him, or the speech that he gave. One could really not wish to have to perform his duties on that day. The position that he held had been a part of the Nazi structure since 1944. It gave him the duty of administering a psychological dose of patriotism, stoicism and illusion, to keep 'everyone's finger on the trigger of his gun'. His speech was a mixture of hollow pathos and words of victory. We listened politely, but with scepticism, because he wore the Gold Close-combat Clasp for 'over fifty' recognised actions.

It could not have been easy to uphold the illusion of a still-determined and steadfast Hitler, on the 56th birthday of the man. He was surrounded on all sides, in his bunker deep in the bowels of the *Reichskanzlei*, in what not only seemed to be a hopeless situation, but would prove to be so. But he did his best. We heard that our commander-in-chief was holding fast in a heroic fight against Bolshevism. Whether or not he won a victory, or if he suffered a defeat, his name would be added to the annals of history. The Russians were not to be left out of the birthday celebrations. They chose their 112th Division to deliver the fireworks against the *Wehrmacht* Regiment Mohr that was to be found on a small sector of the front.

It was no coincidence that this very small sector was chosen for a victory. It was confirmed by the Polish military historians, Rysyard Majewski and Teresa Sozanska, in the book, *The Battle for Breslau*. They reported that the 'Hitlerites' of this unit, the battalion commander, two company leaders and 70% of the men, paid their penalties inside an hour's battle. This book written, of course, from the Russian point of view, quoted that Colonel Schavoshkin had taken care that Hitler's birthday had been a very noisy celebration. Not for the first time, we were sent to relieve the now-depleted Regiment Mohr, for they were transferred to the southern sector, which appeared to be quiet, for the moment.

The weather on 20 April, was 'royal' weather which helped the growth of the plants, shrubs and tree blossom in the desecrated gardens of the city. It was 25° in the shade and spring was not going to be deterred from presenting her blooms and blossom, albeit somewhat early in the year. The lilac was in bloom, spreading its perfume into air polluted with smoke and gunpowder. The flowers forced their way through the raped earth together with the weeds. The shrubs in the gardens were now a blaze of colour, red, white and apricot, forcing their faces through the rubble to the sun. It did the soul good to stick one's nose into the lushness of blossom and perfume, freely offered, forgetting if only for a minute, the odour of war.

Since the middle of April, our battalion had been engaged in the sector of the Andersen, Steinover and West End streets, in very tough fighting. From the Kipke brewery in the south-west, we were ordered to Striegauer Platz. There is a report about the defence of this section of the city, also from a Polish author, from whom we were to learn many years later that our opponent was the Soviet Lieutenant-Colonel Malinin and his unit. The author quoted from Malinin's own vastly exaggerated description of his engagement with "a very strong company of tough Waffen SS", who were "equipped with the very best of weapons, i.e. hand-grenades and bazookas". That version of events appeared in their 6th Army 'front' newspaper. Either the exaggeration was deliberate, or his memory a little foggy. I remember very well who the better equipped were. The mass of new equipment, left behind after their withdrawal, showed that for every new and shining brass shell-case, still warm to the touch, there were just as many empty vodka bottles, the backbone of every good Russian soldier. Perhaps one was his. But the well-equipped were most certainly not us. This made the success of our counter-attack even more surprising for us.

Only minutes later, our opponents had reformed once more, just a street further on. They were hiding behind broken walls and in bombed cellars, waiting to ward off a further advance from us. We, the 11th Company were the spearhead for the battalion and we dug in waiting for further orders. Darkness fell, and suddenly the 'fortress-brides' appeared with canisters of hot soup and a brew of coffee. They appeared, smiling proudly, their unkempt hair tucked under steel helmets and, far from elegant, dressed in military trousers which were much too wide for most of them. But they were happy that they had found us. At the risk of losing their lives, those Amazons had followed us at a distance and impressed us by their show of guts, loyalty and comradeship. They showed that they were made of much stronger stuff, than being there for a flirt or two. It gave us courage and it pained us at the same time when thinking of their personal fates if or when we suffered defeat.

Composure and endurance had been shown by all the troops in Breslau. Those two human constituents are not innate, they have to be learned. We were spurred on nearly every day with first-hand experiences of personal fates, which brought anger when someone we knew was involved. The personal fate of such as a young comrade from the Rhine, brought us to the edge of frustration, thick-skinned as we had become. Our long-awaited post had been delayed for a long time, not surprising under the circumstances. The joy of receiving a letter from his girlfriend, his bride-to-be, was great indeed. He had proudly shown me a photograph of her. She was fresh, she was pretty and photographed in her labour-service uniform, astride her bicycle. His happiness overflowed at the thought of seeing her again, but three days later he was dead. We had had a night visit from the Bolshevik infantry. The next morning, we found him with his distorted face in the rubble, but he had not died from his splinter-wounds. He had been shot, in the back of the neck. The long-awaited letter, now stained with his blood, was taken by one of his comrades. Whether he outlived the war, to take it to his comrade's girl friend, and inform her of the last few days of his life, is also unknown.

We had now been under siege for three months. One day, one of the messengers from the supply unit brought us news that our troops were fighting "for Berlin". No one, but no one in our besieged city, so far away from our capital, had reckoned on this. We simply had not envisaged an end to the war, and most certainly not at the end of the month of April. Our own situation had not given us time for thought of anything outside of the city, except for fleeting moments and then without up-to-date military information. Why should we? We were stunned with this information and alarmed. The Red Army had still not achieved the success of Breslau's capitulation, after three months of aggressive defence measures from our side. Therefore to hear that in between times they had reached Berlin, after we had engaged, in part, the best of the Red Army troops, was devastating for us. And when Berlin fell?

From the military point of view, we had no cause at the moment to give up the fight. But the situation back home gave us our first serious doubts as the first cracks appeared in our ability to hold on. However, what should we do? Firstly, we had given an oath, one which was 'holy' for us. Secondly, we would rather die than be taken prisoners, at least not by the Reds. Added to that, we dare not think of the terrible fate of civilians, such as that they had already faced in East Prussia and Silesia. We dare not give up. However, for most of us this latest news could not be ignored. It was clear to us that the final battle for the fortress was very, very near.

In the military reports of this time, in what was now stereotyped repetition, it was stated that our,

> troops in Breslau had bravely fought off renewed attacks from the Soviets in the southern and western sectors of the front. It was an example to us all, in view of the fact that they moved fast in face of overwhelming superior masses of material.

Since Easter we had had cooler weather which, on 27 April, returned to the former beautiful Easter weather of 25° in the shade. We had a balmy, cloudless night with full moonshine. The moonlight and single flashes of muzzle-fire lit the sky. We could see through paneless windows the towering ruins making a bizarre and ghostly scene on that relatively peaceful night. But it was suddenly and repeatedly shattered, by exploding bombs of a heavy calibre. The enemy artillery took no consideration of their own troops, who were lying on the opposite side of the road to us.

We could not seal off the front-line, broken at Posenerstrasse, the enemy having barricaded themselves into unusual corners. For this particular night, I decided against using double guards here and there, and posted half of our squad with machine-guns and a good stock of hand-grenades, on the main line of resistance. We could determine if Soviet shock-troops were sneaking up on us by using the rays of the searchlights.

We could hear machine-gun fire from somewhere, as well as single shots from a rifle. Both were designed to keep us awake, and to keep us from our well-deserved sleep, meaning that we should not be fit for the next day's battle. In the diary of the *Wehrmacht*, the report for 28 April read, "In Breslau, the Soviets were successful in breaking through our front in several sectors".

It was at dawn that Soviet infantry, supported by a mass of tanks, attacked our front lines. Because of the lack of ammunition, we had no support from our own infantry. We did have local support from a handful of infantry gunners in open positions, who were guarding one of the city's gates. Their very last shell killed one of the enemy's forward artillery observers, who obviously wanted to defy death. Our losses on that day were simply horrendous. Our battalion had to retreat to Leuthenstrasse and it was there that I was wounded. It was the third time and only eight days before the end of the war. I cannot say that I saw the end of the war in those seconds, but I remember in my unconscious that I was terrified at the thought that I had not lived to see its end. Our group had been in the ground floor of a block of flats badly damaged by tank-fire but which gave us protection. We had a very good view of the enemy. In fact we had the upper hand, except for a sniper who gave us a bad time. We could not replenish the ammunition badly needed by our grenadiers. So I decided to handle this problem myself, without any thrill of victory or the courage of a hero, but because I was just frustrated and angry.

In a series of jumps and leaps I reached the third floor of the half-destroyed staircase and fired a whole machine-gun magazine into the dark windows opposite, in the direction I thought he was to be found. If this action of mine were to be examined under a military microscope, the first criticism would be that it should have only been carried out by one of our snipers, who had marksman experience. The result was obvious. As if I had received a blow from an iron bar, my rifle fell suddenly from my hand. In reflex, I grasped at thin air for support. I felt absolutely no pain. Perplexed, I watched blood pour from the arm of my jacket and I looked at my lifeless arm, hanging towards the ground, without any strength to move it. I had received a shot through my lower arm.

The phenomenon of not feeling pain for some hours after being wounded, is 'not unusual', to quote Dr. Peter Bamm, military doctor and surgeon from the Second World War. "We were to experience this phenomenon time and time again. It is causation. The brain is able to block off the effects from the cause. It blocks the entrance in the middle part of the brain responsible for pain, even during the physical efforts of battle. The pain begins only hours after". That is exactly what happened with me, but after this had happened I was overcome with a dread of dying, almost knotting my throat together.

I found a first aid station in the Andersen School, in the cellar, visible to the outside world with a small white rag with a red cross. It showed us the entrance to which I had been accompanied by a comrade. On the schoolmaster's desk a towel had been spread, upon which an array of instruments had been laid, scalpel, tweezers etc, but I was only to receive two injections here, one in my upper-arm and one in my buttocks. A Red Cross sister undid my trousers which had been newly issued to me. Without any ado, she administered the injections, hung a card around my neck and sent me packing to the nearest surgeon. The impression I received was one of robots working on an assembly line. The wounded were in the school, where the desks had been piled one on top of the other, along the wall, to give space for them. After being attended to they had to wait for transport. The doctor, the nurses and the medics were oblivious of the shuddering walls and floor, when a shell landed nearby. There then followed an epilogue, the moans of the wounded, echoing the suffering of mankind. I was happy to leave that place. We, for I was accompanied by two other walking wounded, made our way in the direction of Schweidnitzerstrasse, to where we all had to go. On the way, near the main line of resistance, we heard gramophone music which became louder and louder, coming from the ground floor of a bomb-damaged house.

One could not call it a pub, but at first sight we saw soldiers and civilians indulging in a release of feelings, emotion or worry, call it what you will. They were drinking and enjoying themselves and forgetting the war. One can really say that they were dancing on top of the volcano, and not very far away from hell! We could only stand, stare and wonder at the paradox of lustiness that we saw. Perhaps my injections had dulled my senses, for I, together with the other two, indulged in a beer. I had just missed death by a hair's breadth. I believe that one can understand that I wanted, just for a moment, to switch off from the gruesome daily routine and enjoy the fri-

The author's medical record from *Sanitätsstützpunkt* 5

volity that we had found in what was a very strange place. It was a 'dive',
perhaps that would describe it correctly and it might have housed deserters.
I did not care about the past, with its examples of composure, or stiff up-
per-lips. I just did not want to know. The wounded soldier is also a member
of mankind, and in the split second that he is wounded, he is thrown from
the warrior's tracks and becomes a helpless creature. A creature who had
given his innermost, making his contribution to world history, giving his
energy in the direction of the enemy without thinking about himself, until
he sees the flow of his own blood. He is then not able to help himself.

We found Medical Centre No.5, between the Church of St Dorothy
and the City Theatre, in the ante-room of the wine cellar of the restaurant,
"The Hansa Cellar". A military doctor, two Red Cross sisters, a medic and
other auxiliaries attended to about fifty wounded soldiers. My arm by now
was really painful and extremely swollen. My dressing was changed and my
arm put into a splint. I was then given a bed in the damp cellar, where the
wounded slept in bunk beds, three on top of one another and I was allocated
one on the top. The cellar ceilings were low and I had to fold myself up in
order to climb into it. Those badly wounded slept on the lowest bunks. My
neighbour, who had a blood-drenched bandage around his head, offered
me as a welcome relief a flask which was against all of our regulations, but
which contained brandy.

After a while I could ascertain that we were a very mixed bunch, from
the air force, army, and *Volkssturm*. Two sailors were there, who at the time
of the siege had been on holiday in Breslau, and afterwards were conscripted

into the infantry. I was the only member of the Waffen SS, despite the fact
that we had had very many wounded.

On the whole, I could build a very good picture from the reports of the
men from different sectors of the front. It did not look very rosy. I gleaned
something else from their reports about mankind. The actions of those
men, in their reports of the situation at the front, were tinged with smoul-
dering anger. What could not be ignored was the furious rage of the attacking enemy, always without consideration of their own men, which was
confirmation of my own experience. We exchanged experiences in cold
facts, almost without emotion and I heard incredible stories, almost unbelievable. That they themselves had been in battle, under primitive conditions for months on end, was spoken in a whisper. It appeared that they had
forgotten that they were former labourers, farmers, clerks or students. That
was all a long time ago, it seemed. Now they were highly qualified specialists
in close-combat. For stratagem, spirit of comradeship and quiet acts of
heroism, when mentioned, were without a hint of pathos.

The doctor and his assistants, despite primitive conditions, attended to
our needs in the damp rooms of the cellars, twenty-four hours a day. They
used their medical know-how and technical guile to save lives, which in another part of the city were being destroyed. Every day the newspaper of the
Festung, the *Schlesischen Tageszeitung*, was still being printed. On the first
page of the edition for 28 April 1945, the conditions at the front had been
reported in detail. In the edition of the following day, the 29th and the day
that I was wounded, one could read, "There was once again bitter fighting,
during Friday night, from the Bolsheviks. After strong artillery fire aimed at
the northern flank of the west front, penetration by them was achieved on a
small scale. They were quickly forced back, almost closing the front once
more. Our troops had a success in another sector, winning back in a counter-attack a block of flats which the Bolsheviks had taken the day before,
and forcing the enemy back to their original positions".

On the same page, in large print, were the headlines, "Stronger support
measures for Berlin". Under this heading was the report that our troops had
turned their backs on the Americans at the river Elbe to start the battle for
the centre of Berlin. "Whilst we in Breslau are busy with the continuation of
a successful defence of the fortress, we look, together with the German people and the rest of the world, at the fierce battle in and around Berlin".

Like an ebb tide, the battle area at the end of April in the rest of Silesia
moved backwards and forwards, to and fro. In the region of
Bautzen-Meissen, the German counter-attacks were surprisingly successful.
We won back our territory of Kamenz and Königsbrück. We won and we
lost, and so did the Russians. The Russians lost on 30 April, in Brünn, so
heavily that they retreated. The day before, they took Austerlitz, where Napoleon in 1805 had won a victory over Austria and Russia. Despite giving

all that we had left to give, rumours of the forthcoming capitulation of Breslau became heated. An ecclesiastical delegation from both persuasions visited the fortress commander on 4 May, for earnest discussion on capitulation. The delegation was headed by the Diocesan assistant bishop, Bishop Ferche, dressed in his bishop's regalia.

The delegation had made their way through the burning city and were clearly dismayed at the sight of Breslau. They thought that now, as servants of God, and "before God and mankind" that it was their duty to approach the General. They wanted to appeal to him that he search his conscience and assess if he could be responsible for the further defence of the city. In view of the measures that these men of the clergy deemed necessary, and who had supported the defence of the city with their 'Samaritan' service, General Niehoff promised them that he would come to a decision, and soon.

It was thought at the time that the bishopric visit was decisive for General Niehoff. When the truth was known that he could have, for his sins, made a confession that he had already made his decision before their appearance, he did not. One does not capitulate with chaos, without thought or a structure for bargaining, in seeking the best from a deal and above all wanting to avoid despotic rule. Only with a front-line still intact, and obedience from both soldiers and the civilian population, was the successful bartering for an honourable capitulation of the city forthcoming. So it had to be kept secret for as long as possible.

The Russians were waiting by the hour. Their bombers still flew their routine sorties. Their artillery still sent their shells precisely according to their grid-map. We were left waiting for the final blow which did not come.

At that time our radio-bugging service overheard a broadcast sent by BBC London, that the British leadership recognised the performance of the defending troops in Breslau. They were very much impressed and had therefore refused the request from Moscow, that British bombers deliver the final blow to bring Breslau to its knees.

Raw unadulterated reality informed General Niehoff's plans for the capitulation of Breslau. His experience and his intuition told him that he faced a *fait accompli*.

CHAPTER 18

Capitulation and Captivity

On 30 April, we were to hear about the unbelievable death of Adolf Hitler, in a radio broadcast. "The Führer Adolf Hitler, who fought against Bolshevism with his last breath, died today at midday". At the time of the broadcast, I was to be found in the remains of the Hotel Monopol, which lay opposite our medical centre. I had become good friends with the cook of the hotel, a Frenchman with whom I often heard the German broadcasts, martial music, and the forbidden enemy broadcasts from the BBC in London, sent in the German language.

I was simply stunned by this news, the Frenchman too. In the moments after the initial shock, came the realisation that it was the fall of 'The Third Reich'. For the French who were to be found in the city, it meant their return home. But for me it meant that after all I had given, all that I had sacrificed, it was now null and void. There was no saving Germany any more. We had lost. Would Germany, would Europe, would the world suffer repercussions? The three questions why, what for, and how come, circled around in my mind like a carousel.

We in Breslau had not capitulated. I was still a soldier and here nothing had changed. We could not imagine anything else but fighting, defending, for as long as there was a German government to issue orders, and above all, as long as there was a corner of Germany that was still unoccupied. Even the Commander-in-Chief and Admiral of the Fleet, Admiral Dönitz considered his mission, as deputy head of state, to be one that was to be executed until the conclusion of the war.

Hitler had with his suicide, accepted the hopelessness of further defensive measures, not only for Berlin, but for Germany as a whole, and had made the way free for capitulation. That was a step that he personally was not willing to take, under any circumstances.

After every shipwreck, everyone has to swim for as long as they are able, in doubt and in hope of swimming to land. We were never prepared to go under, in the current of Russia's flood. At the end of April, and the beginning of May, the propaganda over loudspeakers increased, broadcasting "the catastrophe to be found on the front-line", as well as their already well-worn arguments, repeatedly, throughout the day.

Until the third week of April, Breslau's front-line was still intact. Everywhere that the Russians appeared, they had been forced back and there was not a place in the belt of defences around the centre of the city that had been broken. Berlin had now fallen, and in embarrassment and frustration, Rus-

The last edition of the *Schlesischen Tageszeitung*. In the chaos of the fighting it was printed with a faulty corner

sian forces were drawn away from Berlin and posted to Breslau. The Silesian capital came under increased attack, being the only large city left that had not been conquered. We were honoured with an arrogant victory 'parade in the sky'. It was a warning before the final dagger-thrust. Massed Soviet bomber squadrons flew majestically over the city, without dropping a bomb.

The relatively 'peaceful' hours of 1 May were not to last. Each day until 5 May, the raids on Breslau increased. Massed enemy squadrons killed and wounded as many as 1,000 civilians with each raid, according to the priest Ernst Hornig. There were two raids every day. Russian tanks tried their luck to break through to the centre of the city once more, but failed. Our counter-attacks were just as strong as before. Their conclusions that we believed their empty promises of safe passages home, or that prisoners would be released as soon as the end of the war was announced, and that these would influence us to throw in the towel, must have been disappointing.

The headlines of the *Schlesischen Tageszeitung*, whose 6 May issue was to be the last, read, "The resistance against the Soviets carries on!" It was followed by a report from the *Wehrmacht* regarding the armistice agreement in Holland, Denmark and northern Germany. The article ended, "*Festung* Breslau is still defended with unbroken endurance and courage against continual attack, causing the Soviets high losses in material and men. In Moravia and Slovakia the resistance also continues". The following article appeared on the same page. " German radio announced yesterday that Breslau is a brilliant example to the whole of the German nation. We received a recent report from our soldiers in Breslau, who were proud that they once more refused yet another demand of capitulation from the Soviet Commander-in-Chief. Breslau is standing fast! The heroic defenders of the city are a brilliant example for the German people and have been for some time. For endurance and bravery, in face of overwhelming masses of material, they are an everlasting example for all of us fighting on the Silesian front."

This was followed with the information that Hamburg had been taken by the British who had then ordered a curfew for the civilian population. Radio Hamburg ended their broadcast with the words "Long live Hamburg! Long live Germany! From now on 'Radio Hamburg' is to be assessed by the Germans as an enemy channel".

On 6 May, an interview took place with the well-known Swedish researcher Sven Hedin Stockholm who said, "I will hold deep and unforgettable memories of Adolf Hitler as one of the greatest men in world history and whose life's work will live on. He made Germany into a world power. Now Germany stands on the edge of a chasm, because his antagonism could not carry the weight of his strength and power. A land, larger except for Japan, with a population of 80 million and who opposed the whole world for six years and against a power 25 times larger, can never be erased. The legacy of this great leader of people will live on in the German people".

The walking wounded were allowed outside the medical centre throughout the day and I used the daytime hours to walk, to inspect the city and to be by myself. Not that I went very far away. There were hardly any civilians on the streets. Military vehicles cruised around the man-made mountains of rubble and the craters left by exploding shells. When I met a civilian on the street I was always surprised by their appearance. Despite the catastrophic conditions, all were clean, all were neat and tidily dressed and it was most noticeable. Resigned to their fate, nonetheless they were still proud folk. This also applied to any of the military when I saw them, they were disciplined and greeted each other according to his rank.

Astounded and perplexed at this time, I could only stare in disbelief one day, as a car with both German and Russian officers sitting in it, cruised around the walls of the city moat. I thought they were probably negotiators. Now there were no doubts left for me – the end of the fighting was very near, and I hurried back to the centre. There I was to learn that on 6 May, at 2 o'clock Moscow time (1 o'clock German time) the 'honourable surrender of the city of Breslau, would take place'. I don't think that I have to describe the depressed atmosphere among the wounded in the cellar. Some would just not believe it and many wept, brought to tears after months of tension, and felt no shame. Had it all been for nothing? The years of giving life and limb on the front, of deprivation, privation and of sacrifice, the suffering, the air raids back home? We were face to face with the hopeless prospect of POW camp and for how long? It depressed us all and I, I felt bitter, rejected and defiant.

Gauleiter Hanke, in his national pride and arrogance, declared that he would have General Niehoff arrested for his defeatist decision, and then changed his mind. He very quickly accepted the situation, making the equally quick decision of ordering a Fiesler Storch. The plane was only for the personal use of the city's garrison commander, General Niehoff, but behind his back Hanke used it to fly himself out of Breslau. General Niehoff wanted to share the fate of the city with his men, and was glad, upon finding out, that he and the negotiations for the capitulation were not to be disrupted by Hanke's presence. Perhaps at the end of the day that could have severely influenced events to the extent of disadvantages for the defeated. On 6 May, at around six in the morning, many of the Breslau inhabitants saw the Storch in the air. During the course of the morning, a radio message was received by General Niehoff from Kirschberg. "*Gauleiter* Hanke has landed here, slightly wounded in a defective machine." Nothing more has ever been heard of that man. Rumours circulated, whether based on fact or not, that he escaped to South America. There are others who believe that he escaped to Czechoslovakia, but was shot as he tried to escape from a prisoner transport.

Red posters on house walls announced the surrender of the city of Breslau. General Niehoff announced that negotiations were already in hand for the Soviets to take over the city. The great 'Finale' took place on 7 May 1945, in Rheims. General Jödl, under orders from a new Government signed an unconditional surrender, at 2.41, on the 2075th day of the war. There was a final ceasefire on 9 May at 00.01 hours in Europe. This 'Unconditional Surrender' has never been followed with a peace-treaty, to this day!

The Germans lost more than 4.3 million people in the great wrestling match that was taking place on the fronts. Approximately 600,000 Germans became casualties during Allied air raids. Over 3,000,000 German soldiers died in POW camps under the Western Allies, or in Communist *gulags*, as well as refugees, from forced expulsion from their land. (Information from the Berlin *Wehrmachts*-Auskunftsstelle Berlin)

Estimates of the losses from both sides suffered during the defence of Breslau vary. According to the Regiment's commander, Hanf, the battle for the Silesian capital Breslau took second place to Stalingrad, for the longest and worst siege of WWII. City doctors assessed that 1,000 patients died every day and that the numbers of civilians who lost their lives totalled 80,000. From those 80,000, 13,000 lost their lives working on the provisional airstrip in the city, says Paul Piekert in his book *Festung* Breslau. The previously-mentioned Polish authors Majewski and Sozanska assess that every second civilian in Breslau lost their life. At least 90,000 Silesians died in the hasty evacuation from Breslau in January 1945, through starvation, exhaustion or from freezing to death.

General Niehoff's own assessment from the troops within the fortress was 6,000 killed and 23,000 wounded. Taking into account that we only had 50,000 men in the fortress, then we had a loss of 58%. Having said that, this does not take into account the wounded who lost their lives whilst being flown out of the city, or the wounded prisoners, or the prisoners of the Soviets who died.

The losses on the other side were very much higher. The number of Soviet troops around Breslau was 150,000 men, from which the siege cost them the lives of 5,000 officers and 60,000 of their men. Today one may visit a cemetery in the southern part of the city, where alone 5,000 Russian soldiers found their last place of rest.

General Niehoff received a telegram before the capitulation, which read, "Germany's flags sink slowly, in proud sorrow and homage to the endurance of the brave defenders, and the civilian inhabitants of Breslau". Signed General Wilhelm Hasse 17th Army.

One really cannot speak about 'pride' or 'sorrow' at this time. Other words from our vocabulary have to be used when referring to the mood of the brave defenders within the fortress. They were angry, they were deeply disappointed and full of doubt, especially the men on the front-line. When envisaging the prospects of becoming a prisoner of the Russians, some of the officers committed suicide, men smashed their weapons on the nearest stones, whilst others threw their weapons in sheer frustration into the Oder. For three whole months they had been encircled by an enemy who had not broken their spirit. They had had a constant companion, by day and by night, for the previous five years, namely 'death'. The surrender was a sacrilege in their eyes.

Catastrophe reigned in the city. The female personnel of the *Wehrmacht* changed out of their uniforms and thereafter wore civilian clothes. In the staff offices, mountains of paperwork were being burned, files and important documents being thrown into the flames. The warehouses were opened and supplies issued to the civilian population.

In the medical centre we were forced, under the watchful eye of the surgeon, to throw our pistols and side-arms into a wooden box. A condition of surrender was that no weaponry or equipment was to be destroyed. I, in my frustration demolished the inside of my 7.65mm Walther pistol so that it could never ever be used again. After all those years we all suddenly felt naked and utterly defenceless.

From one day to the next, everything had changed. Now we stood under the laws of the enemy. Now we were the subjects of tyrannical Commu-

Vorschlag: Ehrenvolle Übergabe

Herrn Festungskommandant der Festung Breslau
General der Inf. Niehoff

Entsprechend Ihrer Zusage betr. einer ehrenvollen Übergabe der Eingekesselten
Ihrer Festung und Festungseinheiten schlage ich Ihnen folgende Bedingungen vor:

1. Alle unter Ihrem Befehl stehenden Truppen stellen die Kampftätigkeit am
6. 5. 45 ab 14 Uhr (Moskauer Zeit) ein. (13 Uhr Deutscher Zeit.)

2. Sie übergeben den Mannschaftsbestand, Waffen, alle Kampfmittel, Transport-
mittel und technischen Einrichtungen unbeschädigt.

3. Wir garantieren Ihnen, allen Ihren Offizieren und Soldaten, die den Wider-
stand eingestellt haben, das Leben, Ernährung, Belassung des persönlichen
Eigentums und Auszeichnungen und nach Beendigung des Krieges Heimkehr
in die Heimat. Dem ganzen Offz.-Korps ist das Tragen der blanken Waffe
gestattet.

4. Allen Verwundeten und Kranken wird sofortige medizinische Hilfe durch unsere
Mittel zuteil.

5. Der gesamten Zivilbevölkerung werden Sicherheit und normale Lebensbedin-
gungen garantiert.

6. Ihnen persönlich und anderen Generalen werden Pkw. mit Bedienung belassen,
ebenso die entsprechende Bedienung für Generäle in der Gefangenschaft.

Der Befehlshaber der 6. Russ. Armee   Der Chef des Stabes
der 1. Ukrainischen Front   gez. P a n o w
gez G l u s d o w s k i   Generalmajor
General   6. 5. 1945

The surrender terms for Breslau as printed by the Red Army

nist rule, exposed to their arbitrary justice and revenge, and it was to be so. It began with the delivery of our weapons. The Russians would not believe that we had fought with so little. "You could not have held out for so long with only this. Where is the rest?" Very suspicious, they accused us of hiding weapons.

It was now very quiet in Breslau, deathly quiet. Everyone waited for the Soviets to march into the city. The silence was disturbed however. There were sounds of tank motors, and when one cocked one's ear in the direction from where it came, it must have been sweet music for some, for those who cottoned on, as to what was going on, perhaps those who had been part of a tank crew? Some impudent tank drivers were to be seen driving their tanks round and round, and round and round in small senseless circles, to the observers when there were any, some around the same block of houses, which, when not in the know, made one scratch one's head. The drivers held their tank in first gear, overheating piston and piston rings, to the extent that the tank was then no longer usable.

Despite the conditions of surrender in the whole of Germany, General Niehoff's negotiations for the surrender of the Silesian capital were to be viewed as agreeable, correct and just. They held promises. Promises for the safety of civilians, medical help, guarantees of life and care of the military and above all the return to the homeland upon the ending of the war. The officers were allowed to hold their status symbols, i.e. military decorations and their revolver, without ammunition and, what was more important, all of these guarantees included those from the Waffen SS.

The following was suggested as the basis of the agreement:

The Honourable Surrender of *Festung* Breslau

Corresponding to your assurance of an honourable surrender of the be-sieged Fortress of Breslau, together with your military units, I suggest the following conditions:-

All of the troops under your command, stop military activities at 2 o'clock Moscow time, on 6 May 1945 (1 o'clock German time).

You surrender the total number of troops, weapons and war material, transport vehicles and technical equipment undamaged.

We guarantee on our part that all officers and men who have stopped military activities, the safety of life, nourishment, right to hold private pos-sessions and decorations, and passages home after the official end of the war. The corps of officers have permission to wear their revolvers, unloaded but befitting their status.

All wounded and sick will be given immediate medical help.

The inhabitants are guaranteed the safety of their person and normal living conditions.

You personally, and others of the rank of General, will be allowed your own personnel, and conditions allowing, in POW camp too.

Signed by Commander-in-Chief 6th Russian Army Chief-of-Staff General Panov, and 1st Ukrainian Front General Gluzdovski.

The Soviet Commander-in-Chief of the Soviet 6th Army was General Gluzdovski. He gave his consent to this agreement in the presence of the Russian Chief of Staff, General Panov, in the Russian HQ, a villa, 'Villa Colonia' in the Breslau suburb of Krieton. General Niehoff gave his signature to these terms of surrender in the belief that it was an agreement between high-ranking officers which would be honoured. He was at this time a German Officer who was in full belief that it would be so. Perhaps it would, if left between officers and gentlemen. However, it was not to be.

The Soviets just could not resist the temptation. It was just too much to be denied and so General Niehoff and his Staff were invited to a celebration dinner. The 'victors' and the vanquished sat at the same table, which was bedecked only with the best. It was ostentatious plenitude. Candles flick-ered over the mountain of cold specialities including caviar, complimented with meat, *vol-au-vents*, and vodka flowed. Bottles of it stood by the dozen in between the dishes and General Niehoff's water glass was continually filled to the rim with it, although no one could expect him to enjoy the cele-bration. His military correctness dictated that he suffer this gala dinner and not spoil the fun of the Soviets, but outside, he knew that long columns of his men were being driven in the direction of the East. He had however, as a prisoner of war, nothing to say. So the loud celebrations carried on with long speeches and toasts. Many toasts, with the ever-full glass of vodka, were to Stalin, but also perhaps out of respect from one soldier to another, to General Niehoff and his brave defence of Breslau.

The friendly atmosphere and correctness that the German officers found on that evening, was definitely an honest gesture from the side of the Soviet military. But at the end of the day, the ruling politicians had the last word. From the high-grade political commissioners present, there was an icy reception.

They made it quite clear to the 'guests' that they stood at the door of a future without any rights. The Soviets had no intention of respecting the conditions of surrender that had been agreed to. The soldiers were given no rations, the civilian inhabitants were fair game for the whim and fancy of the Russian soldiers, and the Waffen SS were systematically sorted out from the rest. General Niehoff was to spend in total, ten and a half years as a prisoner of the Soviets. Five were spent in solitary confinement in the notorious Moscow NKVD prison, Lubyanka. The rest were spent in labour camps. The document that was designed to protect him from harassment, bodily search, and abuse, was respected by prison guards at first. It worked like a magical formula, until a German Communist in the form of a new camp commander arrived, and tore the said document into pieces. Niehoff's protests, when bumping into a political commissioner, were answered with a sarcastic comment. "These so-called 'conditions' were nothing but a successful trick of war". He was right.

It was during the night of 7 May that the Russians marched into the inner ring of the city. The first of the Soviet units, with assault troops, marched in at 1 o'clock in the morning and took their positions at the Oder bridge, and other strategic positions. Of the inhabitants, there were none to be seen. They were waiting, waiting in fear in the cellars of the ruins, for the first Russian faces to appear. Outside there was a thunder of motors, tanks and every other imaginable vehicle from motorised units. That thunder increased as more and more vehicles stormed through the city in a disorderly column. In our medical centre, the wounded waited. Sitting or lying, they waited together for what was to come, without words, each one within himself.

The noise invaded the cellars, and amongst the roar of motors, we heard the hooves of uncountable horses on the cobblestones and the victory cry of the drunken Reds. I wanted to imprint a picture into my memory and so I ventured up stairs, to the ground floor empty rooms of the Hotel Monopol. I was enveloped straight away with an uncomfortable bitter feeling. I saw the enemy that I had fought for so many years, so close by, and for the first time I was unarmed.

The scene was similar to a colourful wailing caravan, moving over the rubble-covered streets. Lorries were damaged and filthy and in between were tanks, with large red flags hung from their turrets, and dangerously near the vehicles were the typical Russian *Panje* pony-drawn carts. I really had to wonder at the mass of tanks that we had held at arm's length for three

Two photos showing the author on the roof of the Hotel 'Monopol' in Breslau,
1 May 1945

months. I was not there long, for I heard the cries of the women and girls nearby, and single revolver shots from Soviets searching for solitary soldiers, cut off from their units. I had seen enough and hurriedly returned to my comrades in the cellar.

Not long after, a gigantic fireworks show lit the skies over the dying city from tracers, flares and shells. The trigger-happy drunken Reds were firing salvo after salvo from machine-pistols, and even from light and heavy anti-aircraft guns, into that balmy May night. Some of the shells hit

unexploded mines, for we heard them too. The walking wounded had watched the spectacle from the cellar entrance. Even in our totally depressed state one could imagine a New Year's celebration in Breslau in peacetime being something similar, the people having flocked to the inner ring of the city, to wish their neighbour "Cheers and Happy New Year, good health and peaceful times", on the stroke of midnight. On that May night however, in 1945, the show was a prelude to brute force and lack of rights.

Stalin's 'Attrition' applied not only to the people of Breslau, but to every building of importance left standing that through a wonder, had remained whole in the three-month siege. Everything had to be destroyed, and so a wave of destruction rolled through the city. Bands of drunken Reds tottered through the city burning everything that took their fancy and that was still standing.

On 11 May, it began with the Barbara Church and six days later the Church of Magdalena. They burned them to the ground. Frederick the Great's palace in the city had already been destroyed by fire. This type of war had replaced the one that we knew, and as feared it was followed with plundering and rape. Many in the city asked themselves whether the former was not the more bearable of the two, although they had thought that it was the most terrible that they had lived through, thinking that it could not be worse. They were wrong!

For both the military and civilian populations, 8 May was not a day of freedom, nor one of being freed. On the contrary, it was the beginning of hell, and the realisation of their half-joking phrase, "Enjoy the war, for freedom will be hell".

On the fate of the female staff, we dare not think, for they were fair game. All women and girls were 'fair game' for the Russians, like game running wild in the woods. Even when now and then a decent Russian officer was to be found, who could and did deter single acts of rape, there were hundreds to follow. The women of Breslau fell victim to the same fate as hundreds of others in East Prussia and other German provinces.

According to the reports received in the *Ministerium für die Vetriebenen* it was stated in 1974 "that sadly there are not enough words in the German language to reconstruct for others the experiences written down and sent to us from the people of Breslau. Words are inadequate".

Prelate Lange, the curator of the 'House of Good Shepherds' reported that on 7 May, a group of Russians climbed over the damaged wall of the convent in Kaiserstrasse, where two elderly nuns were to be found. One of them escaped, but the other did not even try, thinking that her great age would save her from any physical abuse. Sister Felizita was overpowered by the group, was shot and then raped. "We buried her in the garden of the convent. She was 81 years of age."

Mrs Hedwig Goering reports that, "At first the Russians gave us a good impression, but we were fooled. My niece was raped by Russian soldiers on the third day of occupation. She was only eleven." Other women fled to their allotment gardens, thinking that they were safer there than in the city. Mrs. A. Hartmann was one of them. "We made a mistake, for we women were raped time and time again, just like the women in the city. I lost my nerve, with the continual cries of the women and ran into the city. I must have been in a state of shock for it was only afterwards that I realised that I was witness to seeing women jumping from the windows of the houses, dying, rather than being the subject of rape from one soldier after the other".

This report contained uncountable pages describing experiences, not only from the suffering of the women, but of children and old men. Every Russian at this time was a Tsar and he could do what he liked with 'the Germans', without repercussions. It was allowed, and from General Niehoff's 'conditions of surrender', the guarantee of the 'victors' was nowhere to be seen.

8 May was also no happy day for the anti-fascists. Even his loudly announced membership of the KPD, did not hinder the execution of Herr Langwitz, in Neukirchen a suburb of Breslau, or that of Mrs. Sacher in the same city. The membership books of both were torn into pieces by grinning Red Army men in front of these 'old Communists' before they were both murdered. The former Jewish mayor Heinzelmann, who luckily escaped deportation, angrily asked, "and we Anti-fascists? We feel betrayed and cheated, and we always promised that Communism would free the population from the yoke of Fascism!"

The author (far right) at *Sanitätsstützpunkt* 5, the Hotel 'Monopol', Breslau, early May 1945. At this time the Soviets had not yet taken them prisoner.

Music from the Russian loudspeakers was continually interrupted with announcements in the German language, ordering prisoners to gather at certain points in the city and then to wait for further orders. Officers who demanded the freeing of their men were laughed at. "*Dawai dawai*, i.e. faster, faster!" was the order and the long field-grey columns marched into POW camps. For some it was to lead to their deaths.

The doctor in our medical centre decided to wait, for there were no special orders for the wounded. We used the last hours of freedom to sit or lie in the sun, in the back yard of the Hotel Monopol. With the three other walking wounded, I climbed on to the flat roof, to take a last look at the city. We were discovered finally, on 9 May.

It was in the morning, as we were suddenly ordered 'to show ourselves' to Russian soldiers not trusting themselves to come into the dark cellar. They were waiting at the entrance, with cocked machine-pistols. "Come out with your hands up!" (*Idi sjuda! Rucki verch!*) The walking wounded walked up the cellar steps blinking at the sunlight. Before climbing those stairs I was a regular soldier. But it occurred to me that in the moment my feet left the last tread, I would become from one second to the next, one of those nameless prisoners of war. It was not to be, at least not on that day, for seeing that we were wounded, we were not taken away, nor was there an examination of our pay-books. We were uninteresting in seemed, at least for the time being.

Once more, for all of us in the cellar, it was not long before a husky cry echoed through the cellar. A single Russian soldier tottered down the cellar steps, like a Russian bear looking for honey. He thoroughly searched in all the corners of the cellar rooms and suddenly his eyes fixed on me, or perhaps it was my bed. We were 'freed' of our personal possessions on that day by this one soldier. My bed was obvious for it was the only one with a blue and white gingham cover plus a white curtain as extra warmth. The pale colour made the presence of lice more visible for me to destroy. For him however, it meant that I was someone special. "*Uri, uri!*" he screamed, and I answered "*nix uri!*". It didn't do me any good for he found my '*Uri*' anyway, for he was on the lookout for plunder. He tore my bedding off my bed finding my knapsack and my silver pocket-watch. Taking it by the chain, he swung it under my nose, waving his pistol at me at the same time. My watch had been a going-away present from my father upon entering the army. It had accompanied me throughout the duration of the war, till now. From the six sons in the family, I was the only one named after my father and this watch had my name engraved in the lid. This 'bear' of a man, because of his ungainly movements, 'freed' all of my comrades from their watches too, adding them to those already decorating his arms, up to the elbows, one on top of the other.

This however was not triumph enough and with his gun in my back, he forced me upstairs. I really thought that my time had come and that I was to be 'honoured' with a quick death, a bullet in the back of the neck under a waving Red Cross flag. In daylight we took stock of one another. He looked at me, and I looked at him. He was a little man, short and stocky. His bow legs ended in leather boots. A grey fur cap, with its red star, was sloppily slanted on his head and sat atop a pockmarked face, which was not shaved and a stubble of red hair which didn't hide the deep pits of his skin. Not a pretty sight! An array of colourful medals adorned his brown shirt, and because there was no gold to be seen on his shoulder epaulette, I guessed that he must have been a sergeant. Upon seeing my own medals he suddenly grasped me to his breast in a bear-hug saying "good soldier". Then, releasing me, he laughingly pointed firstly to his own medals and then to mine. Then this bear of a man kissed me on both cheeks, declaring "*Vaijna kaputt*", i.e. war has ended, and "*Hitler kaputt*", i.e. Hitler is dead.

In contrast to his own dark suntan, I must have appeared rather pale. I swallowed the frog in my throat and tried in my depressed state, to grin at him. He must have seen the runes on my collar, but they did not seem to bother him. As one of the 'victors', when only of a lower rank, even he must have known that my runes distinguished me from the others as 'one of those'. If I am honest it did not, at that moment, occur to me either that this would most definitely distinguish me in future.

I then had to go with him once more into the cellars, like a fox in a chicken-run, frightening some women who screamed in panic and fled. It amused him and he let loose a shot or two into ceilings, walls and the tiles in the Monopol kitchen. I was happy that he had not shot at me. Taking a bottle of vodka, he took a long swig, he turned to me and said "Cheers! war has ended, now you can go home". I didn't need to be told a second time and returned to my comrades.

They looked at me in utter surprise thinking that I had risen from the dead, certain that in hearing the shots, that I had 'knocked on heaven's door.' Who can explain this experience? Who understood the Russian character, this almost infantile mentality, spiced with brute-force, naïvety, good-heartedness and unpredictable arbitrariness? Later I was to have plenty of time to learn about the unreasonable and contradictory characteristics of the Russians.

We were most certainly never in doubt as to the influence that alcohol played in the day-to-day routine of the Russians. But we were about to be given undoubted proof it and at first-hand. For our sins, we were much too close to the wine cellar of the Monopol, this treasure-chest being found soon enough by the roaming Reds. We were witnesses to the utter depredation of men, in a uniform, who called themselves soldiers, who drank themselves into unconsciousness, or started punch-ups and then, in their stupor, were uncontrolled in the use of their revolvers. They behaved like animals. We were often collected and forced to drink with them. We used to be landed in '*bau*', i.e. close arrest, for misuse of alcohol when we were caught legless. After that excess, we were nearly all self-confessed teetotallers.

One evening we were forced to witness the raping of one of our nurses. Three drunken Reds tottered down the cellar steps, with their caps sitting crookedly on top of their shorn heads, in search, so we thought, of more alcohol. That was not what they were looking for. With "woman, come here!" they caught hold of Angel, the pretty nurse, with the lovely smile and who laughed so easily. With her cries of protest, her fiancé, a sergeant medic, sprang at the three, regardless that they were armed with machine-pistols, and who beat him to the ground. He was lucky, for they did not shoot him.

We had all been standing in the ante-room immediately behind the outer cellar door and now the machine-guns were trained on us, as they threw 'Engelchen' on to the table. She tried desperately to defend herself, to no avail. We had to witness the shameful scene of rape, from the three, with our hands in the air. Just a few days before, we had been armed and had shown no mercy to such beasts. Now we had no choice but to witness those so-called human beings in face and form. They did not earn the title and we were not able to help. The agitator Ilya Ehrenburg would have been proud of the students of his propaganda. After that sexual gratification, the three then disappeared. 'Engelchen' disappeared during the night too, for the shame and degradation, in front of witnesses, was just too much for her. We never saw her again.

We were sold and delivered, we were 'wares' for the 'victors' and we, our lives, were of no worth. We could live today, but die tomorrow, today or in the next few minutes. We lived with that realisation, day after day. One roaming Red suddenly appeared, and just as suddenly shot at us so that we had to hit the ground or dive for cover under the bunks. Fortunately, no one was hit on that occasion, it was a 'game', a game with only a hair's breadth chance.

We also had visitors who, in comparison, were relatively harmless, such as the up-and-coming 'speaker'. He wanted to practise and needed an audience. So he appeared, waving his revolver nonchalantly in the air and politely asked us walking wounded, to go with him into the ante-room. There he stood on a chair and started to deliver his speech, in Japanese, for all that we knew. He must have noticed that his words were falling on barren ground, for we only understood the words, Communist, Lenin, Stalin and Russian culture, without showing any resonance. He asked for a translator and one of our chums from Upper Silesia was given the job of translating his preaching of political propaganda. He waited in the pauses, wiping the sweat of stress from his brow and taking strong swigs from his bottle of vodka.

Our Silesian friend gave us an evening that we could hardly forget, for he translated the very opposite of what was being said. We listened, we applauded at the achievements of the Communists in their Soviet paradise. We laughed, and our speaker thought that he had the audience of a lifetime and why not, for he had been very polite in asking us to attend. We were a very patient audience and we let him speak, until he fell off his chair, full to the brim with two kinds of Russian spirit, the intellectual and the liquid sort. There he stayed until the next morning. He was then found by one of the officers, and with a leather whip forced into consciousness, on to his feet and then outside, being brutally beaten as he went. In comparison, we thought that a couple of days in German '*bau*' was not so painful and we could feel sorry for him.

For some time I ignored the well-meant advice of my chums, to discard my uniform, not wanting to march into POW camp in hospital clothes. As more and more of the Russian soldiers began to take a closer look at my runes however, I exchanged my *SS-Untersturmführer's* uniform, for that of a *Wehrmacht* NCO. At the same time and with a very heavy heart, I burned my pay-book, with all of the entries of my army career in it, plus details of close-combat activity within the city. I was not only thankful to have survived those battles, but was also more than a little proud to have been a part of them, to have made my contribution. Therefore, I kept my medals.

According to my diary, the medical centre was closed down on 18 May and we were transported to Herrenstrasse, to provisional POW quarters. There we said a sorrowful farewell to everyone, with the now common Breslau expression of goodwill "stay healthy", and "stiff upper lip"! We had no idea if we would be kept together, or if we would meet again one day. It was noticeable that the shiny eyes of the successful defenders were now cloudy and sad, like tired wolves.

My mind was plagued with thoughts of escape, but my splinted arm was a disadvantage. There were no chances of success. But, to end my days as a convict in the unending swampy Taiga forests of Siberia was not for me. I had no illusions about the type of POW conditions that were waiting under the Soviets. I knew that they had refused to sign the Geneva Convention of 1929 and also that many of the German prisoners taken by the Russians between 1941/42 had been executed. I had no other choice but, for the time being, to wait for an improvement in my bodily movements. However, I would be on the alert as soon as the possibility of escape arose.

Other thoughts rushed through my mind. In my gratitude for my survival, I asked myself if there really was a war-god who guided the bullets when he chose. Perhaps, although invisible, he was now looking after me and us?

The sky was a deep blue, the clouds puffy and white that May day. We left the centre and started our march as POWs, joined by other units of the garrison. The wounded who could not walk were transported in German ambulances, under guard from the Russians. Those able to walk made up a column of silent, miserable souls, without the customary in-step march, without a happy song on their lips, and without conversation. They went where their feet led them, behind the man in front, exhaustion in many cases having taken control. We were joined by those from the infantry, air force, *Volkssturm* and Hitler Youth. The boy-soldiers' uniforms were much too large for them. They quickly sought the nearness of the older men as comrades, which was where they belonged.

We wore or carried only the necessary, or at least what we had left for possessions, a mug and plate, wallet for necessary papers, and a bundle of underwear. Others carried a blanket, despite the warm weather. It was very cold in Siberia! I did not even possess a coat. Our guards carried cocked machine-pistols across their chests, typical for the Russians, with a circular magazine of the sort that we had collected by the dozen. The guards were nervous, some so much that they let loose a shot or two, just by fingering the trigger, although we had given them no reason. Those unable to keep up with the column and who attempted to fall out for a pause were attacked with rifle butts and verbal abuse. They were forced to the extreme limits of physical reserves in order to put one foot in front of the other, and carry on. Sometimes the instincts of animals can be more human than the human being, for I remember that one of the horses carefully picked up its hooves to avoid a fallen soldier, although its rider had manoeuvred to trample over the unfortunate man. One of the guards tried, in broken German, to show us some compassion, to pump some optimism into us, declaring "war, not good, you go home, that good"! This naive sort was however few and far between, but his intentions were well meant. Those in the column, who were still aware of their surroundings, noticed a torn poster advertising the new film, in colour, of the film-star Kristina Södermann. We noticed that the top half of her laughing face was torn off, but also noticed the title, and felt the pain of disgust in the pit of our stomachs. The newest film of the blonde, laughing lady was entitled, *Sacrifice*.

We had only reached Striegauer Platz as it became dark. Striegauer Platz was where my friend had died in a bunker and where there were already long columns of men. The remainder of Regiment Besslein were to be the first to leave the city, perhaps because of fears that they could still pull a trick or two out of the hat. In the light of tank headlights they stood, like ghosts, their abnormally elongated shadows stretching over the rubble-filled square to high on the walls of the bunker.

We were continually counted by the Russian soldiers, "*Odin*, i.e. one, *Dwa*, i.e. two, *Tri*, i.e. three". An officer asked me if "wounded?" to which I replied "it's nothing much", for I did not want to be parted from my chums. "Ospital" was his curt reply. So with other wounded who had been separated from the rest, our next stop was the medical quarters for POWs in Herrenstrasse.

Standing at the entrance were gruff-looking 'Ivans', with fixed bayonets on their long rifles. They gave me the impression that they were troops from the communications zone, for front-soldiers would have been a little friendlier. They ran their greedy eyes over us, shouting "*Uri, Uri*". They must have been disappointed, for how can you steal from a naked man, who has no pockets? We had been "freed" of everything that we possessed.

The Russian soldier was given privileges, in that they were allowed every month to send home "bounty parcels", or 'plunder packets', weighing up to eight kilos. The regulation for officers was even more generous, double the weight, to allow for their collection of "militaria souvenirs" as the Russians called them. That regulation was clearly an encouragement to steal. And the little soldier when not so fortunate, not having so many opportunities, coming too late? What did he have to send? The bandages from his feet or the remainder of his ration?

The bed allocated to me was still warm from the previous occupant and the blanket smeared with blood, but it was at least a real bed. During that first night in Herrenstrasse, the paratrooper in the next bed to me died and I witnessed his struggle with death. I lay and watched all the stages of tetanus leading to the terminal stage. The tragedy of it was that of all of us he was the slightest wounded. He had only had a graze from a passing bullet. All that he had needed to live was a tetanus injection, which he never received. He had to lie for nearly four hours, stiff in cramp, the only movement coming from his pale eyes which looked at me. He, just as I, had been one of the walking wounded and yet he had to die. During the night, the stillness was broken with screams, screams from those waking bathed in sweat, from nightmares of their most recent battles.

In Herrenstrasse I had time to look over my new room-mates. They were young, very young, being in school just yesterday? But their schooling had not equipped them for what they were today, old men of war. They had certainly believed that their schooling had equipped them for the important things in life. I was sure that it had not taken long for them to ascertain that it had been useless for war. This education had had to be replaced with another, even more important, a desire for life itself. That lesson was simply to shoot quicker than the enemy, and be even quicker to hit the ground for cover in order to live, to survive. As I looked at them, it was clear that they had been robbed of their freedom before their lives had even begun. I believed at that point, that there must be another purpose to life, other than that which my life had revolved around till then. Surely life consisted of something else other than schooling and shooting? These lads would certainly have other experiences in life, after this, and hopefully ones which would produce laughter one day.

I went to war as a boy and I became a man, one with clean hands. That was an achievement in total war, and because of it I personally found imprisonment unfair. I was not the only one who shared that opinion. Others had to and did accept their fate. Most of them, tired in mind and body, acquiesced to that 'truism'. They played cards, or tried to relax themselves and others by telling jokes, most of which we had all heard before, but laughed at nevertheless. Only now, the laughter had no echo. This artificial 'stiff upper lip' behaviour showed itself amongst the officers by the dissection of their tactical mistakes. "When we, or if we had", who now knew how they could have won the war. Some were obsessed with food, and titillated their palates and that of others, with imaginary meals, explaining how they were cooked. "Take so many ounces of butter and two eggs"! Perhaps because we only had lentils as a good square meal, every day!

There was another theme which wove itself into our daily conversations, women. And why not? We were all in the prime of our manhood. We all without exception, admired Sister Susi, the nurse from Hamburg. She was young, very petite, had red highlights in her dark blonde hair, was scrubbed and left a sweetness behind her of soap and face-cream, which we followed, one after the other with our noses. She was the epitome of womanhood for us, myself included, and was the nearest to our dreams that we had. We all held a secret love of her to our breast, no *amour-fou*, but more of a platonic nature. This sweetness in our lives did not last long, for we became unwilling members of a 'Wandering Club', as our cross-country wanderings began. Instead of the usual coach-house stops, we went from one prison hospital to another. One of those I remember was the bombed Scala Cinema in the former Employment Exchange, a huge building on the edge of the Oder, in Saltstrasse.

Up to that point, my blood-group tattoo, despite medical examinations, had not been a disadvantage for me. The knowledge of this significant and distinguishing 'mark of Cain' had obviously not filtered through on a large scale, but at some time it would. Mine had to be erased, at all costs. This was easier said than done. Some of the other WSS patients tried with burning cigarettes, or continual abrasion with a rough stone. It was even said that it could be done with milk. I did not believe the latter of those solutions. In any case, where on earth could I lay my hands on milk?

The assistant doctor Markwart Michler wanted to help me and arranged an operation. His equipment was rather primitive. The operation itself was to be performed in strict secrecy, away from everyone. He procured a razor-blade as a scalpel and ice as an anaesthetic. At the agreed time, we met in one of the large rooms in the cellar and I prepared myself for the worst, with guards at the door. I bared my arm and it was duly iced. We then had an interruption, with the result that the area around the tattoo was no longer anaesthetised, but "ten minutes pain, or 25 years in Siberia?" And so with the light from a candle, the operation began.

It could not to be compared to the seconds that a foreign body sears into one, such as a bullet, shrapnel or glass, producing the numbness of shock through causation. This was deliberate, so my mind reacted accordingly! It was hell! I ground my teeth, for I had no other choice, or one that I did not contemplate. And it bled! I tried for some minutes to stem the flow by sucking it away. Then, after urinating on a shred of an army shirt, Michler wound it around the wound to sterilise it. At some time later, this was exchanged for a plaster, after it had scabbed. Now my fears were allayed. I was no longer named 'Cain'. Thus I hoped to evade the hunt for members of my organisation. I escaped with only the faintest of scars, which can still be seen today.

I held the highest rank of all of the wounded in the group. Therefore I had the responsibility of reporting to the doctors and non-resident doctors on numbers present, and other things that interested the Russians. The very first time that I performed this duty, it caused smiles from the German doctors and nurses who were standing behind the Russian team of doctors. I clapped my heels together, which was the custom when in the presence of higher ranks or personages, together with my arm salute in *Deutscher Grüss*. I very slowly rested on my cap, in doubt. Habit is habit! The Russian team did not bat an eyelid, ignoring the rebellion against the new regime.

Poles in Breslau, 1946. A drawing by the author from that year.

In comparison with those conditions to be found in prisoner transports, in cattle-wagons, and under way to the East, we could not complain. We could move around on the banks of the Oder. All day long we lay in the sunshine, watching it shimmer on the water's surface. We were thankful for small mercies. Others, fallen into deep depression, lay on their bunks the whole day. Others walked to and fro over the few metres of their room, like caged cats looking for a quiet corner where they could be alone in their despair.

One day in the middle of August 1945, this was all very rudely disturbed, as mighty underwater explosions from the Oder sent fountains of water high into the air. The hot summer sun had reduced the level of the river's water, exposing unexploded shells and other ammunition, as well as weapons from the German soldiers who had thrown them into the river. All had reached exploding point with the increasing heat. The force of the blasts threw to the ground those wounded who were walking the promenade. It caused already weak walls to collapse, and resulted in damage to buildings, and to the furniture in the hospital. The Russians were in pure panic and believed that we were breaking out on a large scale, with the help of explosives. We were just as much in the dark as they. We had no idea what was happening. They ran wild over the hospital yard, screaming as they ran criss-cross in all directions, with cocked machine-pistols. To see their cool command broken to such an extent through a false alarm gave us a lot of pleasure, for there was not much entertainment in our everyday lives. One could nose-dive into deep depression, when busy only with one's self.

I tried to wile away the time by reading every book that I could lay my hands on, to put some distance between myself and reality, to forget what was going on around me. I had to sort out my feelings and my mind, for some objectivity. Mainly I needed peace, peace after the din, the loud, unpleasant and prolonged noise of battle, and the months of strain. The books in the Employment Exchange were plentiful, in the attic and cellars, and I helped myself. To my joy I even found some in my mother-tongue, which must have found their way from the lending-library, perhaps for the foreign labourers. I read everything that I could find, gladly reading about journeys into foreign lands, plus everything that had been formerly uninteresting, including the poems and works of Schiller.

I perused the world once more, soaking up every minute detail of it, the warmth of the shining sun, bird-song, the fascinating flight of the butterfly. I followed the route of the beetle in the sand, like a small child. I did so despite the stifling worry in my breast about the fate of my family back home. I had to work up some optimism and clarity of mind, and not become a sacrifice to the 'barbed wire syndrome'.

I sought conversation in every corner of this band of brothers-in-arms, from different units, from older comrades, to help strengthen my courage to face life. They discussed their experiences with me. I found their philosophy of life was all the more surprising, in the short time since the end of the war. Among those were engineer Karl-Heinz Corfield, who had grave leg injuries, and assistant surgeon Markwart Michler, with whom a very deep friendship developed over many years.

The war had already been over for some months and the fanaticism and brutality of the 'Ivans' had relaxed. They were even lenient with the prisoners, some showing sympathy for our situation. We even formed an orchestra at that time, with self-made instruments. The qualified musicians among us played from their personal repertoires. We had a magician among us too, who made one of the prisoners disappear from his wooden box. "Where is comrade? The box is empty!" What would happen to them when one of us had failed to turn up at the count, the next day? We laughed our socks off. Afterwards, as they cottoned on to how it was done, they laughed too, at themselves!

We had moved once more, to Hedwigstift, a church boarding-house, to be shorn like lambs. One could never have failed to notice the varying degrees of the hair-cut of the Russian soldier. The 'men' had their heads shaved, the sergeants were shorn to ear-level and the officers were not shorn at all. Such were the medical measures against lice. Nonetheless we protested. It was of no avail for our protests fell on the deaf ears of the grinning Russians. "Shaved heads,no lice, *dawai, dawai!*" Those who refused, were physically brought to the barber by force. I found it all demoralising and so I refused to move too. In the palaver that ensued it was overheard that I was Dutch. This saved my hair, but I had to report to the Commander.

Two Russian soldiers appeared, to escort me to the Commander. They wore blue caps. Blue caps meant that they were certainly from the NKVD and with granite-hard faces, they conducted me for interrogation. "What is your name? You are not German, but you are SS?" Now I knew what he was after and I played dumb. My repeated words in Russian "I don't understand," brought the Captain who was sitting at the wooden table to a rage. Then he ordered me to remove my jacket and shirt, which I was not allowed to lay on his field-bed, for fear of lice. I explained freely that the scar on my arm was due to shrapnel, but he chose not to believe me. "You SS!" With that the two granite-faces had turned to grinning ones, and their owners took me to the barbers, where I was shorn just like the others.

I had hoped that that was the end of the matter, but I was wrong. I was now branded. I was now 'one of those', and treated accordingly, being separated from the rest. It was however not long before I was joined by the others. For a witchhunt had begun for other SS soldiers. All had to bare their left arm and show their tattoo. The Commander had been informed and the information had filtered through. Now the guards wandered through the building, searching. Some were able to hide themselves, in the attics and the cellars, and the Commander made good use of the incident for another purpose.

Up to that time, individuals had escaped. It was clear that as there were now 25 in my room, that the commander wanted to use us as pressure to stop those attempts. It was announced that for every one who tried to escape, one of us would be shot. We hoped and prayed that we could rely on the solidarity and comradeship of the others. We were under special arrest for six weeks, six weeks when our comrades never let us down. No one tried to escape in that time.

We, under special arrest, as well as all in the Hedwigstift, were moved once more. Following that move the witch-hunt for the SS was forgotten for a short time. The pressure on sorting 'us from them' eased and we were moved to the Cloister of Compassionate Brothers. For me it was to be the last stop in Breslau as a prisoner. There was no compassion from the Soviets in possession of this house of God. The cloister was the sorting house for Siberia. The fate of every man inside its walls was decided by a commission of Russian doctors, male and female. The cloister was very strongly guarded and the compassion came not from the guards but from the monks. Most spoke Polish and with this language tried to communicate with us.

After a while, the word went round from the others already there, that when a certain doctor was on duty and sat in the president's chair, then few escaped the journey to Russia's paradise. Fear struck every man whose name appeared on the list on the same day as that doctor, who was a female major. The accent being more on 'major', than on 'female'. When this was confirmed, the word went around the prisoners like wildfire, and there was no escape. The said 'lady' could be described as a typical Russian. She wore a tight high-buttoned blouse stretching over her more than ample bosom. There were fist-thick epaulettes on shoulders and neck, and she looked as if she was growing out of it all. She was never, even in high summer, to be seen without her *Schapka*, with its red star on the front, covering the military cut of her short dark hair.

She was as hard as granite. Not fever, nor a bad stomach, would qualify anyone for exemption from Siberia. For of course the weeks of the long, long journey would act as a 'cure' whilst underway! Those prisoners belonged to Group One and would be shipped off to Russia. That woman had a rather doubtful method of delivering her diagnosis as to whether one was healthy or not. Disregarding the symptoms, she would give every man a good hard pinch on his backside! Many doubted if that method of testing the flesh on this area of the male torso had been medically founded. But she believed in it, or wanted to. Under her scrutiny even those on crutches, or with wounded feet, were classified as Group One.

I celebrated my twenty-second birthday on 4 September 1945, but there was no joy on that day. According to the entry in my diary it denoted utter depression. My thoughts were back home. I asked myself if anyone was thinking about me on that day. One thought led to another, as to whether they or any of my family were still living. My entry also tells me that because of malaria, or dysentery, many of my comrades were no longer with me. They had been sent in massed transport to Hundsfeld, the transition camp. From there they went in the direction of the East instead of, according to General Niehoff's conditions of surrender, returning home. Home? One upset oneself by saying the word out loud and so it remained in one's thoughts.

The day came when I had to go before the commission, when my name was on the list. There must have been all of a hundred men who had assembled. We queued like lambs for the slaughter on that day, in the dark, tiled, cloister corridor leading to the doctors' room. There were amputees among us. In circumstances such as those, one could almost be jealous of their very good chances of escaping this plight. But there was no escape when the scales tipped in your direction. Even those who had received a bullet in the lungs, which no one would ever wish to have, gazed with interest at the beautiful frescoes decorating the cloister ceilings. Their optimism could not be overlooked. However, that did not interest us, for we were too busy with ourselves.

The queue moved slowly, too slowly. The hours ticked by. The tension built up inside everyone. Would it be Siberia or our homeland? German medics accompanied the Russians with their long lists. They controlled the queue, together with a very young Russian woman in uniform. Her appearance distracted our thoughts. She was the only thing that could have distracted our thoughts, nothing else! It could have been very amusing under any other circumstances. Even so, this very feminine apparition replaced our thoughts with others. They lasted only for seconds. She was blonde, with obviously long hair that was twisted into a grandmother's knot at the back of her neck. When she undid this knot of angel hair she must have been beautiful! Every time she passed us, we all looked. Our mouths fell open, one after the other, and our eyes followed her very shapely legs encased in soft Moroccan leather boots, which caressed her legs like stockings. She wanted, with her short, brisk military steps, to give another impression. But conscious of her attractiveness, she pursed her red lips as she went, as if that could detract from her beauty.

I began to feel really sick in the pit of my stomach, as the queue slowly nudged its way to that door where my fate would be decided. When I landed in Group One then I would try my luck at escaping! Perhaps I could find a trusted comrade, one whom I could rely on, and we could use our chances of escape on German soil. One way or another, they were not going to send me to Siberia and that was for sure! Suddenly, we were no longer needed. "Come back tomorrow". The commission had not managed to examine the numbers on that day. A move from 'Lady Luck' or that 'God of War'?

That night was long and one that brought no sleep for me. It was one of tense agony and apprehension for the second act. The next day, far quicker than I thought possible, I was standing before this committee. It was a room filled with blue cigarette-smoke, with German and Russian doctors, a translator, and who was sitting in the middle at a table? This beautiful apparition! So, she was a doctor, which explained her rank, but from her appearance she could have been a medical student.

To examine me, she carefully undid my sling and, just as carefully, felt the area around the bullet holes on my arm, which by now was almost paralysed. Although I was tense, I felt the soft touch of her long slim fingers on my skin, like a caress, but let out a loud yell, "Ouch!" as was rehearsed with our assistant doctor during his 'simulation course'. My arm had not healed quickly without the use of a sling and so I saw to it that I had not used mine very often. In that way I stretched the healing process for as long as possible, and the result was now, at that moment, to be seen. I could hardly be called 'whole', although I was not in as bad a condition as others. A discussion began between all of the doctors. In the months of contact with the 'Ivans', however distant, through repetition one is forced to recognise words, until you ask what it means, or you are informed, and so I recognised the word good. Did that mean good enough to work? Was I not going to be released? This angelic female could not release me on medical grounds? I watched her whispering for some minutes with an older colleague in a white coat, and then she turned to me and smiled, saying "*Du domoy*", i.e. I was dismissed!

Only upon leaving the room did I understand her words. I was going home! Had it been the tuition from my doctor friend? Had it been the sympathy of this woman, of the same age as I, which had spared me from Siberia and saved my life? I will never know. Numbed but happy, I wanted to share my news with my chums and returned to my room. Most were Group One. Suddenly it was clear to me that to have shared my joy with them would have abused them emotionally. I could not console them, for I could not find any words. As I stood there, the melancholy sound of a harmonica filled the air, coming from the cloister garden. The melody hung in the air. It was one known to all of us who had worn a uniform. The musician interpreted what we were all suffering, what we all needed, interpreting the despair in most, and the hope in others. The music of this soldier's philosophy was far better than any words of mine could ever be. *Es geht alles vorüber, es geht alles vorbei.* "Everything changes, changes to yesterday".

CHAPTER 19

Illegally in Poland

Now the war for me was definitely at an end. The last act of the Silesian drama was simply a matter of enforcing the resolutions of the Potsdam Treaty which took place on 2 August 1945. From then on, Breslau was no longer German territory, but Polish. Already in the middle of May, a Polish flag could be seen fluttering in the breeze over the City Hall. Breslau was no longer Breslau. Breslau was given the new Polish name of Wroclaw. A seven hundred year old culture sank in a flood of Poles and Polish government. The 'blooming' capital city of this part of Germany had been given away.

The fate of the German eastern provinces had already been decided between the Western Allies, by February 1945, in Yalta. This 'bounty' of war was divided. Although Poland lost territory to the Soviet Union, Poland's borders were enlarged by 250 kilometres, stretching into Germany like soldiers 'falling-out' to the side. It had been a subject of discussion however, as early as 1943, at the Teheran Conference, when Winston Churchill's dry comment was that "No one can do anything about it, when this treads on German toes."

This 'falling-out' action brought compulsory seizure of property, following the forceful expulsion of 15 million German inhabitants. As a result, three million people lost their lives. "A land of death, from the Oder to the

Paper given to the author on his release from Soviet captivity. The later official German translation read: "It is certified that Verton Heinrich [Hendrik in the original Russian], 22 years old, from 20 September 1945 is limited to the physical work deemed suitable, according to the resolution of the medical commission of the hospital of Unit 25472.
Diagnosis: Damage of the left elbow nerve.
The chairman of the commission, Captain [signature unreadable]."

Neisse, for the outlawed", was the description from the journalist Robert
Jungk, on 26 November 1945, in the Zürcher newspaper *Die Weltwoche*.

I was a free man on 20 September 1945. I was given my discharge papers and a 'pound-loaf' of bread. As a stranger, I was allowed to stay in
Breslau, just 24 hours. I was still there 12 months later. "*Du domoy!*" The
Russian doctor had said to go home, but where was that? I could not and
did not want to return to my 'home' in Holland. I knew that the 'old'
régime was allied to the Communists during the war, and allied now to the
'new'. I could only expect reprisals against the 'volunteers' from my homeland. That was confirmed at a later date. No! I must find myself a new
home.

I cannot describe the utter joy that overwhelmed me with the first steps
I took into freedom. I was free at last. Free! There were no more Russian
guards and no locked doors. The military discipline, and the ever-present
fear of death over the last years, was no longer there. I was totally alone.
There were neither accompanying guards of escort, nor any of my reliable
comrades to give me their company. I felt the isolation. The realisation
came that I must fight my way through a strange survival strategy that I
knew existed, but that I had to discover for myself what it was.

My uniform was tattered, making me feel like a vagabond. But because
of it I blended into the tattered city. It was a city of debris and ruins. I made
my way to the home of a young nurse from Breslau. She had been discharged some time before me, and now lived with her mother on the outskirts of Carlowitz. Upon her discharge, it was possible for her to retrieve
my personal effects, under difficult circumstances, and smuggle them out of
the hospital. She buried them, like a dog burying a bone. They were waiting
for me. My diary and old photos were all the possessions that I had.

After dressing in a borrowed suit of her brother, who at that time was
missing, I could go out into the streets. It was dangerous, because the terror
of the Poles raged. Everyone in my age-group immediately aroused suspicion as having been a soldier. If you gave them the opportunity, they would
tear your discharge papers to pieces.

At the end of the war, the Polish state police, or to give them their official title 'Organ for Public Safety', were installed as supervisory officials by
the Communists. But they possessed a high percentage of criminal elements. They made a business from plundering. They dressed in leather
jackets, or had the gall to dress in German uniforms and carry German
weapons. They elbowed their way through the population, stealing from
them by day and by night. Under the protection of the Communists, they
had never even had a whiff of gunpowder. But they were the 'victors' and
now behaved just like the 'Ivans', although they had never been friends. It
may be somewhat strange to understand, but the Communist leadership
which now reigned, was very often the saving grace for many of the German

nationals to be found in Breslau, simply because of their relationship with the Poles.

The Breslauers knew how to help themselves in this situation. A 'jungle-drum' system, using saucepan-lids, became the communication system in calling for help when the Poles forced their way in to where the Breslauers lived. The signal warned the neighbours, every one of whom joined in with a clash of cymbals, the din of which reached a crescendo, stretching from house to house. The commander then sent jeeps and soldiers. He simply enjoyed getting to grips with the Poles, between whom there was no love lost. The 'Ivans' showed no mercy, and very often shots were to be heard.

The Russian/Polish relationship had never been good, but at that time, when the Russians had 'freed' Poland from the yoke of Fascism it was, of course, worse than ever. Both sides were contemptuous of the other. Murder and manslaughter between the two occurred daily. This 'peace' after the war produced even more of a psychological crisis in many people. Suicides were at an even higher rate than during the siege of the city. The total result, including the high death-rate among both young and old, in appalling conditions including epidemics, was catastrophic.

Normal hygienic conditions were non-existent causing the high death-rate. It was not to be wondered at. The civilian population died off like flies, from typhus, typhus fever, dysentery and diphtheria. Babies were the first 'sacrifices'. The deaths of very many infants caused by malnutrition was also not surprising.

It did not take long for the Poles to fill the central prison in Kletschkauerstrasse with people who were arrested under false charges and delivered there. For most that meant a gruesome death. A German railway-worker was taken there, on trumped-up charges that he was the Chief of the Breslau Gestapo. It appeared that his railway identification card, picturing him in his railway official's uniform, proved this! His protest produced a forceful kick in the abdomen or genitals, and blows from truncheons. That lasted until the unfortunate candidate signed a (false) statement confessing to the charges.

The patrols from prison guards during the nights disturbed not only the sleep of the prisoners, but they had to report, standing to attention, that 'our cell is occupied with German swine'. The nights were not only used for control, they were used for the most brutal of interrogations, accompanied by very loud music from the radio, to try to cover the screams of the tortured.

After the Poles took over the control of Silesia, they organised concentration camps where Germans were starved, beaten to death, or died from other methods. One of those camps was in Lamsdorf. The 'Attrition' called for by Stalin, was now replaced with that from the Poles. In this camp alone,

6,488 Germans were shot, hanged, burned, or died from the consequences of being forced into barrels and rolled 'for as long as it took for them to die'.

In Breslau, as in the whole of Silesia, to be German was to be worthless. As such you could be driven from your home and used as forced labour. More and more soldiers, who were discharged by the Russians for any reason, were immediately re-arrested by the Poles and transported away. For me, that was a very big worry.

One could not fail to notice that international flags flew from various houses. Those ensured the safety of their occupants, being respected by both the Russians and the Poles. There were French, Italian, and flags from other nations, which gave me an idea. Even as a foreign worker, this would not give me 100% safety. There was a danger that I was classified as a DP, i.e. a displaced person, admittedly coming under the auspices of UNRA to be repatriated. That was not what I wanted, but it was worth the risk. I simply had to have false papers. Until I had them, I made myself an armband in the colours of the Dutch national flag and attached it to my lapel. My false papers, with a stamp, stated that during the war, I had been forced to work for public transport, the BVB. This vital piece of paper was procured for me by one of its former employees. For that life-saving gesture I was able, some years later, to return the favour. I testified at the 'denazification' of the said man, in the western zone. I confirmed that during the war he had always treated his foreign workers as human beings, and without any harassment.

The unconditional willingness to help each other, apart from those termed as 'flexible shoe-cleaners' was among the Germans second to none. People could trust their past, and also their origin to anyone German, without repercussions. The terrible experiences springing from the siege soldered them together into a brotherhood of conspirators. They formed a piece of German homeland, a colony in the middle of a very hostile world.

At all costs, those Germans wanting to return to their homes that they had left were not welcome and had to be outlawed. The Poles had set up control points and guards very early on. Even by the spring of 1945, a post was set up on the river-crossing at Görlitz, on the river Neisse. Some escaped at that crossing, increasing the housing problem in the city, which by now was acute. The Poles were organising 'ghettos' for the Germans, in an ethnic-cleansing programme. The Germans could be controlled better in that way. Perhaps it would be better to say that it would be easier to steal what possessions they had left, to say nothing of an uncomfortable level of harassment.

They started this ethnic-cleansing programme in the autumn of 1945, in Carlowitz, where I lived. I had been there since my discharge. The inhabitants had been given 90 minutes to pack 20 kilos together, and had to leave their keys in the locks upon leaving. They had just one and a half hours to decide what would make up the 20 kilos, what they wanted to take from among their possessions, and what had to be left behind.

Before this happened, I made my way into the city, to my friend Markwart. He was the assistant doctor who had been discharged at the same time as I. The relationship was a good one, for we were of the same age. We had the same ambitions of surviving and always having a full stomach. He lived with a nursing-sister, in a bomb-damaged house, under the eaves in attic rooms. It was a house of flats into which the Russians and the Poles did not like to enter. Most of the remaining bomb-damaged houses were close to falling down, but that did not worry us old warriors. That was the least of our worries. We were left alone to try to live, or simply to vegetate would be a better description. Our daily bread was bought on the 'black market', paid for in Polish z³oty. Meanwhile the German mark had disappeared. My doctor friend made some money from the treatment of ill Russians or Poles, and from army medical reserves.

There were many Germans who made themselves voluntary prisoners in their homes, not daring to go out on the streets. I became a middle-man between them and the occupiers of Silesia, making good business and exchanges, using articles for sale or exchange. My 'foreign status' made this possible. There were usually a few z³oty left over for me, and therefore food could be bought. It was swings and roundabouts, for sometimes business was not so good. Then, of course, we went to bed hungry and could not sleep. There were other times when we lived like 'kings in France', and were full of Polish sausage and cream torte.

There was a very strange incident during this time, but one that is representative of the political relationship between the Western Allies and the Communists. Markwart was approached and asked to act as a spy. He came home one day and told me that two strangers had approached him. They were two Americans who offered him a large sum of money to inform them of the political situation in Breslau, under the Poles. To spy? To spy, and for the Americans who were our enemy? To spy against the Communists who were also our enemy? The Americans were already spying on their Communist brothers-in-arms? That was a double-edged sword, even a double-edged political sword, and Markwart said 'no'. There was no question of him getting involved, although the thought of the money was very attractive.

Markwart left Breslau, his place of birth. I left in the November of 1945. He saw no prospects for his future medical career, in staying in a city reigned over by Slavs. Shortly before he departed, he wrote down his thoughts about his birthplace, in a poem.

My Home Town

Dear, old and beautiful city, I loved you as a child.
Within your walls each day, Spring's wind warmed my face, so mild.
Walking your cobbled paths, my way I found.
In mews and courtyards, the hidden nooks and crannies I found.
Each new day the sun shone on your cobbled ways.
Patrician house, house of hearth and hall,
From each stone, I heard your heartfelt call.
Dear, old and beautiful city, in ruins and rubble, what have they done?
From your torn and painful, tear-stained face, I want to run.
Your dress of fine old filigree lies torn in shreds around you,
But, I promise, my love will always be strong, always be true.
In my prayers I will pray, that on another sunny day,
That old heaven you once knew,
Will rise again to protect and comfort you.

Markwart was never ever to see his old home-city again. We met some years later in West Germany and I met not only a family man with children, but also a Professor of Medicine.

I did not have to be alone for long, for there were many Breslauers who would have taken me in, a young man on his own, and useful as a protector. So I lived for a long time in Klosterstrasse, in the house of an old lady. In order to prevent the plundering raids of the Poles at night, I barricaded the doors with stout wooden planks. They tried many times, but they were unlucky. When this lady, married to a Belgian, finally received permission to join her husband, she made me heir to her house, which didn't please the Poles very much. I had it in writing that I now owned her house. They found the loop-hole they needed and told me that this 'Will and Testament' was not legally signed and sealed by a solicitor, so it was not legal. It was therefore not mine. I could however let it, or rent it to students, which I did.

One could not be too fussy at that time. Half of the house at the back had been shot away by artillery fire, and that included the toilet on the second floor. Those using it had a lovely view of the mountains of debris and rubble. Such conditions were ideal for insects, not one or two, but a whole plague of them, which robbed us of our sleep.

A family called Laska lived not far from my house, at number twelve in Lützowstrasse. Their house had been spared any drastic bomb-damage. The daughter of the family with her infant, the daughter-in-law, and two aunts lived there, complete with their possessions. The daughter's husband returned from POW camp and together with him, we combined our talents for survival, for ourselves and the family. At that time it was not known if Mr Laska and the two sons were still living. So in close association with the family, I became a provisional son and brother, not only because I found and chopped firewood for them, but also because of my business talents on the 'black' market. With a chosen article from their possessions, I could and did barter for something necessary or useful.

The centre of this 'black' market was the Scheitniger Star, between the Kaiser and Fürsten bridges. The area, having been utilised as a provisional airstrip for the airport, was large, with lots of open space and surrounded on all side with ruined houses. It could perhaps be compared to an oriental marketplace for it buzzed with Polish handlers, and farmers' wives in their white headscarves, offering their wares from stands or from the back of pony-drawn *Panje* carts.

Everything precious to the German national that had made up their former standard of living was to be had there. But to buy it, one either had to be a millionaire, or be prepared to give one's last shirt for it. Butter, eggs, chocolate, bacon, and coffee-beans were offered, but one could not pay the required prices. One could recognise the poor Germans amongst the throng, for amongst the handlers and the Polish civilians, they stood out as thin and anxious. In expecting their exile at any time, many German women sold or exchanged everything from their household, even the suits from their fallen husbands or missing sons. Most accepted the most miserable of prices, not being brave enough to barter with those who had no scruples.

I was more resolute in my dealings with the handlers, as a male, and a foreigner as well. I let them know that business was business and that their stated price was not for me. I bartered in Polish, for as long as it took, until the price was what I had intended, i.e. reasonable for the wares offered. I soon became a 'king' of this market. When I appeared, I usually offered articles from the Laska family from before the war. Such items had become costly, but were of good quality and could no longer be obtained. I had leather shoes, wool coats, suits, bedding materials, inlets, women's brassieres. All were sought after goods and brought the highest of prices.

When business for the day closed, I allowed myself a visit to the *Piwo and Wino* stand, where I downed a vodka and ate a sausage in a roll. I was usually not there long before being joined by one of the many prostitutes. It was the custom when meeting members of the opposite sex on the street, to greet them with a kiss of their hand. This included them, even when they had black fingernails!

After successful sales, we were able to add pancakes and potato fritters to our daily nourishment, but both had to be fried without fat. Sometimes we even had smoked meats. At Christmas 1945 for instance, we managed to have typical Silesian dumplings, with roast pork and pickled cabbage.

Someone had the idea of visiting the now wild and overgrown nursery gardens in Gandau, to harvest some apples. It was a long way on foot. So one day we decided to take a short cut through the churchyard, which lay between aerodrome and Pilsnitzerstrasse to. The first time that we took this route, we could only stand and stare in disbelief and utter disgust at the sacrilege that we found. Graves had been plundered. Mausoleums had been broken into. Slabs of stone and marble had been smashed, in order to plunder from the dead. Wedding rings, other jewellery and gold teeth had been stolen from the open graves, in greed that stemmed from non-capitalists? We could only stand on this 'acre of God's land' in utter disgust at the sacrilege, presumably from Russian soldiers.

I did not hurry to register myself as a DP, for I was not so keen about being repatriated back to Holland. My BVB papers satisfied me for the time being. So that with luck, nerve, and more than enough deceit, I hoped that I could survive that rather unstable time. There had been more than enough dangerous situations, any of which could have been my undoing.

One of those was a surprise house-search from the Poles, particularly dangerous for us when I was found at the Laska's house. Once, the Polish security officers, including an arrogant chap, in an ultra-chic uniform and typical square cap, searched the whole flat in a show of self-importance. Luckily for me, they did not think to test for hollow walls, for I was hidden one time in a very well concealed wall cupboard, used for bed linen. The Laska family could think themselves lucky that they were not sacrificed by Polish businessmen. Such men were those behind the militia, who were sent by them on plundering missions.

Despite it being a time when there were days when one did not how to survive, to live through the next day, I also had comfortable times. One such was a rendezvous on the river Oder, which developed into much more. The weather was lovely early in 1946 and it was bathing weather. The Breslauerw did not succumb to this, for fear of the Russians and the Poles hiding in solitary stretches of the Oder. I just could not ignore this pleasure and made use of the privilege that I had, as a non-German, to bathe in the river. That I did, alone, for several days, until one sunny morning, when I was joined in this idyll, by a 'mermaid', who could not possibly be German.

She was 18 years of age, blonde, and spoke in broken German, and to my surprise, this was laced with Dutch words. A Dutch worker in Lemberg, the city of her birth, had taught her. The joy of bathing soon became a liaison, which was balm for my loneliness and boredom. She was, according to the song we had always sung *das allerschönste Kind*. Was a man in Poland to find the loveliest child one could find in Poland? Whether the weather was good or bad, we met regularly and we met now on the Ole, a lonely tributary of the Oder. Not long after, Elzbieta invited me for a meal with her parents, who lived in Mollwitzerstrasse. My fears were quickly allayed over the meal of maize and *piroggen*, a form of ravioli. The friendly, open-heartedness of this Polish family called Markowitz, who came from the Carpathians, was welcoming. It was only the grandmother who was not enamoured of me, sitting there in her white headscarf and eyeing me with suspicion. She told her granddaughter that I was a spy.

Mr and Mrs Markowitz were Congress Poles, or national Poles, who were forcibly moved from Lemberg to Breslau. They did not like the life-style of the city, where they certainly did not feel at home. They had noth-ing against the Germans and actually heavily criticised the shameful behaviour of their own people. The militia in Wroclaw were not regulars, but were family members from criminal backgrounds that had now jumped on the bandwagon. The Markowitz family had had no bad personal experi-ences with the Germans, in contrast to the Russians, with whom they wanted no contact. This attitude had angered the Russians, in particular soldiers who had made certain advances towards Elzbieta and been given a rebuff. They had then tried to rape her. She had managed to escape them at the last minute.

The sight of Breslau troubled one's soul and it became nauseous for me. I wanted to leave, and visit the countryside, which was a dangerous under-taking. Elzbieta told me that she would accompany me, to protect me, which was a brave decision for her to take. Our visits took us to Deutsch-Lissa, to Leuthen and Saara. The new Polish names I have now forgotten, but not the former fields of slaughter, where I lost many of my comrades. I could not talk about it then to Elzbieta, for I was to her a foreign worker from Holland, and it had to stay that way.

On our way we met the new Polish settlers, who on the whole were not happy with their new circumstances. Some from the town had been moved to the country, and those from the country had been moved to the town. Elzbieta spoke to the sinister-looking Poles who moved around us in suspi-cious interest. They soon determined that we were Polish, whilst I remained dumb and smiling, i.e. a Polish pair! We still had to be very careful. There were criminals who were roaming the streets having been released from pris-ons, but who were not political prisoners. When we heard Russian voices we disappeared as quickly as we could, finding roads over the fields to the woods. We bumped into Russian troops one day, with cars, mounted riders and *Panje* carts, all having flags flying from them in the wind. There were no nasty words, just grins as if they knew that we wanted just to be alone, as they saw us sitting on the edge of the woods.

I felt really free there in the lap of 'Mother Nature' and I lived the hours intensely. Those hours under blue skies, listening to the bird-song, were cleansing. I realised that I saw the countryside reverting to the way it had been. The fields were no longer tilled or cared for. Nature's wild flowers were taking possession of the fields, not the wheat and corn, which strug-gled to ripen in that wilderness. The lovely wild flowers, the weeds, how-ever, stood triumphant over man's daily bread and hid a deathtrap. Whoever wanted to harvest the corn from those acres, would tread the fields of death and mines. I knew that the roots of this corn nestled side by side with the remains of German and Russian soldiers. Their bones had been washed by the rain, dried by the sun and were now turning 'earth to earth and dust to dust'.

After those country visits, I had to ask, "does peace really reign here?" No, something was missing. The country idyll was not complete, for it was totally still. When one listened, did one hear the moo of a cow, or the crowing and clucking of chickens in the farmyard? The stillness was the stillness that one found in the churchyard. The war had taken the cows and the pigs from the villages. There were no strutting chickens, no warning bark of the farmhouse dog. There was no straw in the cow-stalls, which the farmhand had cut for the welfare of the animals, for there were none.

Once, a German soldier approached us coming from the other direction. Had he been discharged? Had he managed to escape? He walked with the aid of a walking-stick, which one could see had been a broom-handle. His bread-bag hung from his uniform, which was in tatters. He did not want to draw attention to himself. He passed by not giving us, the Poles, a glance. 'Oh comrade, if only you knew', was what I thought. He blended perfectly into the countryside, the changing countryside, which had once been as proud as he, a grenadier. We were both sacrifices of a changing world.

We always returned to Breslau as the evening came, returning to the suffocation of the city, tired from the day's outing, leaving the wide open spaces of the country, to return to a city of ruined facades. Sleep often evaded me, after those trips, for I was always reminded of those former battlefields of Deutsch-Lissa, Leuthen and Saara and my comrades who I had left behind. I had up to a point successfully veiled my military past from the Russians and the Poles. I knew that even when my German friends and acquaintances were told, that my past was safe with them. They would never give me away. Elzbieta also believed my version about my past, at least she behaved as if she did.

There was however, someone who began to doubt my story, probably because he was a young member of the militia. He knew that I should have registered myself as a DP long before. Another reason that he had a 'pique' of me, was because of a woman, an acquaintance in whom I did not have the slightest interest, but he thought otherwise. He wanted me out of the way. He saw a rival in me, he was jealous, and that was a dangerous situation. He was convinced that she liked me more than him. But when the truth was known, she was not interested in his advances. He accused me of being one of the Waffen SS. I had no choice but to treat him to some aggression and tell him to accompany me to the local commander, to clear the matter. At that point the said German lady intervened, and threw out the lovesick gallant. I disappeared too, never to be seen again.

The hopes that a peace treaty would ensure that German nationals could stay in the now Polish-controlled eastern territories, gradually disappeared. It did not materialise for those Germans still in Breslau. It never came. The ethnic-cleansing programme carried on as usual and even my friends in Lützowstrasse, the Laskas, had to admit this reality, with a heavy heart even demanding their expatriation. Naturally enough I wanted to go with them when our district appeared on the list, for there was nothing to keep me now in Breslau, i.e. in Polish Wroclaw.

I had of course to tell Elzbieta of my decision. I did this as carefully as I could one day as we bathed in the Ole. She had expected and dreaded it happening. She begged me to stay or at least delay my departure. My brief explanation was not enough to convince her of the danger I was in. So I decided that I had to tell her the whole truth. Perhaps then she would understand. She did not. I showed her the buckle on my leather belt, a part of my uniform. But she had already guessed that I was not just the foreign worker that I made out to be. She made it difficult, she made me feel guilty. I believed that her clinging affection was just a part of a temporary affair between two young people. She could not accept the position that I was in. Not even when I showed her that the eagle insignia on my jacket was not on the left-hand breast but worn on the left arm, as worn by the SS. It made no impression on her. She wanted me to stay. Having done this, I had to beg of her, as a Polish citizen, for my protection. In tears, she swore she would give me protection. Her love and her bravery really touched me, but I thought it could not be real. The situation was decided for me, for us, when she and her family were moved once more. They were forced to return to Lemberg and that ended our liaison.

My worst fears after being discharged as a prisoner became reality on the morning of a warm and sunny day when my freedom ended. I was in Feldstrasse when three uniformed and armed members of the militia stopped me and asked me for my identity papers. One of them held a passport photo in his hands and looked at my face intently and then I was forced to go with them to their commander. The passers-by stopped and looked at us as we made our way through Klosterstrasse. One of the Poles had a rifle over his shoulder and another of them a cocked Russian machine-pistol. Other people just stole a cursory anxious glance at us. Upon being recognised by the Germans, the word soon went around that 'the Dutchman' has been arrested.

We stopped at number 120 in Klosterstrasse, at a large house 'Bethanian House', which was the Polish command post. I was thrown into a dark cellar room, without a word of explanation or questions. The concrete floor was flooded with water, several inches deep. I tripped into it, soaking my shoes and socks. Perhaps it was the first softening-up process for the arrested. It must have been about an hour later that I was collected and taken to the second floor. There I stood in my wet socks and protested, in front of a Pole, who had a cap of Russian origin sitting sloppily on the back of his head. He was sitting behind a large kitchen table, with files on top of it, a newspaper and what else? A bottle of vodka and water glass. His jargon was for me 'double-Dutch' and I didn't understand a single word that he uttered. I only saw that he glanced continually at the passport photo and then at me. It was a man of about my age, but who wore glasses, which I didn't need to wear. I was then suddenly ordered into the next room. It was an ante-room, with people coming and going, all in uniform, all in a hurry, and who took not the slightest bit of notice of me.

I was uptight with worry for days. On that day I had a double identity on me, which could have been my undoing. I had my Russian discharge paper on me, as well as my foreign worker's paper, which had not been discovered. The state security police from the UB had not searched me up to that point. It had to disappear! I decided that I must eat it. Before I could however, a German cleaning lady crossed my path, and I asked her if she would take this *corpus delicti* to the Laskas for me. It was a risk, but the dear lady did what I asked of her and delivered it to the Laskas some little time later.

With that done, I now had to see to it that I left the house. After waiting a while I seized my chance, by walking out casually behind a militiaman, leaving the room as close on his heels as possible. No one noticed. He went downstairs, so did I. He left the house and so did I, with the guard on the door standing to attention, thinking just what I wanted him to think and that was that we were together. For the next week I was in another 'cell' at the cloisters, and was given the best of service from the Father Prior. The Poles seldom enquired after refugees at the cloisters, and when a prisoner escaped, then they arrested someone else. It was as simple as that.

That short spell of arbitrary justice, even only for a few hours, together with the very uncertain future in Breslau that I saw, strengthened my will to leave. My existence there became more dangerous and risky by the day. Far too many people knew that I had been a soldier. One false slip from someone could have given me away, and produced a catastrophe, which neither I nor they wanted. I had, after all, fought against a system which then reigned. I was delivered, but without any protection. In between times not even Jews were exempt from Polish arbitrary justice, and were fair game for the Polish authorities. "Under the Nazi régime in Poland during the war, anti-semitic comments about the liquidation of the Jews grew, with thoughtless approval, at a fast rate. It was not the opinion of individuals, but of the majority of the Polish people". (*Der Vertriebenen*, 1957)

It was about 11 o'clock on 12 June, on the corners of Lützow and Klosterstrasse, that it happened. Everything in my life, at that point, which was dull and cloudy, blew away. I actually thanked my lucky stars, on that warm and sunny day, that 'lady luck' had guided my footsteps to Breslau. In talking to a Polish 'handler', I noticed dark brown locks of hair bobbing on the shoulders of their owner. She was a young attractive girl, dressed in a light blue anorak. In that moment I was spellbound. I was fascinated in seconds, by this slim and lovely being who appeared to be from another world. So much so, that I simply had to get to know her. My bartering came to a very abrupt end and I followed her.

To my immediate dismay, my introductory routine with girls was to prove useless this time. Well, perhaps I should not have been surprised. Convinced that she was German, I should also have known that she could not possibly think that this foreign-speaking nobody was very pro-German. I could not hide my accent, nor the colourful cockade on my lapel. Nor could she know my problems in that precarious time of terror and harassment against the Germans. She had every right to be suspicious and more than a little irritated at my advances. When I had a chance, then I would have to prove to her that my intentions were pure. So why not with my identity? I bared my soul, my past, and my army career in fighting on the side of the Germans, to this lovely maiden. Her mistrust and irritation disappeared. She appeared regal to me, untouchable. I realised that relaxed flirting with her was out of place. I did not even think of it, for this was so different, so very different. I had never been struck so heavily by 'cupid's dart', as now. I was so happy that I could have stormed the heavens. Friedrich Schiller's words came to me, spoke to me, from his verse, "the first love, a golden time, when eyes look into open heavens".

All my experiences in the past, both good and bad, were now null and void, since the starry hours that began since my meeting with Brigitte. That was the name of this twenty-year old. I was underway to fulfilling the intimations of the Laska family, that I should take a 'momento' home with me. It was a 'momento' from Breslau, from the war, from Germany. It was a 'bounty-packet' in the shape and form of a bride.

We met every day thereafter, when Brigitte's work allowed. For like all other Germans, she had to work for the Poles. Her employees were just like Elzbieta's parents. Mr and Mrs Markowitz, Congress Poles, were a very friendly pair, owners of a colonial-ware shop and waiting to go to America. They wanted to take Brigitte with them as an adopted daughter.

I always picked her up from the shop in Feldstrasse, and with every day I knew that I had found my partner for life, beyond any doubt. We sauntered for hours on end, from one corner of her birthplace to another, and in all the surrounding areas.

Those warm June days spent with Brigitte, were the most wonderful of my life, spiced only with a kiss or two, although we became so close that after only a short time, we knew what the other was thinking. There was no need for our love for one another to be put into words. It appeared to me that our souls were totally bound together. Soon, I started to talk about marrying. Later, although under different circumstances, that was to be utopia.

Brigitte's skin was as brown as her eyes, but this did not come from a beauty spa. It came from forced labour in the fields around Liegnitz, under the Russians. It was some 50 kilometres west of Breslau, where she had been evacuated with her mother, in January 1945. She too had experienced the exodus in the snow, ice and 20° below freezing. She had seen uncountable people die, including her mother who died from dysentery shortly after their arrival. Now as a total orphan, Brigitte stood there totally alone and under the 'victors' wrath. The drunken Russian soldiers, frustrated at the long and tough defence of Breslau, often vented their spleen on those defenceless German citizens. Those whom they did not transport away, were put to work in the fields under the old Russian motto "no work, no food".

Brigitte could not forget the plight of the horses when following the plough, for all had wounds, from bullets or shrapnel and their wounds had never been attended to. When horses failed then the Germans were saddled with their work and they had to pull the ploughs and farrows, like Volga boat-people, pulling their barges. She was one of the lucky ones, for she could in the first few weeks of the occupation avoid the raping that was customary, together with other young girls. They could hide themselves, quite successfully, in a hole in a mountain of coke that they made, in the grounds of a nursery. Not only at nights, but also by day they fled to this haven of safety, where they stayed, freezing and still as mice, and were fed at nights by the older women. Only those who had experienced Bolshevism, such as I, with the motivation of leaving my home to fight against it, can understand its system.

In July of 1945, Brigitte returned to Breslau to find her parents' home in ruins. In October she was ill with typhus, which she survived in spite of the fact that medical attention for Germans was a catastrophe. Many died of typhus. One could say that we were both orphaned, for I did not know if my family had survived or not. My last communication from them was at the end of 1944. This ethnic-cleansing programme of the Poles was now to rob her of her homeland.

Far quicker than we wanted, she and all the Germans had to leave their district on 22 June. It broke our hearts and made us happy at the same time, that one of us could turn our backs on that Polish commercial and economic management. Our happiness was however tinged with worry, for the expelled could decide nothing for themselves, including where they wanted to go. They were forced to go where they were sent, be it to the West, or to the Communist Eastern zones of Germany. It had been a journey that decided life or death in many cases. Thousands had already died, in the middle of December, in conditions that could be compared to cattle transport. It was important that the Silesians were sent on their way. 1,600 had been

They found happiness in a city hostile to Germans (and their former soldiers): Brigitte and Hendrik.

given a loaf of bread and a herring as provision for the journey, which had taken a week. In temperatures of 20–25° below, they were herded into cattle-wagons, which were unheated and with no toilet facilities. They arrived in Potsdam, in Brückenburg, in the Western zones with 35 dead. After being delivered into hospital, a further 141 died from the results of pneumonia, heart attacks or the results of freezing.

My hopes for her well-being were realised when receiving a letter from Brigitte from Detmold, which was in the British zone. The journey in goods and cattle-wagons had taken eight days, but she had survived the stress. In

Görlitz and on German soil, but under Communist direction, the wagons were directed on to other tracks, so that the expelled could be plundered once more, of the last that they possessed. My medals, which Brigitte had hidden in balls of wool, had not been found.

In Breslau, things were moving on for the Laskas and myself, for we had registered with the German charitable Organisation 'Caritas'. At the same time, I presented my Russian discharge papers and was accepted as any other German soldier, although I was Dutch. My BVB paper was not shown because of the danger of a DP classification, and deportation to Holland.

For some inexplicable reason, our deportation was delayed and I was already thinking about deporting myself out of Breslau and undertaking a one-man journey to the Western zones. My friends talked me out of the idea, telling me that it was a very dangerous mission and could cost me my life. So I waited. We waited throughout July, August and September, and it was on the 30th that we were ordered to leave. We could take 25 kilos of possessions with us.

With stamps and cardboard stickers on our chests, we left to form a queue under Polish control, and marched to the Freiburger railway station. Before we left, Mrs Laska had run her soft hands over every piece of her furniture in her home. In tears she caressed each piece that had given years of service to her and her family. I, in my happiness at leaving, did not at that time understand her deep feelings at the loss of her treasures. Only later, after slowly collecting my own possessions laboriously together, did I understand. The keys were then taken from the inside of the locks, placed on the outside, and we left.

The Poles did not have enough intelligence to realise that they were expelling the best of their 'milk-cows' and 'cutting their noses off to spite their faces!' They did not comprehend that the industrious hands of the Germans and their knowledge of the economy of their land was something that they did not possess, and perhaps never would.

The militia, armed with German rifles, screamed their orders at the throngs of people, with gestures that drove the column through the streets to the station. They showed no sympathy. The pram of Mrs Laska's daughter was snatched away from her, shortly before she climbed into the train. Most were in tears having sunk to the depths of depression, because of that act, the worst act of man against his fellow man. The Poles drove the people into the wagons laid with straw, but which were now overflowing, then into the goods and cattle wagons. Toilet arrangements were left for them to arrange from inside.

One's wits were a valuable asset in those moments, for we were by now well acquainted with the greed of those non-capitalists. The Laska family and I had the joy of outwitting them, at the last minute, with my plan, 'Operation Janka'. My own baggage consisted of a rucksack and a cardboard box which I gave to the Laska family just before reaching the station. Surreptitiously I removed myself from the throng, unnoticed by the militia. I made my way to one of the exit points at Lützowstrasse, to where another fully laden cart was parked, which I took. I rejoined the last third of the column and reached the first control point, which I passed through without any problem. I rejoined my waiting friends with the additional freight. They were overjoyed at the 'trick of war' against the Poles. It was a grotesque comedy. It was the joy of the 'little' man, that he could rob a kilo or two from the robbers themselves.

Just before the wagons started to move, a young blonde girl ran along the platform, calling someone's name. To my great surprise it was Elzbieta Markowitz, who was looking for me. Being Polish, she had been allowed to enter the station briefly and she looked so happy at finding me. She had found out somehow that I was among the deportees on that day. "Till we meet again, Hendrik", she said, giving me packets in which I found pork-dripping sandwiches and cigarettes. It was all so hurried. Rather choked by her gesture, all I could say was "farewell little Elzbieta", as the over-long train gave a jerk and started to steam out of the station.

The train puffed its way through the suburbs, spraying sparks into the air as evening started to fall. We chugged past masses of green-covered ruins, in the direction of the West. We had fought so bitterly, not so long ago, in those streets. We passed churches in whose graveyards the past generations of my fellow passengers slept under centuries-old stone crosses.

Our wagon was full to overflowing. There was very little room to sit. In the past I was accustomed to the usual military phrase 'the wagons must roll to victory' when we used them as our military transport. But we had it far better then, for we could and did open the door, dangle our legs over the side, and move around freely. We could not do it on that journey, which could take perhaps a week, because the Poles had sealed the wagons from the outside.

CHAPTER 20

In the Eastern Zone

The sound of the wheels was a monotone taking the exiles with every turn of those wheels, further and further away from their homeland.

From a small ventilator in the roof our wagon, I could see the flat fields, green woods and the decorative farmhouses, now threatened with dereliction. I could understand only too well, the bitterness of my fellow passengers, for this land had found its way into my heart too. The fate of Silesia had been a turning point in my life, particularly in Breslau. There I had fought my last battle against Bolshevism, been wounded, taken prisoner and became a civilian once more. The 24 hours' respite had grown into a year, one with falsified papers, and an adventurous one at that. Above all I had met a young woman whom I could not wait to see once more, and who, with luck, would become my wife.

We made a stop in Sagan, another in Forst, where we were deloused, and then again Görlitz. After another two days, we reached Zittau, but we were not in the Western zone. Our train rolled over the railway bridge spanning the river Neisse, into the farthest most easterly corner and the Soviet zone in Zittau, in Saxony. Lorries, one after the other then drove us to a regimental barracks, a transit camp. Not even rested from the stress of the journey, we had to assemble on the square the next morning. There we were forced to hear a welcoming speech from the representative of the Socialist Party of Germany, the SED. Worn out, cold and apathetic nearly 2,000 of us stood, huddled together and surrounded by Communist red flags. Degradation was on the agenda that day. After all that we had been through, we were forced to hear that we should be grateful, grateful that we had been freed from the yoke of Fascism, and by the peace-loving Communist Josef 'Uncle Joe' Stalin. This Saxon had perhaps more to say but his insulting comment had met questions of disbelief from the brave as they asked "Freed from WHAT? our house and home!" So he cut his speech short, but not before he turned the knife and welcomed the future German/Soviet friendship, before he disappeared and we were put into quarantine. We were therefore not allowed to leave the camp for the next fourteen days.

It was on the second day that I found the hole in the fence and took myself off on a one-man recce into the city. Once upon a time Zittau had been a beautiful city, with its Renaissance and Baroque architecture and buildings and their decorated portals. Now it could only be described as something similar to 'a worker's paradise'. The shops were empty, and I mean of goods. They did have window decoration, made up of empty boxes, offering the thick layers of dust for free. The Zittauer went on their way, when they were to be seen, in streets that had not seen a street cleaner in many a month. The women did not appear to be any different to the Russian women except that they were not so stout and round. In fact, when you took a glance at their faces under the headscarf that they all wore, you could see sad and empty eyes, small mouths and hollow cheeks. They were quite haggard. I bought and wrote a postcard to Brigitta, and then made my way back to the camp, using the hole in the fence once more.

All of the deportees wanted to leave this camp as quickly as possible, for here in Saxony it was situated far too near the Czechoslovakian and Polish borders, but they had no say in the matter. The occupying forces were responsible for our distribution. Just as the 'little soldier' was never informed of military strategy, we for instance didn't even know the destinations of the transport, when leaving that transit point.

In 1946, on 29 October, a National Census took place, and alone in the western zones, 1,622,907 Silesians were to be found, mostly in Lower Saxony (626,087) and Bavaria (434,281). In the Eastern zones there were 1.3 million.

The results of deportation, evacuation, and illegal transportation of east Germans, were even beyond the imagination of the occupying forces. So much so, that Sir Orme Sargent, State Secretary of the Foreign Office in London declared that "it is unbelievable that the Germany of today can solve the resettlement problem of 14 million of their starving people. For me, it is beyond my imagination".

A Commission, the 'Papal Protectors for Refugees', declared that "the Germans have to master a problem, the like of which has never ever before existed in world history. Such an exodus robbing such a mass of people of house, home and existence has never ever taken place, and at such short notice".

When one assesses that 8,000 people can occupy a small town, then one can imagine that a small town arrived every single day, somewhere in Bavaria. In Hesse alone, 67,000 were counted in one month as 'new citizens'. The transport brought the dead too. The Councillor of Control, attached to the German Evangelist Church, and the Allies, described the situation as of "half-starved, exhausted to the point of death, they arrive, having been robbed on the way of everything that they possessed". And it happened in peacetime!

Germany performed the impossible, however, due to the discipline and will to work of the war generation. Germany absorbed all of the refugees from the east, not in a day, but in a few years. Their industriousness also produced a boom. It was an economic and industrial wonder.

This massive absorption was not without its problems. There were many who were irritated, overworked, and tearing their hair at the organisation belonging to this enormous overwhelming problem. It was particularly serious in the Western zones, where four million houses had disappeared. There were so many refugees who had to be given a home in amongst those who already existed. This was not very diplomatic, particularly when you did not have a 'say in the matter'. In his book *Die Vertriebenen*, Siegfried Kogelfranz reports that particularly in Bavaria, a wave of 'religious pilgrimages' started. That meant that without the owners at home, their houses could not be inspected for spare rooms, or space for refugees or house-mates. When the dear Lord did not 'help' those unfortunates, those stout believers in Jesus Christ, then they 'helped themselves' out of their plight and bricked-up spare rooms or excess space, wallpapered over, and were therefore not encumbered with 'guests'.

The situation had to be resolved by force from the local mayor or the police, so Brigitte reported to me. Such was the situation in the village where she was evacuated, near Detmold. The very sorry truth of the matter was that upon arrival, and as fellow-Germans, in Germany, they found that they were not wanted by their own people. "What is mine, is mine!" was the attitude, and those who possessed nothing were ostracised by those others who had plenty. The Westphalian farmers were well nourished. They had survived the war without drastic bombing raids in the region. They viewed the eastern deportees as 'lousy gypsies from the East', interlopers, who should have stayed where they were. Such behaviour was however, not the rule. When there was a hard case of resistance, Allied Regulation No.18 came into force. It allowed the refugees to occupy a place to stay in the absence of the house-owner.

Our quarantine period was coming to an end and immediately the Laska family was transported to Taucha, near Leipzig. That was not where I wanted to go, in an area for the masses. I myself had no ties at that moment, so I decided that perhaps I had to give my fate a helping hand. The farewell to the Laska family was very hard for me, for they had become my beloved family.

The experiences of the last few years washed over me. I had met brave and frightened people. Friendliness, faithfulness and the dark side of human nature, all had been mixed with suffering, destruction and death. In the middle of it all, I had found love, founding the very strong will to survive. This will, in the striving for a little luck in life, could not be broken.

Before I had left Breslau, Inge Rudolph, the wife of the company commander that I had had in Pomerania had offered me a home, in her birthplace Finsterwald. That was in case we lost the War and I could not return home to Holland. I had written to her as soon as I had arrived in Zittau, and by 13 October, her husband, Hermann, brought me the necessary settlement permit for the area of Finsterwald. At that time, this permit was the most treasured and necessary that a man could possess, for without it you did not receive a ration-card.

Hermann lived with Inge 'in sin', or a 'wild' marriage which had nothing wild about it, for it was one without a marriage certificate, and he lived there under another name. He had escaped from a POW camp following some dangerous adventures. No one knew that he was not Inge's legal husband (in those times it would have been a scandal) or that he had been a former Waffen SS officer. We had no inhibitions in deceiving the absurd and bureaucratic 'collective' régime that masses of others also sought to avoid.

The excessive number of criminals now found within the Communist authorities was just as much of a scandal. It did not need a very high intelligence on our part to hide our identity or our past from them. In my case, I had been a Dutchman under the Poles and now, I was a German with the Christian name of Heinz.

I lived with Inge and Hermann in a room at the back of their house, which was warm and comfortable, the warmth coming from the traditional tiled stove. Inge was well-known since her childhood, which was not so surprising, for her family's textile business could be found on the market square. It had been one of the leading businesses for the last 100 years. It was highly respected, the reason for the very quick settlement permit when one had contacts!

It did not take long for me to find a circle of friends who shared my own tastes. Tastes? With that I mean in beliefs and convictions, all having been part of the young war generation, growing up in the Third Reich, and not being able to throw off its fascination. On top of this, the shock of losing the war ran deep. They would tell you that they did not feel freed, or even agreed that they had been, but that they had been betrayed of their ideals. Added to this was the brutal régime of the Soviets, which did nothing to bridge the gap between them and their convictions, and most certainly did not make them change sides! The continual defamation of the German soldier from the occupiers hardened their attitudes, beyond any doubts. We were soon to become just as much of a conspiratorial band, a corps bound together, as that which I had found in Breslau.

This new chapter in my life did not bring a new routine into it, for we were all hungry. When you needed something as nourishment, then your empty stomach had to groan until you found something to eat, which usually meant travelling for miles around. It was a catastrophe when the distance to the local farms was just too far for a bicycle ride. It sometimes resulted in going away empty-handed, because the farmers had nothing themselves. Then you had to take the train, which meant special permission. I had no trouble in obtaining this special permit for a long train journey in 1946 in those Eastern zones. I obtained a permit at the office of the 'Antifa', because I was a representative of the firm of Inge's parents, and I went on buying trips for them. This process was not however possible without a certain 'denazification' procedure.

I travelled with a rucksack and a cardboard case filled with textiles as exchange wares, just as I had in Breslau at the junction of Scheitniger Star. I was once more 'king' of the road and the barter business. My expenses from the firm did not run to anything like a good square meal on the way. It was nothing more than a potato cooked in its jacket and spiced with a little salt. This *pomme de terre* was cold, the carriage was cold and my fingers were blue with the cold. I ate it usually just after the train rolled out of the station, in the hope that I could replace it with something edible from the farmer, on arrival. There was no heating in the train, for many a window was broken, or did not have any glass in it at all. Many were provisionally repaired with cardboard or wood but the wind whistled through the carriages nonethe less. Others could not be moved, up or down, because the leather strap for this had been cut off by passengers and taken away, most probably to sole a pair of shoes.

The whole population was now a caravan of merchants, all travelling hundreds of miles for corn, flour, potatoes or apples, anything to fill those groaning stomachs. Perhaps if one was lucky, one took possession of a bundle of dried tobacco leaves, for a puff or two. In every carriage of the train, small textile or household businesses were represented with tools, saucepans or an iron, rugs, underwear or suits as exchange wares for the farmers.

Such train journeys were not without danger and led to many accidents. A permit most certainly did not ensure you a seat. Every inch of the train was used as one, be it by climbing on to the roof, sitting on the buffers, or clinging for dear life on to door handles whilst standing and journeying on the running-board. All the ways were as dangerous as the other. For those on the roof, a tunnel meant lying flat and holding on tight in order that you were not blown away. For this far from luxurious method of travel, I invested in a pair of motorbike goggles against the soot and black smoke from the steam-engine, not only to protect my eyes, but in order to see better. When I found that there was no seat for me, then I always favoured the buffers between the carriages, where there was a little protection against the wind.

A situation that I experienced in Berlin is burned into my memory. For me it represented the basic instincts of man and took place in the almost destroyed transit station. At 11 o'clock at night, the station looked like something out of the Balkans, or a soldiers' camp. Everywhere were bodies, men and women snatching sleep, with their arms tightly holding the treasures of that day against thieves. All were waiting for the next train, which departed at three in the morning.

As the train slowly rolled into the roofless station, there was an eruption of movement and a flood of people stormed the train. People shoved, people were pushed, elbowed and all fought for a place on the train. They screamed and fought one with another like animals. One man I saw paid the penalty of using his ingenuity, climbing in through a window, half in and half out, someone saw the opportunity of a lifetime and, from behind, helped him out of his shoes. Decent behaviour or consideration, if brought up with it, was in this situation worthless. One had to reduce yourself to that basic instinct just like everyone else.

Another time I had to journey home on the running board of the train and experienced at first hand the depths that basic instincts sink to when hungry and in need, from people in despair. I hung on, with my precious bundle strongly held between my knees. The quality of coal was not the best and public transport suffered. Second-grade coke fired the furnaces of the steam-trains and this poor quality showed itself when pulling a heavy load uphill or around bends. The train puffed its way nearly to a standstill. Those standing with their treasures on the outside of the train, were subjects of attack, from people who had reconnoitred and were standing at those points, armed with long sticks with hooks. They tried their best to snatch whatever they could away from you. Many a bundle changed hands this way, in trying to ward off the attacks with hefty kicks.

One of my journeys to Berlin forced me into the lions den, i.e. the Dutch Consulate. I had enough cheek to ask for one of those CARE packets, even as a bogus 'displaced person.' It was dangerous being on 'Dutch soil', so to speak, I could have been arrested, but nothing ventured, nothing gained, and I was not asked for any proof identity. As a German soldier I had no right to this treasured parcel, a 'generous gesture' from America. But my cheek paid off and I walked out of the Consulate with one under my arm. So it should not be wondered at, when some time later I was ordered to register myself in Berlin, for my name was on a wanted list. I was accused of entering foreign service without the permission of Her Majesty. That 'Her Majesty' had deserted her land and her people, whereas I had defended both from Communism, would not be a debatable point or argument, and so I ignored this.

I was deeply moved by the sight of the city of Berlin, the old capital city of the Third Reich. No matter in which direction one looked its destruction stretched for miles and miles. In the Zoo there was not one tree standing. It was nothing more than the bones now of the capital that it had once been. Bones that had been licked clean of its charm, culture, and its beautiful facades. Stripped of its character it stood derelict from horizon to horizon. Berlin had died, been mercilessly killed. The former American Consul for Germany, Vernon Walters, on a visit in October 1945, declared that "Not even the war damage that I saw in Italy can compare with that which I have now seen in Berlin. It resembles a crushed skull".

German discipline and industriousness came to the fore, an example shown by the *Trummer-Frauen*. They were the women who for nearly six years, had hidden in cellars by night to survive the bombing of the Allies. They had taken over the important work left behind by their soldier husbands. At the same time they brought up their children. They showed the world that it was time for a new start. They sorted half a brick here, a whole one there, and threw them into piles. From houses that had once been, they were now symbols of reconstruction.

I only learned later about the battle for Berlin. I heard from French volunteers, who had like me, volunteered to fight against Communism and who, in Kolberg and especially in Berlin had given their last drop of sweat and blood for the cause. Their sacrifice is without comparison. In the centre of Berlin, it was the 'Charlemagne' who fought to their last man and destroyed sixty enemy tanks. The American historian Cornelius Ryan reports in his book, *The Last Battle*, that nearly 100,000 women were raped in Berlin, by Russian soldiers. A further 6,000 committed suicide rather than live under the rule of the Bolshevik régime. At that time the 'missing persons' list increased out of all proportion, as the people of Berlin were dragged from their homes by the Reds and transported away to the East.

I was to experience the extreme contrast of misery and amusement at that time. Hundreds froze and starved in the extremely cold winter of 1946/47. The old people were the sacrifices, not having the strength to trudge cross-country with a rucksack for their needs. That was one side of the picture and the other presented itself in the amusement of the newly presented American way of life. I ventured one evening to the area around the railway station, 'Berlin Zoo', to take a look for myself. Already in the early evening I heard the 'swing and jazz' oozing from the murky underground bars and clubs. It was an offence to the ears of every normal German. They were newly formed in the cellars of the houses. In those bars, a bottle of whisky cost the princely sum of 800 marks. The well-nourished 'kings of the black market' enjoyed the spoils of their unscrupulous business deals. Needless to say, there were the highly made-up madams, who were willing to hop around, to 'jitter-bug' with the crew-cut styled and sweat-bathed GIs in an ecstasy of wild movement, which released all their inhibitions.

The 'black' market in the Scheitniger-Stern was harmless in comparison to Berlin, for it was strictly forbidden. Forbidden or not, it flourished. The people were in dire need and already there were new selling spots for one's dealings, be it in house doorways, or an abandoned bus, or a cellar. Once more everything was there. Once more, the 'man in the street' could not afford the prices. When one was caught scheming and dealing, then one could expect the hardest of sentences from the authorities. Everyone took the risk, for they had no other choice. It was a code of honour to procure what one could for the simplest or the most urgent of needs. Prison was the result. More than once I came close to this, although I never had any 'hot wares' on my person.

This happened in Berlin, Dresden and in Leipzig, where police sirens were to be heard. Police in old *Wehrmacht* uniforms dyed black stormed out of lorries, together with Russian soldiers in jeeps. The streets were very quickly cordoned off encircling the innocent as well as the scheming dealers. One had to be like the wind to escape. One had to be fit in order to be far quicker than they. I thanked my lucky stars for my sports training as a soldier, that life-saving training for the battlefield. This was also a battlefield, but of another sort and the ruins gave plenty of cover.

One should not be too critical of the 'black' market, however much one thinks it criminal and unjust. It was however the only possibility one had of surviving the drastic conditions that reigned, and more drastic they could not have been. This 'black' market forced the last ten pounds of potatoes or carrots out of the farmers' cellars. The only commodity one could not buy for one's welfare was coal.

It was a very hard winter, with polar conditions in 1946/47, with the same below freezing temperatures of 20–25° that we had experienced in Silesia and Russia. People not only starved to death, but they froze too, some not being able to fend for themselves. They died by the dozen. The goods section of the railway station in Berlin was guarded like Fort Knox, to avoid the theft of fuel brickettes which were now worth more than gold. The thieves, professionals and or simply fathers of children, were now forced to thieve whilst the goods train was in motion. Sometimes they found outlying stations where they could uncouple a whole wagon on a dark night, and empty it of its contents. Those goods were meant for the Russian Army and the warmth of their soldiers. The joy of the 'little German man' was therefore doubled and trebled, for why should they be the only ones who were warm? So they joined the bands of thieves, wheelers and dealers, who were to be found in the whole of the land. "Steal what you can" was the word in those days.

The normal citizen yearned for an orderly way of life. The Soviets put the pressure on, spraying the land with psychological terror, in the form of political propaganda, such as "learn from the Soviet Union to be victorious", or "Long live Stalin, the best friend of the German people". The media were also involved in this brainwashing, particularly in films, in which the German soldier, the *Wehrmacht* was always the cowardly rogue. Russian actors roared in mime, depicting simple and naive Teutons with helmets sitting crookedly on the backs of their heads, in a stupor from alcohol. Was it an interpretation based on their own behaviour? The Waffen SS were to be seen in the field, in their black parade dress, naturally with white-blond hair, their eyes in a bestial gaze as they took part in erotically sadistic torture of a lovely lady member of the Russian partisans. Naturally enough this lady held the Russian flag high in not giving anything away. It was distasteful and the worst sort of propaganda, but so apt coming from the Communists. They however were not the only ones.

Already at the end of the thirties, incitement against the German race started in America. They too used their film industry for their propaganda, with one of 'those nasty Germans' replacing one of 'those nasty Red Indians'. Uncountable numbers of those films flooded the screens in the western zones after 1945. Everyone could see spine-chilling and gruesome stories on celluloid, for the brainwashing had begun on the screen!

The American high command possessed, of all things, a Psychological Department! The Chief of this department readily admitted having manipulated and falsified stories, including parts of Hitler's speeches.

Upon her arrival in Detmold and before I had left Breslau, Brigitte had written to my parents on my behalf. Her letter was the first contact with my parents in which she could but did not mention my name, although she informed them that I was alive and well, and that we were befriended. One must remember that letters were censored. It was in September 1946 that she received an answering letter, from my younger brother Cornelis. He had written that every member of my family had been interned. He wrote that under no circumstances was I either to return to Holland or even write to my family. Those few words confirmed my fears and my opinions of the political situation back in my homeland. A second letter was to arrive in Detmold. This time it was from my eldest sister Louisa and contained very sad news for me. Brigitte had to inform me that I had lost two very dear members of my family, my father and one of my brothers, the eldest.

My father had died just a few weeks before she had received the first letter from Cornelis. He had died in the Dutch Internment camp in Amersfoort on 27 August. There were only bare facts because of the censorship. Therefore there were no details on the death of my brother Jan, other than that he had died eighteen months before in Assen, on 3 March. I had seen both, for the last time, two and a half years before, but had heard nothing from my family since the end of 1944. My brother Jan was just 27 years old when he died. The news was very bitter for me, very painful. My father had died in an internment camp at the age of 62. For days I could only read and re-read those few lines. I turned to stone trying to imagine the cause of his death, for those lines filled me with fear. For days this brought me to tears trying to assess the cause of death of both my father and my brother. And I could not go home? I could not write? I could not give any support in what had to be a terrible time, for the ominous warning from Cornelis had been clear enough. It was only later that I was to learn of the dimensions of the tragedy, of the Odyssey that my parents, my five brothers and my two sisters had had to suffer in my absence.

My longing to go to my family was replaced with that of wanting to go to Brigitte and it gave me no peace. However, she warned me against a visit to her in the British zone. It was too dangerous. Thousands however had managed to escape from the Russian zone, and from the organisation of their distribution. They wanted to escape from Communist rule, and did so in such numbers, that on 5 July 1946 the borders were closed. One could only travel from one zone to another with a special permit and by train. This 'inter-zone' permit was impossible to obtain.

Despite being trapped 'behind the Iron Curtain', a term first used by Joseph Goebbels and which was thereafter used also by Winston Churchill, there were escape routes, but one had to find them. I had to find them, for I was not going to be deterred from my visit to Detmold. With a map, and advice on a possible route, I started an illegal journey over the border, to an area that was called the 'Green Border' and checkpoint. It was still dangerous, despite its description, but did not have a minefield, barbed wire, or the wide coverless strip called the Death Strip, in full view of the guards. There were however patrolling Russian guards.

Such spots were well-known to the German Police on the other side, and by criminals too. Particularly in the winter of 1946/47, there was heavy criminal activity at the checkpoints, leading even to murder. Criminals, released from German prisons and concentration camps, returned to their former professions that had put them there in the first place. They lurked in the darkness to rob the refugees of all that they had. They were all using the protection of the popular 'politically prosecuted' status.

I had not known any of this as I arrived in the British zone at the end of October. My route had taken me through Berlin, Magdeburg and Halberstadt. There, prior to reaching the station, the train stopped, having used up all of the coal allowed for the journey. The passengers had to alight from the train and walk the rest of the way along the railway tracks. So far, so good. I was in the Harz region and the next stop was Dedeleben, which I reached through thickly wooded slopes, on foot. In the railway station there I had a wait of ten hours, before the next train left at two in the morning. In order to hold on to the little that I had with me, I hooked my bags through my trouser belt as I slept. Dedeleben was the end of the line, with no other connections to the West, and so there were few using the train. Those that did, were like me, on their way to the 'green border'. I found out the way after requesting directions from the railway porter, on leaving the train at five in the morning.

We were a group of around 30 people. All were heavily laden, like mules, with bulging rucksacks, baby-prams and little carts. I looked, with my coloured and checked coat from Breslau, like a pauper in contrast. It just seemed to happen that I became group-leader, possibly because of my orienteering talent. I warned the others of obstacles and Russian patrols, although I did not know exactly where we were going. Our route away from this 'iron curtain' was not easy, and more than once some stumbled into holes in the ground, and our shoes and socks were wet through, for it was still dark. That was all the better for one's target, when shooting at something or someone, was harder to hit.

When on the road through the woods we could hear the sounds of motors, long before the Russian patrol lorries reached us, we had time to hide. We hid from the strong searchlights mounted on the lorries and after the pause I gave the order *Gepäck aufnehmen, ohne tritt marsch.* Not in parade-style of course, but it did not take them long before they behaved like a regular army recce patrol. Once a Russian soldier saw us, as we crossed a well-lit open space, and we heard Halt! come here!" which we ignored. The group followed my order not to stop, but to disappear as quickly as possible into the woods on the other side. There were two shots and then silence. He did not attempt to follow us, possibly because he was on his own.

We then, unbeknown to us, walked in a complete circle, not knowing that we were so close to the British zone, which we entered, and left to return to the Russian side and where we were seen by two Russian guards. The unbelievable happened, for they looked, saw and indicated with a nod of their heads, that we should continue on our way! We did.

One of the group, a woman, was much older than the others, and was exhausted. The journey and possibly the tension were so great that she wanted to give up. So I supported her for the rest of the way, while others pushed her small wooden cart, with her possessions in it. At daybreak and with the rising of the sun behind us, I knew that we were nearly at our destination. We saw a farmer on his bike, and as he approached us we asked if we were already in the British Zone and he answered in the affirmative! Not long after, at around seven in the morning, we reached the transit camp in Jerxheim, where we had a friendly reception, not from soldiers but German police, once again black-dyed *Wehrmacht* uniforms. They inspected our luggage for 'hot wares', i.e. cigarettes and alcohol. One man in our group was a handler, he was the man that had his hands already in the air as he had heard the two shots when in the woods. He had a good stock of vodka in his baggage, which was immediately confiscated.

The rest of the journey needed a lot of patience with hour-long stops between stations, ten hours in Jerxheim, and another four, via Brunswick to Hannover. It had taken the whole day until after dark. And dark it was, for the trains had no lighting, or heating. The passengers standing or sitting were cold, frozen through, and silent. Those sitting could at least warm themselves on the stranger sitting alongside. Upon looking through the window, it was dark outside. There were no lights to be seen in the country-side houses. As we chugged our way through the towns, there were no lights there either, just the ruins rising into the night sky as ghosts out of the darkness.

The main railway station in Hannover was very dimly lit, but the masses of travellers were the same, just as they had been in Berlin, with hollow cheeks and in tattered clothes. They drifted over the platforms, perhaps with hope in their heart that things would normalise, that "everything changes". Perhaps it would be today. But on that day, they appeared to me to be the driftwood of war.

I saw British soldiers, for the first time, in their khaki uniforms, walking comfortably through the grey throng, well nourished and chewing gum, as I went on my way to a bed. It had been offered to me by Jan Reilingh, the brother of my fallen friend Robert. As a student in Dresden, he had managed to land near the 'Brits' in Hannover. He now worked in a hospital, which was where he found me a place to sleep, in the boiler room in the cellar. It was not very comfortable, but it was warm! The next morning found me under way once more.

I sent a telegram from Hannover to Brigitte and it worked. Brigitte was waiting for me on my arrival. It was now nearly six months since we had seen one another and it was a very happy *wiedersehen*. Despite the food problem, Brigitte looked just the same, and at least she had found some luck over the last few months. We were happy that we had both survived the evacuation. Her first quarters in Horn-Oldendorf, she told me, had been primitive. She was given work, like all the others, in order to be given a ration-card. Her work was in a factory making wooden lamps, in Detmold. There she caught the eye of the factory owner who took her away from the factory and she now worked in his house. It was a villa where she had her own room. She was taught to cook and was well looked after.

During my stay I had a guestroom in Heiligenkirchen and we spent a lot of time walking and talking and when I accompanied her home, it was always after dark. Our feelings for one another had not changed. They intensified and there were no doubts in either of us that we were meant for one another. At the same time we both knew that I could not stay. I had managed the dangerous journey into the British zone, but I did not feel safe with the close proximity of the Dutch border. I did not feel safe with the thought that I could, when caught, be classified once more as a DP and handed over to the Dutch authorities. I had neither that very precious settlement permit in this situation, or an Inge to procure one for me. No settlement permit and no roof over my head. No roof over my head, no work, and no work meant no ration card. Brigitte had all of these in Detmold, in the land of the river Lippe, and the British zone. I had all of these too, in Finsterwald, in the Russian zone. With heavy hearts that is where we knew that I had to return. We had no other choice. We had been patient for so long, and knew that we had to be just as patient for a little longer, to see what the future held. It was cold reality and we could not alter the situation. I returned after those wonderful days in the land of the Lippe, using the same route by which I had come.

I was once more in the land of the 'Ivans' on 13 November. My return trip, on my own, had not been a problem. I had had no companions. Who wanted to return willingly to this 'Red paradise' on the other side of the Elbe?

Once more in Finsterwald, I came to the conclusion that life in the Western zones was not all that the German refugees had hoped. They did not find the quality of life that they were used to or expected, in comparison to the Stone-age 'Nirvana' to be found here in the Russian zone. Although there was no arbitrary deportation in the Western zones, 'power to the full' was well practised over the vanquished.

The power was soon to be seen in all its force, beginning on 20 November 1945 in the form of the Nuremberg Trials, which lasted for nearly a year, until October 1946. The Germans looked, waited and hoped for the truth, the whole truth and nothing but the truth, plus the resurrection of rights. They were treated to the wrath and revenge of the conquerors, decorated with a 'holier than thou' attitude in a 'show trial', in which the laws were made by the 'victors'. The prosecution was made up of the 'victors', judge and jury were 'victors' and the hangmen too. We returned to Medieval laws that were now wrapped in modern, new, and the fictitious, accompanied by the guiding principle that "those who lost the war must forfeit their lives".

Orders and obedience were crimes. The breaking of our oath was, perhaps, a mitigation. Denunciation was rewarded with the 'closing' of your case. All of the principles of law were not only ignored but were trampled into the ground by the feet of the 'victors' in Nuremberg. For example, "No sentence without lawful rights, or carrying out of orders under force", meant non-conviction. One could not be sentenced for the actions of others.

In many prisons under the Western Allies the use of torture was allowed. It was on the daily agenda, be it physical or psychological. The means justified the end. The use of manipulated gallows to 'hang' the said prisoner was one of those psychological methods. Spinal injuries and irreparable damage to the vertebrae of the neck were the result. Torture continued until the said prisoner signed a confession that had been dictated and typed beforehand by the 'victors'. No one questioned the self-same format of the hundreds of prisoners presented as evidence. Illegal Courts Martial were held within prison walls. There was blatant disregard of Church Law, using soldiers disguised as priests to hear the intimate 'confessions' of the prisoners. Nothing, but nothing was sacred and all entered the court as wrecks, with broken bones, broken spirits, abrasions or burns, to take their places in court or in the witness-box. Defence lawyers who protested at the lawless justice, were whisked away under arrest. Insight into the prosecution documents, bringing clarity, was refused. They were shipped off by the ton, to disappear and in many cases to be destroyed.

Outside the courthouse, people were starving to death. Inside the 'victors' were judging Germany's crimes against humanity. Outside, hundreds of thousands sat in prisons without any proof their crimes. Inside the 'victors' sat and judged the arbitrariness of the Germans. The sweet odour of epidemics wafted over the victims of the bombing of the 'victors' outside. Inside an International Tribunal judged the behaviour of the Germans. Meanwhile, thousands at that time were being dragged out of their homes and deported as slaves into labour camps. There they worked until they died. All of which happened in the Malmedy trial.

A Transitional Agreement was drawn up in 1954 in Paris, on 23 October, after the Declaration of Sovereignty over the *Bundesrepublik*. It stated that German jurisdiction would not be allowed to judge the crimes of the Allies. Rights? Revenge? "Don't do what I do, do what I say?" What cannot be denied is that it was not a case of "Rights for all". One has to ask what did the Nuremberg Trials alter? The answer is nothing. Most certainly it did not affect the number of wars that have taken place since 1945, and with far more sacrifices than in the Second World War. Most certainly not for the 'victors'. No one however has brought the warmongers into court.

It took twenty years before the former American Minister of Defence could admit to the world that the American government had made "a terrible mistake" with the Vietnam war! Robert McNamara used the term 'mistake' in that 58,000 American soldiers lost their lives in fighting for their fatherland. It was a 'mistake' that cost two million Vietnamese their lives? Two million?

The historian Dr Golo Mann, declared that "To research the crimes of the Allies against the Germans in Germany, is absolutely necessary for German history". I will do that.

The Americans held over three million German soldiers prisoner in the summer months of 1945, in Europe. The American General, and Commander-in-Chief of the Allies, General Dwight D. Eisenhower, who later sat in the top-most seat of the government, that of the US President, said it all when declaring, "We did not come as liberators, we came as conquerors". He never said a truer word. Liberators have no need to torture, have no need to rape and have no need to harass. Liberators possess the self-esteem to keep to the rules of human rights. They have no need to plague, or deliberately let people starve, as he did.

Dwight D. Eisenhower begrudged the prisoners a roof over their heads, begrudged the prisoners even the simplest and most meagre portion of food, even though huge reserves were available. Prisoners were given less consideration than animals that had a burrow to keep them dry and warm. Out of the rain? Protected from the sun? The prisoners on the meadows of the Rhine had none of that. They lived in holes in the ground and were forced to go there. Holes that filled with rain produced a bog. They did not even have the most primitive of sanitary conditions, which in turn produced epidemics and death, adding to that of being left to rot. Many died in the Rhineland between Remagen and Sinzig. It was a deliberate programme of extermination. It happened not only in the Rhineland, but in other places as well. Places of extermination!

An article in the magazine *Der Spiegel*, in their 40th edition from 1989, reported, "Foodstuffs, although in huge reserves, were deliberately withheld, so that the interned died. They also died from lack of hygiene and sanitary conditions, both leading to epidemics which killed". "Ten times more than those Germans who lost their lives on the battlefields of Normandy, and from then until the capitulation, died in POW camps". A quote from the former candidate for the US Presidency, Pat Buchanan said, "Nearly a million prisoners died, not only in American POW camps after 1945, but in French camps too". That quote is from the bestseller by James Bach,.

The figures are only the official ones and most certainly could be added to, but the official figures should not be used to judge or for revenge, conquerors or not. They should be used to add weight on the other side of the scales to achieve a balance that was not done in Nuremberg. There, morals, conscience and most of all justice, were non-existent, and also deliberately ignored. Can we now interpret the words from Carl von Clausewitz as, "The prisoner of war status is another form of the progress of politics"?

The war had now ended, but not in the POW camps. The German people have the key to unlocking the door of the past that is necessary for German history, necessary for the future. But those who stay 'mum', together with those who will not take a look into the past, are lost. One-sided accusation, one-sided "researched facts", and one-sided withholding of documents of historical importance in their archives, plus those who keep silent, all that has to end.

For me, it was at that time important not only to have a full stomach and a roof over my head, it was a daily battle to stay incognito and not to become one of those POWs. There were however always checkpoints and inspections of papers. It was all too easy to be noticed at these inspections and arrested. Between 1945 and as late as 1950, 122,671 Germans were to become prisoners of war. 43,000 of those died. 776 were sentenced to death, and that happened in peacetime.

In Finsterwald the same situation slowly evolved as in Breslau. The longer that I stayed, the more well-known I became, and that I had been a Dutch volunteer for the German Waffen SS. What if someone were careless with this information? This fear was always breathing down my neck and so

I moved away. I moved very near to the Laska family once more. But I was to spend the next few weeks and months in the northern part of the East zone and not in the suburbs of Leipzig.

The eldest sister of my fallen friend, Robert Reilingh, had been married to a German soldier, an officer who fell in Russia. Now being widowed, Eva Gahrmann lived in Greifswald with her parents-in-law. A circle of very nice people, her friends and family members welcomed me with open arms. Greifswald lay on the coast and had surrendered to the Russians. It had remained undamaged, possessing the oldest University in the whole of Germany, dating from 1465. It lay in a romantic setting with old gabled houses. Extreme want or need was not to be seen here, for the Gahrmann family, just like that of Inge, were the owners of a large furniture and textile business. They were respected in the vicinity. They had contacts with the farmers in the country, the academics in the University, and with the chemists in the city, who possessed alcohol, for the 'black' market. Yes, I was also the executive here, in Greifswald, in the wheeling and dealing business. I undertook the long and uncomfortable train journey from Saxony to Mecklenburg.

I had, in both the pre-war and post-war years, experienced from many people evidence of unity, and of help and support. That included the medical care of a doctor upon falling foul of malaria. It was during my second visit to Brigitte in May 1947. I detoured on the way back, calling in on friends of the Laskas and from a very short visit, I had to stay for five weeks. I was cared for by those very dear Laska friends as a refugee, and also cared for free of charge, by their doctor, Dr Schuler. The summer months of 1946 had wandered into the summer months of 1947 in the East zone. I spent wonderful days on Germany's largest island of Rügen, in the very large summerhouse belonging to the Gahrmanns. We arrived with more than enough 'black' market provisions, with friends who had journeyed with us on the train, over Stralsund and the Sound of Rügen, to Germany's largest island.

It was paradise! It was a paradise of flat land, steep cliffs, calm and raw angry seas, woods of beeches hiding moorland and labyrinths of reed. The long, long sandy beaches I remember were empty of people, and were guarded, as we bathed, by towering chalk cliffs. We never saw any Russian military. Tourists? There were none. I thought of Rügen as sitting under a large glass dome, which resisted the disturbance of the occupying government. But even there in the north there were moments that sickened and saddened, such I was to see in Bad Kleinen in the railway station.

There was a column of German prisoners standing on the platform and after counting, it was found that they were one man short. One had obviously escaped. Without much ado, one of the Russian guards snatched one of the other travellers and forced him into line with the other prisoners. Now the numbers were correct! The shocked man made no protest and neither did the passers-by who witnessed what had happened. They remained shocked and 'mum'. I protested to a German railway policeman who did not want to know. He didn't want any trouble with the army and was annoyed with me that I had the privilege of travelling the way I did, as a disabled person, i.e. war-wounded, so he took away my permit.

I had lived for a whole year in Silesia under the yoke of Polish Communism, and nearly a year under Russian Communism in the Eastern zone. But had I a future? There would never be one for me here. My intuition was at work. More than ever, I feared for my safety with each day that went by. My intuition had never let me down. I was therefore more than overjoyed when receiving a telegram from the West that was to end my 'guest status' under that 'red flag' flying in the wind.

CHAPTER 21

In the Western Zone

I received the news from Brigitte that my brother Evert had suddenly appeared in Detmold, having escaped from a forced-labour camp in a Dutch coal mine in Limberg. He had gone straight away to Brigitte. The case that was to be made against him, as a Waffen SS officer, was something that he was not going to wait for. The 'special courts' of hate, revenge and reprisals was not for him. With help from the civilian coal-workers, he managed to escape, without wire-cutters or a ladder. He was shown the way over the darkened border by Dutch smugglers in return for some 'hot' wares, i.e. cigarettes.

Now my decision was to be made, and had to be final. Brigitte was in the West, Evert was in the West, and I? The friends I had on this side of the Elbe were dear to me, but Brigitte and Evert meant far more. My decision was without any doubts. With a determination that was stronger than ever, I knew that it was time and that I must leave. My landlady in Taucha had only the minimum of trouble with my change of abode, for she did not inform the authorities of my leaving or of my true identity. They now knew who I was. Her penalty was the refusal to give her a new coal oven. My instincts had been 100% correct. Had I stayed I would had have been arrested in no time at all. So I escaped that forced-labour camp. I had had a piece of good luck, and left that worker/farmer's 'paradise'.

Without map or compass, I arrived in the West, in Detmold. I cannot describe my joy at seeing Evert and Brigitte. I had not seen Evert for several years. He had quarters with a Dutch couple, Mr and Mrs Snüverink. Their two sons, both in the Waffen SS, were both reported missing with our troops in Russia. So they were in the same situation as we, for they feared reprisals against themselves in the absence of their sons. They had left everything that they had owned and escaped to Detmold. Evert and I were now welcomed with open arms and became 'provisional sons' for them. We both owed much to this couple. Mr Snüverink had had a large and successful building firm, and it was to be assumed that he would again, one day.

Most important for Evert, was for him to have a new identity, without it he would have no ration card. So as I had more experience in this, I presented myself before the authorities as Evert. He was three years older but this was not noticed. I had explained that my papers were lost upon fleeing from the Russians, but this was not acceptable. "No, Sir, you could be Hitler's son for all we know!" They were friendly, but a solicitor was more helpful. We found one who believed the story and for a fee gave me the needed

Untersturmführer Evert Verton (front centre) marches with his company into Canadian captivity, Netherlands 1945. The soldiers belonged to 34th SS Division 'Landstorm Nederland'.

documents, attested and sealed. I presented them to an Eton school-boy-type British officer, who smelled of leather and whisky. "Documents, all correct, goodbye!" Evert and the Snüverinks waited for me with impatience. He had never trusted himself to go out on the street before I returned with his identification. But now he could, with papers declaring that he had been born in Finsterwald and had fled to the West. And I? I did not know who I was anymore, for I was now my brother!

In Holland, Evert's escape and my non-return would mean our deaths, if we were to go back, for there was now 'ethnic-cleansing' at home. Families of those who had kept Communism away from their door were penalised. 'Ethnic-cleansing of traitors' was also happening in Western Europe. The families were persecuted and mobbed. I find it difficult to write about the behaviour of my own people, about their crimes, that were similar to those of the Soviets in east Germany, and which I would never have believed of them.

The German people were to feel vengeance. But they knew nothing of the crimes against the non-Germans, the friends of Germany who had fought for a federalised Europe, with autonomy and rights of self-determination at their side. The younger generation had been the driving force behind that 'voluntary' sacrifice. The Germans were busy with themselves in the immediate years after the war. So it is not to be expected that they were interested in the personal fates of those beyond their borders. Revenge was now the order of the day. When the sons were not present, then the mob vented their spleen on the family members, not only the male members, but female members and their children too.

This applied not only to 'the man in the street', but also to the Prince Consort, Prince Bernhard von Lippe of Biesterfeld. He came under the scrutiny of MI5 and the CIA, even during his asylum in England. His past record, i.e. his position with the IG Farben firm, plus being a member of the SS, gave Eisenhower's staff differences of opinion. An army in exile was formed by Dutch Government officials in London. Prince Bernhard von der Lippe of Biesterfeld was its commander.

The principal offenders and agitators were those exiled members of the BS and OD, i.e. *Ordnungsdienst* administrative authorities or public policy officials. Their orders were carried out by uniformed bands of men, with an orange band around their arm and carrying Sten-guns. There were decent but disapproving Dutch police, reserve-officers and former resistance fighters, Prince Bernhard too. But they did nothing to interfere with the shameful atrocities of those mobs on their own people, the political misfits and others. The conservative members of the exiled government in London, in 1943, had enough forethought to form new laws and resurrect old laws, in case of public unrest. At all costs, they wanted to avoid the workings of Communist and Socialist infiltrators/agitators, in the chaos after a possible defeat of Germany, and the possibility of them taking control, although at that time, one could say that they actually supported Bolshevism. Some laws were backdated, and some were changed. For instance, the law on freedom of action, some actions formerly not being punishable offences before 1940 were now an offence, for instance.

Unqualified judges could now sentence Dutch citizens to ten years in a concentration camp. Other judges were given special jurisdiction to give the death-sentence, which had not taken place for centuries in Holland. Sentences included having one's nationality taken away, having no right to vote, and one could have property/possessions taken away.

The revenge was planned, and former volunteers and collaborators were the targets of unimaginable and inhuman behaviour. Wives of German soldiers, girls who were engaged to German soldiers, or even if they befriended one, had their heads shaved, had swastikas smeared on their foreheads and were then hunted through the streets. The homes of former NSB members had their homes plundered, as were those of any linked associations.

In comparison with the unending flood of literature on the 'heroic acts' of the resistance against the Germans, their crimes against their own countrymen were never written about. Virtually nothing was published, for no one dared. One of those who attacked this theme was the Dutch theologian Dr. H.W. van der Vaart-Smit, who interested himself as early as 1949. He wrote a book *Kampteostanden 1944–1947*, on the atrocities taking place in prisons on political prisoners, all of which were recorded. It was a horror. The foreword to this book was written by Professor G.M. Russell, who states that "The truth of this black chapter in our post-war history should not stay silent, nor be denied".

One cannot say that this behaviour was spontaneous. It was a merciless and bloody revenge, practised on defenceless people. The 'crime' of these people was having been a member of the NSB, or a German sympathiser. In a free thinking society they were now criminals. They were penalised with methods that surpassed the ecclesiastical torture methods of the Inquisition of 1232, in particular on women (page 22 of Dr. van der Vaart Smit's book). On the next page one can read of other atrocities. The female jailers of those women were no better, maybe even worse than their male counterparts, for all were jail-bait for them. They beat up the prisoners at will, reverting to medieval methods, or locked them for days in cages in which they could only stand. When one of the jailers lit a cigarette, it was used as a method of torture, one of the 'harmless' sort (page 33).

On page 34, there is a report on the transport of amputees and the behaviour of guards upon reaching an internment camp. The guards threw the amputees from the vehicle like a load of ballast. One was an eighteen year old who had lost both his legs, and was severely injured. An accompanying nurse lost her temper. She received a bullet in her thigh. Many of those prisoners were psychological wrecks after such experiences and were sent to the Institution for Psychiatry in Franaker. They were treated as demented, not "demented patients", but to quote one of the treating doctors, as "demented criminals".

The jailers were members of the shooting clubs. It was "Schützenfest time" and lasted from July to November of 1945, until Canadian troops stopped the massacre of prisoners. Prisoners were murdered at will, or badly injured and then the necessary medical help was withheld. Even stretcher-bearers when help was available were fired upon. Notorious for its system of torture, was the internment camp in Scheveningen. A total of 45,000 Dutch citizens were accused of collaboration, 170,000 of them being interned. Holland had a population of 8.2 million inhabitants at that time.

One could ask, "Are we talking about the same peace-loving Holland that fiercely clung to and defended its neutrality among the nations, but that was more than ready to wage war in this fashion on their own people?" Thousands of individual fates are not known, have never been recorded. Women and girls stayed silent, in fear of reprisals when the sexual crimes against them became known.

When parents were 'classified', their children were torn away from them to be put into homes, and they were interned. Visits to their children were forbidden and their contact completely severed. The children of political prisoners were very badly treated in those homes, where they vegetated. As many as 300,000 children were suddenly without parents, and were continually brainwashed that they were the children of criminals. It should be of no surprise that eventually many were ashamed of their own parents. Psychological pressure and ill-treatment of those children resulted in many of them becoming ill and sustaining psychological problems.

For the last fifteen years, an association called the "Herkenning Work-group" has existed in Holland, to help children with this dark chapter of their lives. They were the persecuted political sacrifices of discrimination. It remains in existence today. The association had to fight very strong resistance from the administrative authorities. It is only in the last few years that they have become known as a 'charitable association', and deemed worthy of support.

When their own people were subjected to this wave of revenge, then how did the German citizen on Dutch soil fair? In the preoccupation of hunting the 'fou' and the 'volunteers', from the German citizens still to be found in Holland after 1945, 203 were sentenced. Eighteen were sentenced to death, six were executed, six were sentenced to life imprisonment, others received sentences of between three months and twenty years, but none served more than 13 years of their sentences. The forthcoming economic boom, to be found in Germany, played a very large role in this, for Holland was very much dependent on their neighbour. There was an economic boom to be seen on the horizon, and the legendary business-sense of the Dutch soon came to the fore.

It was in Detmold that I heard from Evert of the martyrdom of my family. It probably would have never happened, nor been so tragic, had they stayed in Germany, to where they had fled in the last few months of the war. They were evacuated, with the wives and children of NSB men or German sympathisers, or as the families of 'volunteers'. Those measures followed after the French practised the same lynch-law on their own people, after the retreat of the German *Wehrmacht* in 1944, and as the Armed Forces from northern France neared the Dutch borders. As the Allies marched through France, an aftermath of executions, without a process of law, surged through the countryside. It happened in Belgium too. The Belgians, wanting to see blood, killed around 1,000 of their pro-German people.

The 5 September was a Tuesday in 1944 and three months after 'D-Day'. "Radio Orange" broadcast from London, that Breda would be the first Dutch city to be liberated by the Allies. It was to be a day of significance for the annals of history and known as 'Wild Tuesday', not from the uncountable arrests but from the very loose bullets from the guns of the OD.

In the same month, 65,000 Dutch Nationals, including my parents, in danger of the waves of terror, left Holland for exile in chartered railway wagons. Not all arrived in Germany in one piece. More than once the passengers had to alight from the trains and take cover under the wagons, or find any other sort of shelter. There were low flying aircraft attacks by the Allies, although it was not military transport. Most of the refugees settled in Lüneburg.

The Verton family however, in Hildesheim, in a former one monastery, joined my sister, who was married to a Dutch 'volunteer', an education officer in the SS division 'Wiking'. I had already visited my sister there, and on that occasion had met British 'volunteers' of the Waffen SS. Yes, they were members of the 'British *Freikorps*'. They had been former members of the bomber-crews, had found themselves in German prison camps, but had declared themselves as 'volunteers' to fight against Communism. My family enjoyed the next seven months in Hildesheim, a city of 80,000 inhabitants, until 22 March 1945, a lovely spring day. It was chosen for a bombing raid by 200 four-engined Lancaster Bombers. They destroyed this jewel of a city, with its half-timbered houses, which had been spared up to that time. A 5,000 metre high mushroom of smoke, from fire and high-explosive bombs, could be seen from 300 kilometres away. The city and the monastery were left in ruins. The need for a roof over their heads, and the longing to see their own home again, sent them once more back to Holland, to agony and suffering. There was no military or strategic reason for the bombing of Hildesheim.

Upon their arrival in Holland, all were promptly arrested by the OD. They were responsible for law and order, and wore orange arm-bands. My one year old nephew was torn away from my sister and taken to a special home for NSB children. A notice was attached to the children's beds, "Child of the SS" or "Child of the NSB". They were 'orphans', but not orphans. Much later, after my sister was released from internment camp she recorded a tape saying that she had managed to sneak secretly into the home and was devastated at her son's apathetic and neglected condition.

After two years of internment, she was one of the lucky ones for she could claim her son once more. At three years old she found that he could not walk. Her son was also deaf in one ear. One can assume that he had had painful inflammation of the middle-ear which had not been treated. My sister was lucky that she could collect her son from the home, for many had been adopted. Many of the children were presented for adoption.

Through this sad and sickening time, a thin thread of decency showed itself, from one of the brave. He was one of those brave enough to criticise, to rise above his own experiences of war and take up the sword of decent social behaviour. One such was the Dutch journalist W.L. Brugsma, who had been a resistance fighter and one who had served a spell in a German prison. He criticised the inhumane treatment of these children, and asked, "how clean are those responsible for the Ethnic-Cleansing?" The articles from this man are still suppressed. They belong together with the very sparse literature to be found on this chapter of Dutch history.

On top of the suffering of my family in the internment camps, news reached them of the death of my brother Jan. There are to this day unanswered questions concerning his death. He died on his way to work. He went to work on his motorbike every day, to the German aerodrome where he worked as an electrician. Assassination from the resistance was rife at that time, practised especially on those working for the Germans. It would not have been difficult to acquaint oneself with Jan's daily routine. In our opinion, he was either the victim of an air raid, from low-flying planes, or the subject of an assassination, from a sniper, just like the father of my friend Robert Reilingh.

For my mother it was a sudden shock. To hear of his death in the circumstances that she was in, was very hard. She was at that time 55 years old. She had fought tooth and nail for the liberation of her family, until she played on the nerves of the camp directors. They then put her into a psychiatric institution in Assen. The Russians too did this with their dissidents. Locked in with the mentally ill, my mother soon became ill, both physically and mentally, as a result of her surroundings, as well as from the separation from her husband and children. She suffered from harassment and very bad nourishment, eating mostly mouldy bread and cooked potato peelings. She had just got to grips with the death of her beloved eldest son, when she then received the news of the death of our father.

My father had had a hernia operation, which was not post-operatively treated during his internment. Instead he was put to work. He had by that time written many letters, optimistic letters, with plans for the future, for when they were released. Some weeks later an obituary circulated amongst the prisoners. It was of my father, an obituary of 59 lines describing his heartfelt longing to be re-united with his dear wife and children. His funeral could not have been simpler. We were thankful that one member of the family was present, Evert. An exception was made and Evert, under armed guard, attended the funeral of our father.

Evert had been captured in the area of Arnhem, by the Canadians. They then delivered him to the Dutch, who delivered him into the notorious Harskamp prison. Before he could be sentenced he was put to work in the coal mine. With his escape he avoided the torture that was on the daily agenda. Allied war correspondents took many photos of the war. They took one of Evert, marching at the front of his men as company-leader, upright and marching into the POW camp.

My family were finally released, one after the other in 1947, after two years of internment. Nothing but skin and bone, covered in lice, and care-worn, my mother was also released from the Institution in the same year. She spoke unwillingly of her time there. She had a very strong, iron will and

'Homecoming', a drawing by the author made in 1946.

this helped her recover, helped her on to her feet and back to her place as
head of the family. The youngest of my brothers who was just twelve at this
time had spent the two years in different homes, not knowing where any of
his family were. He had no news and no visits, which were forbidden. One
is duty-bound to mention those who kept to good social behaviour during
this misery. One was a doctor who secretly helped my mother. Another was
a Jewish jailer, who was sympathetic to one of my brothers and was humane
in his behaviour towards him.

Robbed of house, home and possessions, the family found a new abode
in Woudenberg, in the province of Utrecht. In the countryside, they were
surrounded by straightforward and helpful people. They had a very friendly
farmer as a next-door neighbour, who even hid my letters to my family.
Gradually the family almost returned to normal. Very soon the local police
started to pay visits. They wanted to catch either Evert or me on our visits,
particularly on public holidays, when they were sure that we would be fool-
ish enough to return. One official would simply have loved to catch us. He
accused the family of spying, having found a photo of our model aerodrome
that we had built as children in the garden, complete with model planes. We
were supposed to be spying on military establishments!

The pressure on the civilian population gradually decreased which cannot be said for the 'volunteers'. A further 5,000 were arrested and interned,
without 'due process', for all the difference that would have made. Five
years later, in 1950, Dutch soldiers who returned to Holland, having been
released from Russian POW camps were immediately arrested and sentenced! The final insult came for those men, when they were visited in their

cells by officers collecting information and experiences of the Russian-front soldiers, because of the 'Cold War' with the Communists. An anachronism of history? Upon being released from prison, those men lost their nationality. Holland made displaced persons out of their own countrymen.

It was no better in other countries. The Norwegians too sentenced 7,000 of their 'volunteers' with a sentence of up to four years' imprisonment. In Denmark it was more, with 7,717 men sentenced. The Belgians sentenced 3,193 'collaborators' to death. Even when the death sentences were not carried out, for the 'volunteers' it meant years of imprisonment. Switzerland was no better, with 1,300 men brought before courts martial. The sentences were harder than for the fighters in the Spanish Civil War in the 1930s.

As late as 1952, 2,400 French 'volunteers' were interned for their part in fighting Bolshevism, which they could avoid by then fighting in Indochina, or serving in the French Foreign Legion. From the 'volunteers' from the Balkans and the Soviet Union 11,000 Slovenian 'volunteers' were liquidated by Tito's partisans in May of 1945. Then a further 90,000 Croatian soldiers of the *Ustascha* Army were sentenced. The British delivered 35,000 Cossacks, without consideration of asylum, or of international laws, to the Russians. They were either shot on sight, sent to forced-labour camps, or into mines. The same applied to neutral Sweden that had profited so much from German trade. They gave their German prisoners, and those from the Baltic divisions, to the Russians.

The hate-laden atmosphere of this European ethnic-cleansing did not allow for objective argument or explanation of motives. Only years later were approaches made to repair the association, without condemnation, between the Russian front-fighters and their accusers.

Hans Werner Neulen, in his book *An Deutscher Seite*, asked the question, "Were they the best that prevailed at that time, or captive slaves in Prussian straight-jackets? When, between the Communists with their universal aims of remedial teaching, and the National Socialists with their expectations of Germanic control, the ideals of liberation did not materialise, then the foreign 'volunteers' chose the side of the German Reich".

Till today in the Netherlands, no one will accept that there were far more 'volunteers' wearing field-grey than those of the Allies wearing khaki.

CHAPTER 22

Constructing an Existence

For a very long time after the war, Evert and I did not realise that we both belonged, due to our birth dates to an age-group that suffered the highest casualties during the Second World War. 'Lady luck' however, had decided that we would both survive and now we had to build an existence for ourselves.

We both now had an identity, even if threaded with untruths, tricks and deceit, nonetheless it enabled us to live in the British Zone. It was far better than the alternative, but still not easy. So as not to starve we both needed work and a permanent roof over our heads, and neither was at a premium in Detmold. It meant looking elsewhere.

We gleaned the information that miners were needed in the Ruhr area. It would be the hardest of physical labour, but every miner was sure of 2,864 calories per day, i.e. a full stomach! There were no other offers of work, so we used this as a springboard for our futures. Work in the mines was top of the list, as hard physical labour of course. Another perk was that accommodation was offered with the job as well. There was a little fly in the ointment inasmuch as, in this still conservative time, you had to be married before you received accommodation together. Brigitte and I could not bear the thought of another separation, and so there was no other choice, we had to marry. That meant waiting until the bans were hung in the local Registry Office which took three months. Due to his contacts with the local council, Mr Snüverink managed to have this three-month wait waived. The advantage was that no one had the time to snoop into my true identity or nationality. The only truth in the matter was my name of Verton.

The date was set for 12 December 1947. It was a cold winter. Inside, the cold demeanour of the Registrar was just as ice-cold as it was outside. However, he married us, with Mr and Mrs Snüverink as our witnesses. Our romance had begun in war-torn Breslau eighteen months before, in the summer months. We sealed our fate together forever, giving our word to one another in the extreme of winter months, in Detmold. We are, after 55 years together, still as much in love as on that first day in Breslau.

We neither felt the cold nor saw the greyness of the mist as we left the Registry Office. Our wedding breakfast was a stew with runner beans. For those times it was *cordon-bleu* and relished as such. Our honeymoon, of one night, was spent in the Railway Hotel. It was rather meagre, for despite it being December, the room was not heated. The next morning in wanting to leave, a dog baring its teeth barred our way, warning the proprietor of our departure. The dog was there to stop those crooks of society who had no intention of paying for their rooms.

Our wedding was to prove to be the reason that the whole of my family left Holland and came to Germany. My brothers found their wives here, and in the words of Geothe, "we formed a chain" of Vertons, a new one, which now stretched from France to Holland, and from Holland to Germany.

The three of us then made our way to the Ruhr, the epicentre of coal-mining. Both Evert and I were engaged straight away by the Essen Coal Company in Dortmund-Dortfeld, which owned two-thirds of the coal works in that area. Brigitte and I were given a warm furnished room in the Karl-Funke Strasse. Only a couple of streets away Evert was given a room by one of the medics of the company. Among Evert's duties was first aid to the injured in the mine. The medic was a Marxist and although he had never seen the Russian Steppes, a bronze bust of Lenin had its place of honour beside the highly polished coal-fired stove. Evert was to be found most evenings in our room, where we cooked and ate, and had to sleep. Brigitte knitted us pullovers from shredded parachute silk, and cut us trousers from tenting material.

The whole nation heard about our record output in the tons of coal that we dug out of the earth. We were the heroes of the underground, but the population still froze. "Every ton is useful. For death lies in empty hands, for no coal, no food, no transport, therefore no production". That was the declaration of the British military command, who urged for more and more, because more than a quarter of our coal was for their usage. Dismantling and demolition was now the order of the day. There was a hive of industry, for what the Allies had not destroyed with their bombs, they destroyed with explosives, such as the tall chimneys on industrial sites. Everything that was of use was dismantled, brick by brick. It was a 'cold war' and the continuation of war, but by other means.

The increased pressure on the coal-miners did not ensure the upkeep of safety precautions in the mines. On the contrary, the training of new workers was simply not what it should have been. Evert and I belonged in that category, being fully-fledged miners after just three days of training. That was how we started. Our production was still not enough, and so POWs were released from the prison camps on the condition that they worked in the mines. The accidents underground increased, and at a shocking rate. 178,000 tons of coal daily was the record, 50% more than in 1936.

We, together with a dozen other colleagues, entered the cage. It took us down below at a rate of 20 metres per second. But we were still not at our place of work when we reached the bottom of the shaft. We had two kilometres to walk, that meant being bent almost double, and having to step over rail-tracks and electric cables, and always knocking our heads as we went. It was unexpectedly vast. In our pit alone, there were 200 kilometres of tunnelling. In total it was 5,000 kilometres in the west German mines, longer than the flight-path from Hamburg to Cairo!

I was plagued with a vision at the beginning of this work, of a worm being crushed from an avalanche of earth and stone. We were after all, a thousand metres below the surface, under towns, under cemeteries and to say nothing of rivers! Claustrophobia at this time, was the last thing that I needed. So it was nose to the grindstone and get on with the job.

The pressure of this work played on our nerves at times. Some miners were liable to this more than others. It made them argumentative to the point of disputes, as Evert found to his cost one day when he landed on the wrong side of one. It really had started from nothing. It resulted in a punch-up and Evert and his opponent waltzed in the coal-dust, with blood on their bare chests. I was held back forcibly by the others, when wanting to help him. It was the 'Inauguration to the Association of Moles', for like animals, we had to learn who had the say, who was the boss and where our place was, which we had to keep. The supervisor of our seam separated the pair of them and the whole dispute was then forgotten. We came to be a close-knit band, for were we not all in the same boat? We all gritted our teeth, we gave sweat and blood. We soon learned to depend on the experience of our colleagues who had been miners for far longer than any of us. They saved our lives, more than once, from avalanches of earth and stone, which was my nightmare. We did not recognise the 'stretching and groaning' of the mountain that warned them far earlier than we realised.

Somehow the sounds of the underworld were just the same as those of the war. There were pneumatic drills, replacing the machine-guns, and dynamite replacing the exploding bombs. There were injured and the dead, just as on the battlefield. The safety of the miners was not an important factor. It was not on the investment plan and there was a lack of the most experienced of the miners, for there were still very many of them sitting in prison as Nazis.

Two years before Evert and I enrolled for this new work, there had been a loss of 411 men from the neighbouring Grimmberg Colliery. At mid-day on 20 February 1946, a blue and red flame shot out of the shaft, the earth shook like an earthquake as a mixture of methane gas and air caused an explosion. That happened eighteen months after a previous explosion caused the deaths of 107 miners, as the result of an air raid.

We had deaths in our colliery too, and were witness to terrible injuries. Evert and I only ever had a graze or two. We most certainly did not believe in the 'troll of the mountains' and his 'aggressive powers' over those daring to intrude into his world which could certainly be 'spooky'. Often there was nothing to be heard but a monotonous drip, drip of water whose echo mixed with the airwaves. When the old and porous support beams soaked in phosphor glowed in the dark, then the gullible could believe in a 'some-thing' which they could not define, and so were willing to believe in that 'little beast'.

At the end of the day, and as Brigitte picked me up from work, she had difficulty in recognising me as we left the cage to cross the yard to the shower-room, for we all looked alike, like Blackamoors. So she waited until one of those black beings winked at her and it was me. It was like a con-veyor-belt in the hot steamy shower-room. We stood in a long line and soaped the back of the man in front in readiness for a good scrub. We were always about an hour before we could be called clean, and then we all had black rims around our eyes, like women with eye make-up.

One could not ignore the fact that many of the old miners were chroni-cally, even terminally ill. One could hear the hacking, raw coughs of those invalids on the streets. There was no shower that could wash the dust-caked lungs of those men, trying to take some fresh air into their clogged lungs that no longer functioned properly.

One day passed into the next. But one day was not like any other for Evert, for he was suddenly seized with miners' claustrophobia. He simply had to leave the seam in which we were working and reach daylight. He never went underground again. That was not unusual amongst miners. I was not affected in the same way, but I too left some months after Evert. My next job was also underground, but not to the same extent, for it was a vaulted wine-cellar and only a couple of metres under the surface. I climbed inside the giant wine vats to wash and brush them, as I was the right size to climb into the small openings. I washed the wine-bottles and re-filled them too.

We experienced a distinct improvement with the Currency Reform of 1948. Overnight the shops filled with all of the pre-war goods that we had been denied, with a shake of the head, from shop-owners. Every man re-ceived a one-off payment of 40 marks, but the rationing was not yet at an end.

After five years of separation, came the day in the summer of 1949, when I could take my mother in my arms at long last. She arrived by train in Dortmund. It was extremely moving, for I had not seen her since 1944. Some of my letters had not reached her, so she did know that I had served some of my time in East Prussia, Silesia and Breslau. She had not known about my time as a prisoner under the Russians. Now we were all together and she met her daughter-in-law, although at first there were language problems.

The presence of my family rather complicated my life. It appeared for some to have contradictions. As a 'refugee' from the east my mother was no longer my mother but an 'aunt from Holland'. Brigitte and I had moved house since working in the mine. We now lived in a house owned by my former colliery director, who was always very friendly and sympathetic to us. I decided to make a clean breast of things to him. I was glad that I did, although it had not been necessary, for he had guessed anyway. It was however a relief to no longer have to hide the truth.

I was glad to have my work in the wine cellar. But it was not for life as it held no future, no advancement. With the land in ruins, the building trade offered work that did hold a future. The future Federal capital city, Bonn, seemed to be just the right place to look.

We were very impressed with Königswinter and its district. On a visit we made, the countryside of the Rhine and the Siebenbürge area seemed so much nicer than the mountains of black coal and silhouettes of mine works visible in the Ruhr. Bad Gödesberg in particular, with its tree-lined avenues, plus the style of the old villas, which had been spared the bombing raids, reminded me of the sleepy suburbs of Holland. A Cologne-based firm engaged Evert and I and sent us to Bonn. There we became floor-layers, of every type. With the construction of this new federal capital, there was an excess of work to be found, in new buildings of government, universities etc.

A year later, and with our move to Bad Gödesberg, we changed our work once more, to a firm in Königswinter, very near us. We had ended up with a former colonel who had been a commander in Hitler's HQ in Prussia. He was the son-in-law of the owner of the perfume emporium "Eau-de-Cologne and Toilet-water". He owned an estate, the Wintermuhlenhof near Petersberg and directed firms in different branches. Most of his employees were former officers. Most of his guests too, were from all branches of the former armed forces. They could be seen with him walking around the park. Although many impediments had been placed in the path of former German soldiers, many found their feet again quite quickly after the war. They were helped by having a positive mentality, and discipline from their soldiering days. Their behaviour towards their comrades, their conscientiousness and organisation, all of these were important assets for the reconstruction of the German economy.

The former soldier got to grips with every type of work that was offered. His willingness came from a close-knit comradeship that he had found during the war. The result was that former high-ranking, and some very senior Generals, became successful directors of many of the foremost firms. Later, as the economy improved, we also profited. Together with a former comrade, we formed our own firm in 1953, which had always been our dream. Shortly before the publishing of this book, our firm celebrated its Golden Jubilee. Our firm grew, based on a risk or two. Optimism and improvisation soon found us employing a couple of dozen men, giving them work and their daily bread. To do that we had to give our all, including many weekends, in the first years. The first vehicle in our car park was a pre-war lorry, an Adler with front-wheel drive, and a trailer. It was usually overloaded and gave us many a puncture, but that was how we visited our customers. In winter, when the motorway was iced, or if on an incline, then two of us sat on the front bumpers as ballast and we could continue on our way. That would not be permitted today, but then, we had to know how we could help ourselves. Physical efforts were the foundation of economic rehabilitation.

CHAPTER 23

Comradeship for Life

Evert and I were still living with false identities, which at some time or another had to be corrected. There was an Amnesty in 1954 which enabled us to do just that. We had to appear before a Court that understood the veiling of our identities. There was no case made against us. However, we were stateless, for Holland refused our rehabilitation. It had to stay that way for some years. Even citizens without nationality or fatherland, can be industrious, for themselves and for others. But I was not allowed in Holland with my business. My German colleagues however had the privilege of taking their business there. Seven years were to come and go, before we were reinstated as Dutch Nationals.

I can remember with clarity my very first return visit into my Fatherland after 17 years. I was deeply moved. My feelings were mixed as I drove over the border at Aachen, on the way to Maastricht, which was my first stop. My 'passenger' was my passport, sitting on the passenger seat, for with the safety of my family uppermost in my mind, I travelled alone on that occasion.

I must say that I was rather disappointed at being waved through with nonchalance by the border officials on the Dutch side of the border. Had I

1961: the author (second from left) finally reunited with his brothers

not been on the wanted list for many years? Now, armed with a new passport, and a bundle of correspondence from the Ministry of Justice, and my 'rehabilitation', they were not interested! All the better.

In 17 years things had changed. Firstly, everything appeared to be smaller than I could remember. My fellow Dutch were friendly, but loud. 'Very loud' was my assessment, as I inquisitively watched the people on the street, like a child. They drifted here and there and were casual, and now had a far more leisurely manner. The Maastricht Agreement was not yet in force, but the coffee beans were very much cheaper than in Germany. In Holland's oldest city I filled myself with Matjes herrings, that I had not had the pleasure of for many a year.

On subsequent visits I was able to assess that my homeland was not as it had been. No, it had changed a lot since the war, especially in the large towns. There was nothing left of the Old School mentality, now it was casual and dirty. My wife Brigitte was not impressed with the dirty towns that she saw. In Breslau I had told her with pride that even the exterior of the houses were washed in the annual spring-clean. I told her how orderly and clean my people were, and the streets spick and span. Sadly, not any more, except perhaps in the suburbs where Old School standards still prevailed, just as I remembered them.

Naturally enough there came a time when. I wanted to see my old comrades. But in Holland there was still a problem. The neighbours could not be told. They were very quickly suspicious and they were not to know about one's past. In West Germany that was now no problem. There it was already very liberal. Groups of war-veterans were forming, who helped one another when in need. They were also assiduous in the service of searching for missing comrades. That was an urgent priority, for only in the second half of 1948 were former Waffen SS members included by the American Occupation authorities into Social Benefit laws. In other zones it stayed as it had been since 1950. There were no government social benefits or facilities whatsoever, to show gratitude for our sacrifice, or for our service to the Fatherland.

Later generations were able to recognise the 'yoke' under which the front-troops had bent. They bore no grudge, no ill-feelings against the State. How did we find one another? From my own post-war actions of searching for those that I knew, it was very quickly evident that our troops were widely scattered in all corners of Germany, and in places that I had never heard of. That really didn't need any explanation. Millions had been evacuated from war-torn towns that remained empty for some time. A very happy reunion took place with Georg Haas, the former accountant of the 11th in Breslau. He put an enquiry into the military magazine *Der Freiwillige*, wanting to know the whereabouts of former comrades. This took place in 1956. The joy was great at seeing one another again after 11

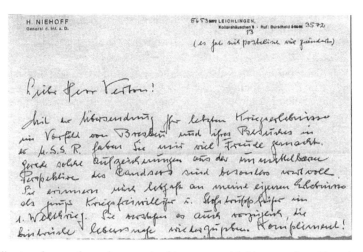

Following the war the author remained in contact with his comrades. Above is the
beginning of a letter from the former commandant of Breslau during the siege, General
(retired) Hermann Niehoff, thanking Hendrik for sending him his war memoirs.

years. He had feared that I had not survived, having been a POW under the
Russians.

In two of the books that he wrote, *Brände an der Oder*, and *Gaben die
Hoffnung nicht auf*, I contributed original photos and sketches. I played a
large role in them under the pseudonym Hendrik Velthoven. Both books
on the 'Stalingrad of Silesia', in which he wrote truthfully and openly about
the bitter battles, and the suffering of its citizens, were successful documents
of the last months of the war.

All of us comrades were industrious in the search for former brothers-in-arms. The Waffen SS were first and foremost in the search, as was
confirmed time and time again by the Red Cross and other War Welfare
services. Eight years after the war there were 3.5 million missing persons.
The fate of 750,000 illegally deported civilians, and 300,000 children, still
had to be researched. This action reached tremendous proportions that
were exclusive to the Waffen SS.

Regularly, the bands of searchers met together to exchange their find-
ings, such as in Minden in 1956, on 5 and 6 September when 10,000 members were present! Two years later in Hamlin, 16,000 turned up. Between
them all, they could solve 600 cases of missing comrades. The director of
the German Red Cross at that time, Dr Pasewaldt, could report that the
whereabouts of a quarter of the former units, 13,000, had been located, all
from the work of the comrades, which was passed on at those reunions.

The speakers at the reunions were none other than commanders from
the Armed Forces, such as General Paul Hausser, and the Generals Felix
Steiner and Kurt 'Panzermeyer' Meyer, as well as politicians and the mayor

of Minden, Dr Mosel. There were absolutely no problems with these meetings at that time. On the contrary, Dr Mosel began his speech of welcome with "My dear comrades of World War II". He told the many who were assembled, that it was an honour for the city to be able to welcome us war-veterans.

The former chairman of the FDP party, a parliamentarian Dr Erich Mende, recipient of the Knight's Cross, and a former major, declared, "We were totally dependent on our brothers-in-arms for our lives. We did not ask, "are you Catholic?" or "are you Evangelist, *Wehrmacht* or the Waffen SS?" We were dependent, as a *Wehrmacht* division, for example, on the Waffen SS holding the Caen-Falaise road." Support and understanding for our troops, came from various directions. Dr Kurt Schumacher, the chairman of the post-war SPD, the German Labour Party, and also Federal-Chancellor Konrad Adenauer, who referred to the Waffen SS at the CDU Conference, in Hannover in 1949, as "Soldiers like every other".

In the following years, as World War II started to belong to the past, and the war generation wandered into old age, they became 'interested parties'. It is forgotten how closely-knit the German population were at one time. According to old tradition, one placed a burning candle on the windowsill, to guide the soldier-lad home, and to keep alive the memory of those, still far away, many in foreign POW camps.

The Waffen SS slowly belonged to the past, and slowly, speeches of regret started to take place, from parties and from the politically prominent. But "out of sight, out of mind!" is not the code that we of the Waffen SS live by. Our code, "Our loyalty is our honour," may be scoffed at by some, but we still live by it today. It is a duty, the duty of unending work to locate our missing. Then we work to give him or them a worthy grave. There are still 1.4 million Germans missing (1995 statistics). We try to give social help where needed. An example is the organisation Paul Hausser Social Work. Up to 1992 it could boast of collecting 4 million marks for social help.

Every land honours their dead. Until recently, everywhere except Germany. The American soldiers returning home to the States had the red carpet rolled out for them. We were de-nazified, the *Wehrmacht* and foreign 'volunteers' too. Old soldiers meet and shake hands over the graves, those from the East and those from the West, in Normandy and recently in Russia. A front-line soldier shares the experiences of others, and each brings respect to the other. They are all eyewitnesses who did their duty. This only applies outside Germany.

Until recently the state did not honour their dead. Only outside Germany did one find a wreath of remembrance on the grave of a German soldier, 'unknown' or not. Until recently, our remembrance services were ringed with police and protestors. We are reminded "to remember not to forget", but can also find upon our arrival, that our memorial service has been cancelled. A comment from a former French President of a veterans' organisation was, "A land which ignores its own history, which lies about its past, staggers thereafter, without orientation".

Post-war meetings with military personages were, for me, a highlight. It was not possible during the war, as there was no time or possibility, since, for those of our rank, such men of high rank were out of reach. Now they were no longer military personages, but were free to voice an opinion and share their experiences with us, their men.

One such was 'Papa Hausser', or to give him his correct title, Commander-in-Chief of the Armed Forces and highly decorated General, Paul Hausser. His name will go down, not only in German history books, but also those of the Second World War. He really was a father to his soldiers, they were 'his boys'. He was the one who sometimes contradicted Hitler when necessary. He visited us in Bonn one time, where he showed not only his humour but his humility as well. One of us in speaking to him addressed him with his full military title. He didn't want that. "But General I cannot call you Paul," as was suggested. "Well, call me *Paulchen* then!" which is an endearment, for someone of whom you are very fond. We met again Stuttgart in 1970, two years before he died at the age of 92.

Dressed in a light coat, similar to the one that he had worn in Russia, the commander of the 'Wiking', Felix Steiner visited us in Bonn. Just like Napoleon, he spoke to his men, one after the other. As a friendly gesture he spoke as if he knew exactly when and where in battle he had seen them before.

Then there was Sepp Dietrich. This old war-horse, this bluff fire-eater belonged to a fraternity all of his own. His strong but casual personality, his laid-back manner, I found just the same in meeting him again. I met Major-General Kurt Meyer, and General Herbert Gilles, who was a sensitive and intelligent man. Despite their former high ranks, both men were humble and approachable. Arrogance was never to be seen.

It was in 1963 that Brigitte and I were in Madrid, for a week, as guests of the legendary Otto Skorzeny. We journeyed together with a married couple who were the book publishers who had published his book, "Live Dangerously". A most impressive man, Skorzeny possessed the typical charm of the Viennese. In 1943, he was to become a worldwide legend for freeing the Italian Duce Mussolini, from under the noses of the Italians, without shedding a drop of blood. He had read both books from George Haas and wanted to meet me. Nearly every day, and everywhere we went in Madrid, we could see and feel the respect that the Spaniards had for Otto Skorzeny. He was always referred to as 'Senor Colonel', and our drinks were always 'on the house'.

In the 1970s, because our daughter Henrike worked for the German airline Lufthansa, we took advantage of her 'personal percentage' for flights.

Brigitte and Hendrik Verton (right) in Madrid, 1963, as guests of the
legendary Otto Skorzeny.

We made a trip to the Eastern-bloc, visiting Moscow, Leningrad, and my
wife's birthplace, Breslau.

Our present and future lives lay in Bad Godesberg, where we felt and
still feel 100% at home. It was where the decisions were made, and where
the politicians argued over the atom bomb, over re-armament and over
Eastern agreements. This 'dwarf' seat of parliament, this post-war capital
was to be treated to a good dose of sarcasm from an American reporter as,
"Half as large and twice as dead as our Central Cemetery in Chicago".

In those days Chancellor Adenauer used the small river ferry daily, to go
to his office from his house in Rhöndorf. He travelled without a govern-
ment-paid limousine, and also without bodyguards. Both would be un-
thinkable today. He would doff his hat in respect to his fellow citizens, and
to those he knew and met on his way. That is all a thing of the past.

There is an old Russian saying, "We come to treasure the things of the
past". Perhaps if we live long enough, perhaps if we have the urgent need
write about it, and if we find the time and leisure to relive our experiences,
we may. Perhaps we will, when the shock and the hope, the suffering and
the yearning for happiness, and when, in remembrance, all becomes 'a
lighter shade of pale'.

Research into the underlying reasons of our personal fates is also very
necessary, in order to be able to correct what is falsely claimed today. It is the
duty of those living to protect the honour of those comrades who gave their
lives.

Sacrifice was the fate of the 'volunteers'. The harvest of sowing their anti-communist seeds was defamation, and persecution was the tragedy of their honour. There will always be 'volunteers', wherever a future of freedom needs them. In the past they were called fantasists, sentimentalists, pretenders, party-followers and even country-bumpkins and of whom history has disapproved. Idealists should constantly protect themselves against the orthodox.

We were born into an era which we could not determine, but which paved the way for something enormous. It was an era in which Communism was lifted out of its local setting and wanted to grow and spread throughout Europe. We banded together as its opponents, in wanting to ensure an honourable place for our nation, within the nations and new community of Europe.

We believed that with our 'élite organisation' of not only upright German, but European 'volunteers' from the north-westerly lands, following the victory against communism, we could produce a reform, a *Perestroika* so to speak. With our participation in the Waffen SS we were treated on an equal basis, as every other. Some of us advanced to ranks above German soldiers, such as the battalion commander who was a Dane, or like my brother Evert, a Dutchman, or I too, on a smaller scale, with 12 to 48 German soldiers under my command.

In Bad Tölz at the *Junkerschule*, the party programme of the NSDAP was discussed amongst us, and dissected and criticised by the European offi-

Hendrik Verton and Paul Hausser, Stuttgart, 1970

cers, without any disciplinary action. What we practised, on a small-scale, gave us hope for the future, with not only Germany destined to lead. Was that to be Utopia, only an illusion? Perhaps, but we thought then that it was possible. 'Lady luck' didn't see it like that. She saw to it that, after a lost war, we analysed and learned from this analysis.

A life without a zenith, a youth without reaching the heights or without ideals, was not for us. We lived in a time that needed the utmost effort. Perhaps it was the best that could have happened at that time in our manhood. It was a probation period for us that we came through with flying colours. Those of us who feel guilty must bow to that guilt. Today, what we fight against, whether as an individual or as a group, is the refusal of individuality, which is unjust and basically immoral!

"Everything that is unjust nurtures the seed of destruction."
Alexander von Humbolt

Epilogue

A saga, that long epic of heroic achievement, in Medieval prose, was a narrative of a long, involved account of a series of incidents. But it is not the same as a fairy-tale in prose. I guarantee that nothing of my account is a fairy story. My feelings and views from that period of my past are also honest.

In my narration I have not tried to glorify, but to present a document that is as correct as an eyewitness from that era can describe. In this present day such a document is a bitter necessity. The past was not always ideal, for us or our opponents. I felt neither wistfulness nor nostalgic longings in writing my book. The facts therein are pure unadulterated facts that are not to be twisted by others for their own false ends. My life was and is worth living.

With this Epilogue I wish to give my heartfelt thanks to my comrade and former Second World War officer and *Oberstleutnant* of the *Wehrmacht* Adolf Kruger, who read my book as a competent editor and corrected it. The same applies to Heid Rühl, another former wartime officer and later senior teacher, who also assessed and gave a criticism on my book. Further thanks go to my brother-in-law, Dip.Eng. Jan Carl van dem Berge, and to Mrs Birgit Guden who typed my handwritten manuscript.

Hendrik Verton, Spring 2003

Federal Republic of Germany
Federal Chancellor
Bonn 17.12 1952
General (Retd) P. Hausser
Ludwigsburg / Wittenburg
48 Asperger Street

My Dear General,
    In retrospect, I would like to send you encouraging information, that in my speech that I gave in Parliament on 3 December 1952, one topic embraced the Declaration of Confidence for the former German *Wehrmacht*, inclusive with the members of the Waffen SS, inasmuch as they fought honourably for Germany, their Fatherland.
    I remain, in deep respect,
                                    Adenauer.

Bibliography

Ahlfen, Hans von and Hermann Niehoff, *So kämpfte Breslau*, Gräfe und Unzer Verlag, München 1959

Bamm, Peter, *Die unsichtbare Flagge*, Wissen Verlagsges., Herrsching 1989

Bacque, James, *Der geplante Tod*, Ullstein, Frankfurt/Main 1989

Barraclough, Geoffrey, *Die Einheit Europas in Gedanken und Tat*, Göttingen 1964

Carell, Paul, *Unternehmen Barbarossa*, Ullstein, Frankfurt/Main 1963

Delmer, Sefton, *Die Deutschen und ich*, Nannen-Verlag, Hamburg 1962

Bundesministerium für Vertriebene (Hrsg.), *Dokumentation der Vertreibung*, Berlin 1957

Groen, Koos, *Landverraad*, Unieboek, Weesp 1984

Gleis, Horst G. W., *Breslauer Apokalypse 1945*, 1988

Haas, Georg, *Brände an der Oder*, Ring-Verlag, Siegburg 1962

Haas, Georg, *Und gaben die Hoffnung nicht auf*, Ring-Verlag, Siegburg 1962

Hausser, Paul, *Soldaten wie andere auch*, Munin Verlag, Osnabrück 1966

Helmdach, Erich, *Überfall?*, Kurt Vowinckel Verlag, Neckargemünd 1976

Höhne, Heinz, *Der Orden unter dem Totenkopf*, Berteismann, Gütersloh 1967

Höhne, Heinz, *Gebt mir vier Jahre Zeit*, Ullstein, Berlin 1996

Hornig, Ernst, *Breslau 1945*, Bergstadt-Verlag, München 1975

Hoy, Werner, *Festung Breslau*, Moewig Verlag, 1958

Irving, David, *Hitler und seine Feldherren*, Ullstein, Frankfurt 1975

Kaps, Johannes, *Die Tragödie Schlesiens 1945/46*, Verlag Christ Unterwegs, München 1952

Kern, Erich, *Der große Rausch*, Verlag K. W. Schütz, Oldendorf 1971

Kleist, Peter, *Auch Du warst dabei*, Kurt Vowinckel Verlag, Heidelberg 1952

Kogelfranz (Hrsg.), Siegfried, *Die Vertriebenen*, Rowohlt, Hamburg 1985

Majewski, Ryszard and Teresa Sozanska, *Die Schlacht um Breslau*, Union Verlag, Berlin, 1979

Neulen, Hans Werner, *An deutscher Seite*, Universitas, München 1985

Paul, Wolfgang, *Erfrorener Sieg*, Bechtle Verlag, Esslingen 1975

Peikert, Paul, *Festung Breslau*, Union Verlag Berlin, 1966

Ryan, Cornelius, *Der letzte Kampf*, Droemer-Knaur-Verlag, München 1966

Steiner, Felix, *Die Freiwilligen*, Verlag K. W. Schütz, Oldendorf 1973

Strassner, Peter, *Europäische Freiwillige*, Nation Europa Verlag, Coburg 2001

Suworow, Viktor, *Der Eisbrecher*, Klett-Cotta-Verlag, Stuttgart 1989

Tayior, Alan John, *English History 1914–1945*, 1965

Telpukowski, B. S., *Geschichte der Partisanenbewegung*

Treffner, Helmut, *Geschichte der Waffen-SS*

Vaart Smit, H. W. van der, *Kamptoestanden 1944–1948*, Verlag Keizerskroon, Haarlem 1949

Vorst-Thijssen and De Boer, *Daar praat je niet over – Kinderen van foute ouders*, Utrecht 1995

Zappel, Albrecht, *Vorträge über die Geschichte Breslaus*, 1993

Zayas, Alfred-Maurice de and Walter Rabus, *Völkerrechtsverletzungen der Alliierten im Zweiten Weltkrieg*, Langen Müller, München 1980
Werth, Alexander, *Russia at war*, London 1964
Zentner, Kurt, *Aufstieg aus dem Nichts*, Kiepenheuer & Witsch, Köln 1954

Stackpole Military History Series